The Iranians slammed on their brakes and skidded sideways as well. We took our vehicle to the side of the road. They were trapped in a cross fire. These guys opened the action, but they never fired a dozen rounds. Time was more precious than ammunition. We could see the headlights of the second car approaching in the distance. We had to finish it fast, without setting their Land-Rover on fire. We let loose. Within seconds, our automatic fire ripped them apart. We tore off across country.

## THE TEHERAN CONTRACT

"Rivals fiction for danger and intrigue, breathtaking escapes, misadventures and bloody mayhem."

—*Publishers Weekly*

Bantam Books by Gayle Rivers and James Hudson

**THE FIVE FINGERS**
**THE TEHERAN CONTRACT**

# THE
# TEHERAN
# CONTRACT

**Gayle Rivers
and
James Hudson**

BANTAM BOOKS
TORONTO · NEW YORK · LONDON · SYDNE

THE TEHERAN CONTRACT

*A Bantam Book / published by arrangement with
Doubleday & Co., Inc.*

*PRINTING HISTORY*
*Doubleday edition published April 1981*
*Bantam edition / December 1982*

*The events described in this book occurred in May-June 1979. The
names of the main protagonists have been changed and their
identities altered to protect their anonymity.*

*It is not the authors' intention to belittle the failed American
mission in Iran. Any similarities are purely coincidental. This book
was written prior to that rescue attempt.*

*Bantam Books are published by Bantam Books, Inc. Its trade-
mark, consisting of the words "Bantam Books" and the por-
trayal of a rooster, is Registered in U.S. Patent and Trademark
Office and in other countries. Marca Registrada. Bantam
Books, Inc., 666 Fifth Avenue, New York, New York 10103.*

*To George Greenfield*

# PART I

★

# THE CONTRACT

# 1

The first contact came in London in early May 1979. I had come up from Geneva on business. I was staying at the Royal Commonwealth Society Club, just off Trafalgar Square. Peter Fox called and invited me to lunch.

I was not surprised that Fox knew I was in town. He was a guy who flitted around the periphery of what I do. I assumed he was looking for some specialist equipment or a supply of ammunition. Nothing too big or complicated. He would be on an open tender from someone or dabbling in a security system. Fox was a security consultant, but not a very successful one.

He had never been a special operative. He had gone in the regular army as a boy soldier and done nearly thirty years before being passed over as half-colonel because of problems with the bottle. Now he was a retired major, making a fitful living with whatever business that rank could generate. Like a lot of retired army personnel, he came out full of great ideas, but the commercial world proved harder than he had anticipated. Fox was not a man I treated very seriously. I would take an inquiry from him on certain items and offer him a straightforward business deal. But when he started talking about "doing a job," that was another matter.

The first time he broached the subject, at a quiet table in the rear at Bertorelli's on Queensway, he was as guarded and cautious as if he knew what he was doing. Would I be interested in pulling off something big? He promised to get back to me on it.

Even this tidbit was offered in a way that revealed his basic innocence in these matters. Fox could not disguise his excitement. He had heard something somewhere and could not hold it back. I saw him laboring to be clever and cool. At least he had not said, "I just heard about this fantastic job . . ." He knew a bit about how the game works.

Leading up to being contacted on these things is a series of backward and forward patter until each side has been long tried and tested and knows the offer is serious. Principals do not ring you up and say, "Hey, we'd like for you to do a job." The system has its own filters; people on the fringes are used to carry away the chaff. Principals regularly use people to contact you who are not really up to the job of doing more. But these filters are led to believe that they are at the epicenter of the affair. They think they are putting the deal together, and the job might be pulled off and closed down before they realize they have been cut out. That, I suppose, is what makes the world go around. Here came Fox, running hard for general.

He stopped in the middle of lunch with an expression of changing gears and asked, "Gayle, can you fly a helicopter?"

"I've flown a helicopter," I said. Fox already knew my credentials with fixed-wing aircraft. He and I shared mutual acquaintances of a more serious bent than himself. He plunged ahead.

"Would you be interested in some high-risk flying?" he asked.

"That depends on what we're talking about." Fox's hints led me to think about East Germany. I expected him to ask, "How would you like to take some people into Austria?" This is a typical chopper pilot's forte; it is happening all the time. I was not ready to lend credence to anything Fox offered. He was full of too many romantic notions. He could have overheard something at the local mess or at his officers' club. I played along with Fox's excited intrigue, but I refused to take it seriously. I did this on purpose; it is part of my defense mechanism. When anyone tries to get a reaction out of me or put me on the spot, I confuse him—it is a natural reaction, not a manufactured one—by dismissing it as frivolous. As if I were not even picking up on the hints and innuendos. I discard it all, as if I am not involved in the sort of thing he is talking about.

"Would you be interested in a special op?" he asked at last, frustrated by my seeming incomprehension.

"Oh, come on," I said, "I've given all that up."

This frustrated Fox even more, but it was an automatic response. I did not do it facetiously. If I take none of that sort of talk seriously, I am never led into a conversation on a particular operation. The only time I start talking is when I know the business side of an op is being done in a business-like fashion. There are too many people who get involved in great romantic schemes, who keep their adrenaline running, and their egos boosted, and nothing is happening. I recalled the American who went all over London telling anyone who would listen he was going to snatch Robert Vesco. He gathered people like Fox around him, and they all beavered away and got souped up on an absolutely preposterous scheme.

Someone just had to ask the question, "Who is going to pay for this?" and the whole thing went down like a deflated balloon. Fox and his ilk would hear a scheme like that and say, "Christ, that's a million-dollar operation." The Yank would have been greatly surprised when he found he could not interest the hard cases, like myself, in it. That is how the circle stays unbroken.

I had made a habit of looking out for myself since I was a kid in New Zealand, hunting alone in the mountains with a small-bore rifle. Early in the New Zealand involvement in Vietnam, I volunteered for the New Zealand Special Air Services. I was still a teen-ager when I survived my blooding in the jungles of Malaysia on operations against Communist insurgents, rehearsals for Indochina. I did a tour and a half in Vietnam, leading Green Beret and U.S. airborne units on RFI missions before walking into a minefield that blew half a dozen good men to pieces. It took a year and four hospitals to stitch my body together again, another year before the nightmares died away. I went to South Africa and worked as a private pilot. A few jobs in Rhodesia brought me the capital to go into business for myself. For seven years I had been operating in Europe.

There are two types who move through the specialized little world in which I live: the serious ones and the buccaneers. The latter are more often used than useful, but you get degrees of buccaneers too. Fox would never get involved in an op, play an active role in the field. He was looking to finagle a job on the management team. On the other hand are the Freddies. Up in Sunderland, Freddie has only to hear about an operation and he has his boots on and is trying to join the team. And Freddie is not even a military man. He is fat and unfit to begin with, the sort of guy I would never let near a mission. Mind you, Freddie can pull off a job. He has done a few, and that is what keeps him in the business. The Freddies of this world exist on other people's "outs." If a third party is needed for a transaction to take place, and there has to be a fall guy, Freddie is enlisted on the deceit that he is controlling the deal. Behind his back, the two principals have already agreed to terms. One takes the deal to Freddie. He takes it to the other principal, thinking that he is introducing the deal. Freddie thus is fed into the pipeline. If the deal goes through without a hitch, Freddie is a hero. Should it go wrong, Freddie finds himself isolated at both ends. Caught sitting. He goes down.

It is on the basis that the two principals want to make the deal that Freddie enjoys their protection. He will never recognize his true position. He winds up thinking he has pulled off a fantastic deal, and he rakes off a bit of change for himself. It is not wise to underestimate him. The Freddies have the ability to do most of the right things and a capacity to suffer a bit of intrigue. Their courage goes without question. Not their intelligence.

Someone comes to mind—call him Dixon—who is so blasé you are not seen in the same company as this man. But he has the gall to go into the Department of Trade to get an export license for a particular piece of equipment, throw some heavy names around, tell the bureaucrats, "If you don't get off your arses real quick, you're in trouble," and gets his certificate. Then he ships the stuff out as batteries and comes back running, shouting, "Look, we can do it again, because I've still got the certificate." So you say, "Sure, Dixon. We'll do it again. I'll be in touch."

At that first lunch with Fox, I never asked a single question. I did not respond with total disinterest, because that would have been wrong too, but a coolness that said I had better things to do with my time. This made Fox tell me more, in hopes of piquing my curiosity and to make plain what seemed to be escaping me—that he was on to something big. Fox was a reasonably sensible guy. He was not a buccaneer of the wrong sort. But he was not really alive to the hard commercial facts of life of a genuine professional operation. He harbored great dreams, I suppose, of being a gun runner or an arms dealer. Even people on the fringes still believe this was a romantic life.

Fox was feeling important, because he was holding secrets. He must have had some sketchy outline of the operation. He could have been told to come to me, or his principals might have known he would approach me and have given him a mandate to go out and find the people for the job. He might have gone to other people as well, but, in the process, he was expected to reach me.

Fox and I talked around helicopters for a while—range and specifications. It became apparent he wanted to move a chopper over a great distance into the mission zone.

"It is better to arrange an indigenous helicopter," I said, "than to bring one in from the outside. Even if it means stealing it or paying someone to leave it somewhere."

Despite their speed and convenience, helicopters are seldom the best way to pull off a job. They are pretty vulnerable things, once they get moving. If you do not know the game, they are the most glamorous and easiest way to think of picking someone up. That is the way the man's mind was working. But when the doers get into planning an op, they usually run way off on a tangent from something as simple as a quick helicopter pickup. The idea is to outthink the basic thinkers. So when you get ready to start, you have a totally unorthodox operation. To an outsider, it may appear a hell of a long way around, but you get it done.

The longer Fox talked, the more he seemed to confirm that the job had something to do with the Eastern bloc. I am cautious these days. When I get involved, I want to control everything from planning and equipment to intelligence and field operations. Fox inferred that my flying services might be utilized on a mission that he was going to control. I would not have raided a sweets shop under Fox's command.

"This is really an interesting one, Gayle," he said hopefully. "I'll come back to you on it."

"You do that," I said.

If Fox was heading this one up, it was pure romance. He had offered someone services he could not provide. I would never be meeting any principals. The whole thing would die a natural death.

I was telephoned several times over the next two days at my U.K. office by a man with a South African accent. He refused to leave a name or state his business. He never found me in, and I did not return his call to telephone numbers he left with my secretary. On principle, I do not return calls to mysterious strangers. If it is legitimate business—or if they want me badly enough—they will find me. But I do not encourage these things. Where the Freddies get all excited and jump at anything that comes along of a secretive or clandestine nature, chase it and try to track it down, the reverse of that applies for the pros. You go around avoiding it. You try not to be seen to be involved in these things, though there are people who know. The genuine article will seek you out and find you. Like direct recruitment, though that works a little differently.

If you are looking for soldier boys, there are pubs and clubs full of them, where they spend every night drinking, talking about the last job and waiting for the next one. If you want to put something together, you go to these places and put out the word that you are looking for some special people. In Marseilles, walk up the hill from the old port to the Green Parrot, and you will find the top Frenchmen in the game. The owner is the girlfriend of Jean-Paul Leveques. Leveques is a mercenary officer—one of the best. Ex-Angola, he was offered the job of cleaning up Kolwezi before the Legion got the call. Leveques' boys are no pie-in-the-sky buccaneers. Most of them are ex-Legionnaires or ex-Indochina; the latter, a rallying cry in France. In Brussels, there is an organization called Freedom Fighters International—I am apparently on their rolls—which recruits for everything but Communist jobs. They can lay on straightforward gun boys or an entire command structure. In London, the Zambesi Club was a hangout for mercs for many years. Most of the action has moved to another place in White Hart Lane. The Red Lion in Camberley is another recruiting pub. A lot of the Belgian mercs hang around the Copper Kettle in Brussels. That is Schram's bailiwick. Schram was the maniac in Biafra, the kind of man who gives mercs a bad name. Schram was a close friend of Steiner. A deadly bastard. His last claim to fame was Angola. He went down there in a great blaze of glory. He was going to do another Congo, be another Mike Hoare. Most of his men ended up dead or in cages. He pissed off, left them behind.

I do not recruit in pubs. I go into the sergeants' mess at a special forces' barracks somewhere in London and talk with old friends. I call in for a drink at a few private officers' clubs. The men I want are not hard for me to find.

Toward the end of the week, Fox called and asked me to see him again. We met at Twiggy's, the coffee bar in the Great Eastern Hotel near Liverpool Street Station.

"We talked about a job over lunch the other day," he said. "We did."

"Would you be willing to meet with some people to talk about it further?"

"Who are they?"

"It's a firm of private detectives." Fox saw that I was very unimpressed. "These people are ex-Special Branch," he continued. "They do government work. Set up bugs in embassies and so forth. They want to talk to you about this particular operation."

"Quite frankly, I'm not interested. This doesn't sound quite like my game." The usual evasive stuff.

"It might be worthwhile, because the operation is definitely going to take place." Out of desperation, he began to tell me what it was about. "We're moving people," he said, looking at me for response. He continued. "A family. Out of Iran. These are important people. A lot of people want them."

"Including the Ayatollah, I presume."

"That's right." Fox was getting excited.

"Come on, Fox. This is the big time. This will cost a fortune."

"Oh, don't worry. We've got the finances. You'll have the whole thing. Backup. Intelligence. The equipment and the men you need. We'll have a helicopter."

The conversation bounced back and forth between fancy and reality. I was being a bit flippant, but Fox was dead serious. He was hanging in on a deal, and I was rejecting it, but the guy was beginning to convince me that there was something going on here. The project was at least feasible. Iran was hot. People must have been coming out every day. We arranged a meeting the following Monday in the City offices of his detective agency. I arrived five minutes early.

The sign on the door read "A.G. Consultants." I am not impressed with private detective agencies. That is real amateur stuff. Divorce cases and men in dirty macs. Fox's man was very ex-Special Branch; fat, suspicious, and tactless. His name was Jarrett. Ex-inspector, CID. I felt very uncomfortable in his company because of past history. He reinforced my discomfort right off the top.

"We know you touch on jobs like this, Rivers," he said in a loud voice. He was purposely rude. He was a bombastic policeman, a man used to power and used to using the system to his best advantage, having the assurance of protection from high places.

"Fox said you're interested in the job," he continued.

"I haven't said I was interested in anything. I simply agreed to come along to a meeting as a personal favor to Fox."

"This is big-time stuff, Rivers, and I'm not convinced you're the man for the job."

"I'm probably not. I can't comment, because I don't know what the operation is all about. A family. Does that mean women and children?"

"They're already out. Four adult males."

"That's not a family."

"Father, two sons, and a nephew."

Jarrett was the first man in the impression stakes. He started to imply that it was a government job, which was quite unlikely at this stage. Besides, if it were government, Jarrett had no business telling me this early on. He continued. Jarrett's scenario was to get these people to a chopper, fly them into Iraq, smuggle them into Baghdad, and send them out on a commercial flight with false papers. Was I interested in servicing part of the operation? Handling the flying?

"You're right," I said. "I'm not the man for the job."

"Who is?"

"James Bond."

Jarrett was annoyed to say the least when I started to pull his plan to pieces.

"There are already too many people who know about it," I told him, "including Fox." That remark did not endear me to Fox. "What are you going to do for manpower? Are you assuming these people won't need protecting? What is your backup if the chopper fails? Are you going to end up coming down in the desert or the mountains and walking people out? How are you preparing your four adult males to come out under these circumstances? Why don't you break the family up? Bring them out piecemeal?"

"No. We've got it worked out where we can get in and get out quickly. Fox has promised us SAS boys for this one. They don't need to break anything up. It will be a cinch."

"The Special Forces won't touch this exercise," I said. I was getting irritated at the amateur way the operation, and the meeting, were being handled. Yet it might have been a ploy to draw an alternative scenario out of me. Our discussion was quickly breaking down. If he was supposed to be getting nibbles from me, like a mouse up against a piece of cheese, he was not succeeding. I was rejecting everything he offered me.

"The range of the Bell 212 chopper you're talking about is just not going to get you that far," I said. "What have you done about refueling?"

Jarrett was talking about a hike of three hundred miles or more. The Bell 212 has a range of that amount under ideal conditions, but mountain flying was going to erode his range dramatically. You do not go flying into the mountains of Kurdistan on the limits of your fuel.

"Have you got a refueling facility in Kurdistan?" I asked Jarrett.

"We don't need that," he said.

"I'm telling you, you do," I said. "You're taking a team of at least six to bring these people out. What are you going to do? Leave the team in Iran? They'll have to come out in your chopper. Your plan stinks. The only reason you and Fox want to use helicopters is your people are afraid of walking. Get your mind off the helicopters, and you might come up with a workable plan. If they're prepared to walk in the first instance, you can work a helicopter in and use it sensibly. But if they're not prepared to walk initially, you're going to do it all wrong. And when it does go wrong, you're going to be unprepared for walking."

There was no reason to continue. Jarrett and I were each speaking a language the other did not understand. When we left, Fox was irate.

"Look, Gayle," he said, "we can get a lot of blokes. We can get anybody for this job."

"Go off and get yourself a pilot," I said. "And when you find him, make sure he's a bloody good one. He's going to have to make a chopper with a range of two-hundred-fifty miles under those conditions go at least four hundred miles. If he can do that, he's a better pilot than I am. Apart from that, your principal is the wrong man to be involved in this business. Are you sure of him?"

"Oh, yes. He's thick with everybody. He's attached to MI-6. He's the right man."

"Well, you go tell your secret agent that he better do things a lot differently."

# 2

I took a two-day break at home with my lady in Málaga before flying back to the Geneva office. The morning after my arrival a man called my room at the Ambassador Hotel and asked if he could see me. He spoke in English with a German or Austrian accent. He refused to discuss details on the telephone but inferred that it was a matter of a straightforward business deal. We agreed to meet that night in the hotel bar.

I arrived early with René, an associate in my Swiss operation. He and I have an arrangement for meetings like this: If I suggest he go pick up his girlfriend, he leaves. If I say nothing, he stays, and we crowd the guy out before he can compromise me by telling me about something I choose not to be a party to.

The man arrived and came straight to our table. "My name is Valner," he said, extending his hand.

He was tall and straight, over six feet, with fair hair and a light complexion. I guessed his age as mid-forties. He wore a well-tailored suit and expensive glasses. He could have passed for a Swiss businessman, but somehow I knew he was not Swiss. He looked fit, but his bearing was not ex-military. His manner was polite and formal.

"We have mutual friends in Germany, Mr. Rivers," he said. "They think you may be able to help me do some business in Iran."

"René," I said, "why don't you pick up Michelle and the car and meet me back here in an hour."

Valner waited until René was out of the room, then came straight to the point. "We have people in Teheran," he said. "We need them moved. Would you consider advising on an operation of that nature?"

Neither of us made reference to my previous contacts with Fox and Jarrett. We were both playing a game. We each waited for the other to mention them, then let it slide. Valner amplified on the job. It was a strictly private affair, privately funded, with no political overtones. His concept of what it all entailed was as realistic as Fox's had been fanciful. Would I be prepared to write an exercise on the operation?

"Are you asking to retain my company to advise on the logistics of such an operation?"

"That is correct."

"My fee for that will be 5,000 pounds sterling."

"Agreed."

"How many people must come out?"

"A family of four."

"All adult males?"

We looked at one another.

"All adult males." Valner briefed me on the basic facts. His organization would undertake to put the family in a "safe house" in Teheran, from which they must be collected and escorted out of the country. Getting involved in Iran was nothing new to me. This was a relatively simple exercise, and Valner gave me license to create my own scenario, with two provisos: The operation must begin by the first of June, and there was a ten-day limit on operations inside Iran itself—beyond that, he could not guarantee me security or intelligence.

"How soon can you have your report for me?"

"A week from tonight. Here in the bar."

I gave him banking instructions for the 2,500-pound down payment.

At noon the following day, I called my banker at the Place Bel-Air branch of Crédit Suisse in Geneva. "This is 300-580-60-C/300."

Fifteen seconds passed while he ran up my balance on his computer.

"Code?"

"BH 100."

The second code was to prevent anyone who had my account number from calling in for a balance.

"Equivalent pounds sterling, 2,500 deposited in Swiss francs this morning."

I took two days to push my other business aside, then turned full attention to the scenario. Assuming, I wrote, that the operation would work in the line of least resistance—that is to say, we would move these people toward Turkey, the closest safe border—I suggested that utilization of a helicopter in the first instance would be foolish. Valner had never mentioned choppers; I wrote this into the report in order to elicit some reaction regarding the earlier contacts in London.

I cast around for three days, then came up with an alternative idea of using two long-distance transport lorries, one to carry the merchandise and the other as a diversion. I proposed to get the lorries in Germany. My report was brief and nonspecific. It ran to three pages, plus an equipment list. It was the best I could give him, based on the scanty information Valner had provided me. Valner arrived five minutes early for our second meeting. I was waiting for him. He read the report several times before commenting.

"You remain opposed to the use of helicopters, do you?" I made no reply. Valner continued. "Jarrett briefed my people on your meeting. He thinks you're totally unsuited for the job. He thinks you're cocky. It was on the strength of what you told him that we decided to contact you."

"What is Jarrett's position?" I demanded.

"He's out."

"Peter Fox?"

"Out."

Valner had eliminated in one stroke the elements that made me question the seriousness of the whole affair. Jarrett was a hired hand, a supervisor, a man without authority. Valner was a confidant of the principals, if not a principal himself. Though he persisted with the story of working for private industry, his modus operandi told me he had done these things before. Valner was connected, somewhere, with intelligence.

"Your scenario is acceptable," he said at last. "The balance of your 2,500 pounds will be in the bank tomorrow. However, we would like for you to carry it a bit further. Circumstances have changed slightly since you did this."

"You've got what you paid for."

"Will you meet some of my people?" Valner asked.

"When?"

"In the next few days."

"Call me when you've got a firm date."

I spent the following morning in Adelboden, and when I returned to the hotel, I found a message to call Valner at a local number. We arranged to meet three days later in Munich. An air ticket, he informed me, was already waiting with the hotel concierge.

Valner met me at the Munich airport with a black Mercedes and a silent chauffeur. We rode out to a distant suburb. At an uncluttered office, a secretary gave us two air tickets to

Zurich and an apology from her employer. We returned to the airport. By early evening, we were at the Zurich Hilton. Two men awaited us in the dining room. The four of us proceeded to a hotel suite and, without further preliminaries, started talking about the mission.

There were no names or pack drill on any of us. The other three knew me and knew each other. Of the two newcomers, one was most certainly Israeli of Central European extraction. He had the suntan, the accent, the white short-sleeved shirt with wide lapels, the abrupt confidence of an Israeli operative. The other man was American or Canadian; intense, almost worried-looking.

The meeting opened awkwardly. We sparred for forty-five minutes. We were playing a delicately balanced game. They had to tell me they knew enough to have confidence in me, without saying they knew so much that it would frighten me off. It was imperative for me to know how serious and how qualified my principals were, and from what level this operation was being mounted. Regardless of Valner's protestations, I had to assure myself that Jarrett and Peter Fox were out of the deal; if these people were of that caliber, I wanted no part of it.

The American began to talk a bit too much about my personal history—Vietnam, South Africa, the Mirage deal in Egypt. I grew edgy. Valner spotted this and cut the American short. I noted that no one was in charge here. Valner was at least of equal rank with the other two, which was important, because, as my contact, I wanted to know that he was more than an errand boy.

I satisfied myself that all three were professionals, but we were still dealing in hypotheses, because no one had reached a final decision about the other yet. They were as good as I was at playing the game, and the meeting reached the point where it was in danger of breaking down.

We shifted gears and started talking about the conditions one could expect to encounter in Iran. The Israeli mentioned things he had done there, in the desert. This boosted my confidence in the man enormously. He would have been clandestine, and the Israelis do not pick second-rate men for that. I knew the Shah had been close to the Israelis, but this was my first encounter with an Israeli network inside Iran, admittedly a presumed one on my part. The CIA was thick on the ground there, but the Israelis must have overlapped in case politics there or elsewhere threatened their exchange of information with U.S. intelligence.

We talked for two hours, not even stopping for a meal that was brought to the room. The Israeli and I picked at our food, while the American devoured half a chicken. The meeting dragged on; all four of us were trying to hold back as much as possible but still go forward just enough so that we could finally make a contract. Contracts for mercenary work are unwritten—verbal agreements—but they are surprisingly specific; each party expects the other to honor the terms and conditions. Before I went out to gather a team, I had to make sure that these people had the backup to support me in the combat zone. The best way for me to learn this was to test their intelligence feedback. If they knew what was happening in Teheran at the moment, they were strong. But they could afford to give me very little of substance on their intelligence network without compromising themselves. We reached an impasse.

"At least," I said in exasperation, "you can tell me about the target family."

"The head of the family . . ." the Israeli started.

"Name?" I asked.

"No names," he snapped. He continued, "The head of the family is a businessman. Immensely rich. Very close to the Shah. A longtime friend of the U.S."

In the Middle East, it is hard to stay neutral. You gamble. One side or the other. He had a long run on the winning side. Now it was my job to retire him.

"We feel quite certain," said the American, "that you might recruit people onto a team who are so sensitive that their government—the British, for argument's sake—would know about their going."

"Men do not disappear from their regiment without someone knowing what they are up to," said the Israeli.

"We've been talking in certain circles, Gayle," Valner said, "about the people you're likely to use, and I can assure you there will be no objection to the type of team you would bring together."

"How can I be sure of that?" I asked.

"Need I remind you of other teams you've put together with Americans and Brits on them that were tacitly approved?" the American asked. "All you can do is take my word for it.

You have a way of working that does not seem to embarrass people."

The men I planned to take out of active-duty units would never know any of this. They simply would not be stopped. The merc who hired on for the action got to see a very small corner of the whole picture. I would go along to the barracks and talk to him about the job. Afterward, he would not get the word: "Don't have anything to do with it. That's a bad one." The reason he heard nothing was that someone had talked to someone else, and a decision had been made to sanction the mission. If the decision had been negative, no order would have come down from above: "Take this one, and you're in big trouble." It would have been a quiet word in the mess or the pub from a major in his unit or his regimental sergeant major. Intrigue at this level cast a wide net. If a man did not hear that he was to stay away from a job, he knew he had silent approval.

Even while our conversation was going on, I was working out my plan of action for the mission; its final form would have to wait for intelligence briefings when I knew where the dangers lay. The three men liked the idea of the long-distance lorries, so I led them to believe I intended to do the entire operation that way.

"The drop point will have to be in Western Europe," I said. "Borders mean nothing on missions like this. If the Turks pick us up, unless they want a horde of terrorists swooping down on them, they'll send us straight back into Iran."

I did not add that there was no way that I would close this operation inside Israel. If this were a Mossad job, they might eliminate us just to wipe the traces clean.

"Western Europe," I repeated. "It's your choice where, but I must point out that none of us are safe until we've reached the end of the line. Till you have the people where they are going."

The three looked at one another. A moment passed.

"Germany," said the Israeli. "Frankfurt. We'll instruct you further."

"I need an operational briefing," I said. "How soon can I get one?"

"Within the next few days."

I was already getting input on the team I would gather, weaponry, logistics. I needed briefing by their principal's intelligence-gathering organization, but already my mind was running off at tangents. I needed every bit of information they could give me. You do not plan a mission without knowing what all the possibilities are.

And that is when you start using your head.

They would furnish me with two or three safe houses in Iran. A choice of routes and border-crossing points where officials were sympathetic or susceptible to bribery. Clearance into all the countries along our route. When I had all that information, I would start working away from it.

Unbeknownst to the principals, when I created my scenario for the mission I would build in a secret eleventh-hour factor, which would allow me to change the plan anywhere along the line. I would agree to the operation ending by our turning the family over to them, but when the time came, I would put us in our own safe drop spot and call them to come pick the family up.

I do this because I trust no one.

The American started offering me facilities from their end—two trucks from a company in Germany, drivers, logistical support on the journey. I heard them out in silence.

"No," I said, when he had finished, "we'll come to our own arrangements and our own deadlines and keep you informed. I think it's time, gentlemen, that we stopped talking about a mission and started talking about a deal."

I had estimated the job before I came to the meeting, but the principals were not to be privy to my costing procedures. I wanted a team of six men besides myself. The six would each draw 400 pounds a day, plus a 25,000-pound bonus at the end of the mission. I calculated on a maximum of fourteen days for the job from the time we left London until delivery in Germany. The men drew their bonus whether they lived or died; that was insurance against someone running out in a tight moment or getting sidetracked to blow a bank. A fourteen-day life insurance policy for 60,000 pounds for each man would cost 3,500 pounds each from a Lloyd's underwriter who specialized in this sort of thing. A merc's life is not a negligible commodity. If a man went down, he knew that his family would have 25,000 pounds cash in hand to tide them over until the insurance claim was settled.

I estimated the trucks would cost me 2,000 pounds each for three weeks' rental—they would be sent a week in advance of our party. Six thousand pounds for my expenses flying about, putting the deal together. Forty thousand pounds for arms and a special piece of equipment I was considering. A 70,000-pound fee for my company.

"My company will take the job for a contract price of 326,000 pounds. Plus a half-million-dollar float in escrow to which I have access before the operation begins. If I use the float outside the operational perimeter, I file expense documents, and the bank pays out against them. If I use it on demand within the operation for a bribe or any other justifiable reason, there is no record. Understand that the budget I'm giving you is the absolute minimum. If the operation expands in any way whatsoever outside my responsibility, it could double. If that happens, you'll be expected to cover with ready cash."

A long silence followed.

"My price is firm," I said.

The people had access to far greater sums than we were talking about. I did not intend to haggle price, then worry about the money running out halfway through the mission.

"You buy us now," I said, "the financial side is taken care of in a proper fashion, and we can get on to the military side."

"Let's see how that 326,000 pounds breaks down..." Valner began.

"It doesn't for you," I said, cutting him short. "This much you can know. I'm taking six men in addition to myself. Each man receives a 25,000-pound bonus at mission end. I tell you this much because you'll have to deposit 25,000 pounds in six individual escrow accounts before anyone moves."

"Twenty-five thousand pounds is a very hefty bonus," the American muttered.

"Specialists command top wages. I'm going after the very best. If I wanted the thickos you people sent to Angola," I said, looking hard at the American, "I could get them for a thousand quid a month. When the mission was over, we'd pay a million dollars in ransom... for the ones who lived."

Paymasters are the richest people in the game. Typically, they are on a deal whereby they keep the difference between the real costs of an operation and what a principal is willing to pay. I have known them to make a million dollars on a two-million-dollar deal. I always offer a tight budget but never move without a substantial float. There are factors in every operation that can never be calculated. If you're not protected financially, and a deal goes sour, people write you off very quickly. You find yourself stranded, forgotten in some funny place. This lot knew there was no negotiating on my price, but it was worth trying on for size.

"Let's see," said the American, "you want half down..."

"And half when I find you? No thanks. Remember, you people came to me."

A lot of guys do a one-off, abuse the budget, and say to themselves, "That was great." Then they wait a long time for the next job to come along. I have a reputation for not taking advantage of principal or paymaster. My services come high, but my price is fair and justifiable.

I have a company to run. If I was going to spend the next month or six weeks doing this job, I was going to be paid for it. The 70,000 pounds would be far from pure profit for my company. When you run an operation like this, you are responsible for the men until they are home. I might have to pay for repairs to a Marseilles brothel, bail someone out of jail, cover medical expenses if one of us got hurt. Taking care of your men is the first order in this business. While I was on this job, I would be earning nothing elsewhere. And my company had overhead just like any other business—salaries, telex and telephone bills, rent. "Half later" is something you try on for size, but no one takes it very seriously.

"You drive a hard bargain, Mr. Rivers," the Israeli said.

"I have responsibilities. I have men to look after. I have to guarantee that the mission will be a success. My company's reputation is on the line. You may have been expecting a cowboy, but we do not do business like that."

The three looked at one another.

"We've got a deal," said the Israeli.

They rose and forced a smile. I shook their hands.

"Money down, money advanced, money guaranteed," I said. "I want 6,000 pounds now. Deposited to my account before I leave the room. Within five days, 170,000 pounds in an expense account to which my Third Party and I will have full access."

"What is your Third Party?"

"An associate of mine who has power of attorney over my signature. Let's call him my agent, in whom I have vested full authority to act in my behalf. As soon as I have assembled my team, I want six times 25,000 pounds deposited to individual escrow accounts with guarantees that the money will be released on instructions from my office. I'll give these

instructions on our return. In the event of my death, or
detention, my Third Party will do so. My men will know that
their money is safe even if we are all killed. The half-million-
dollar expense float will be held in another account, to which
my Third Party and I will have full access. If Valner is to be
my liaison with you, I want him to oversee the opening of all
accounts and to get the banking instructions so that you can
know exactly what is happening with your money."

There were no objections. We had no contract, but the
principals were now locked into the banks with me for one
and a quarter million dollars. The American got on the
telephone. Half an hour later, I confirmed with my banker
that the 6,000 pounds was on deposit in my account.

"Gentlemen," I said, "I must go to work. There are two
more small points. To avoid conflict and confusion, I want
only one liaison with you."

"That will be me," said Valner.

"In order to save time, I would like to hold all future
meetings in Geneva."

We shook hands again.

"Good luck," said the Israeli.

"We're counting on you, Rivers," said the American.

I caught the train to Geneva to give myself time to think.

# 3

I was more than pleased with one aspect of our agreement.
By knowing from the outset what my men were going to cost
me, I did not have to go to them and negotiate a price. I had
only to tell them what they would earn. Any good man would
jump at this deal.

A mercenary's salary demands are usually directly proportionate to his ability as a soldier. I could have gotten a
regiment of second-rate guys for the four hundred quid per
diem alone. The poor blokes in Angola were getting slaughtered
for four hundred a *week*. They were not mercenaries; one day
they were hospital orderlies or mechanics; the next, they
were playing soldier. In the Tripoli Hilton assignment, the
bonuses were only $10,000, and those guys did not even get
out of Italy before they were arrested by the carabinieri.

A good mercenary's salary demands are more often directly

proportionate to his debts. And the upper-echelon boys talk big money. The guys I had in mind used their service checks to pay their club bills. Four hundred a day meant nothing to them. They might spend that in a brothel in Hamburg on the way back. The 25,000 would be their operating capital for the rest of the year. That was one reason these blokes came to work for me. Once we left on a mission, the money was forgotten. We would all be back on active duty, in a battle zone. But they could depart in the secure knowledge no one was going to cheat them out of their wages, that life would be pretty good when they got back.

I could have lived off these jobs alone, but I had a company with other business interests, so I looked on these assignments as business investments. I saw to it that there was a profit to take out of my company at the end of each year.

But the top mercs lived from one big job to the next. They trained all day long with their units or in keep-fit gyms and drank all night in their clubs and pubs. And they earned more than the average company director by doing one or two ops a year. One man I wanted was off in Greece, doing a bodyguarding job at the wedding of the daughter of a shipping tycoon. He was getting 2,000 pounds for three weeks' work. That would keep the bailiff from the door. Keep his name from being posted at his club.

It is a popular myth that all mercenaries get killed in the end. Not so. What they do is just like being in the army for a twenty- or thirty-year stretch, only they see a little bit more action. When they get on in years, they start thinking about a final score, to buy a pub in Cornwall or a boutique on the Côte d'Azur.

Take Howie Hill. Howie is my arms expert—ex-small-arms instructor, regimental sergeant major in the SAS. He is not quite fifty. He runs a small company which is a cover for dealing in sports firearms. Howie took leave from the regiment off and on for twenty years to do special ops. Now he is a happily retired man with a pleasant Dutch wife and a house on the cliffs overlooking Brighton beach. On his army pay, he would not be driving a BMW. His wife would not be driving a Mercedes Sports. Howie lives quietly on his soldier's pension, with everything around him owned and paid for. If I need some range work, I go to his range club. If I need a special sniping weapon put together, Howie does it for me.

But he spends most of his time fishing in the surf. Howie knew how to make the game pay off for him.

I know other guys who used to win or lose a thousand quid in a poker game and now work as security guards for Purolator. They spend their nights talking about old adventures.

I do not give a damn how they handle themselves or their money or their lives. I cannot get involved in that. All I want from a man is that he be in a certain condition and a certain frame of mind when I call on him.

The next day I took the train along Lake Geneva to my office in Valles. Valner called me before noon, and we met that evening in Crans. We had dinner at a restaurant, then worked through the night in my chalet on details—telephone and telex communications, bank account numbers, banking procedure. Valner gave me a contact number for himself in Munich. We worked out a fall-back liaison through a personal code. Early the next morning, we took the train together into Geneva and separated at the terminal. I spent two days in Geneva and Valles on business, then flew to England.

I was in my U.K. office when a long-distance call came through. It was Valner. "I must see you at once," he said. "Meet me in London tonight."

We met at the Dorchester Hotel.

"How soon can you schedule your bank introductions?" he asked.

"Why?"

"Because the operation has basically changed," he said.

"What do you mean?"

"The head of the family is no longer available to come out. The others are not in Teheran."

"Where the hell are they?"

"Outside Teheran. In a safe house. But they can't hold their position long."

"What does that mean, 'the head of the family is no longer available'?"

"I can't give you any details."

"You have to. We're not going into this deal blind."

"He was executed yesterday. The other three are fugitive. Can you and I go to Geneva at once and sort out the banks, so we can start the mission? I'm going to have to disappear soon to coordinate this thing. Can you speed the whole thing up?" Valner was trying to remain cool, but the urgency in his voice betrayed his anxiety.

"Let's stop right here. I want a full briefing right now. Before I go any further. From what you say, my scenario is no longer valid. If I'm going to write a new one, I have to do it from the latest intelligence available."

"Tomorrow," Valner promised. "The whole story."

We took off at once for Geneva. It was eleven o'clock before we got into my bank, where my banker was waiting for us. We sorted out everything in the bank within an hour; confirmations would come through the next morning. The bank knew how to contact me through my Third Party in Geneva. By one o'clock we were aboard a flight to Munich.

We spent the night in a small rest house in the heart of the city, then returned early the next morning to Munich airport, where we were met by the Israeli and the American. There was panic in the air. Things were changing rapidly. Something obviously had gone wrong.

We drove in total silence to a vast estate in the Munich suburbs. We passed a guarded gate and climbed a gravel drive through an avenue of trees that ended at the base of a gentle hill crowned by a nineteenth-century Gothic mansion of fifty rooms or more. We parked amidst a dozen Mercedes and BMW's, most bearing diplomatic plates, and walked the last hundred yards to the house. The place was buzzing with activity; middle-aged Germans in conservative suits talked earnestly with young Arabs in Levi's and jerseys; olive-skinned men from the Mediterranean, whose carriage bore the invisible mark of officialdom, brought bulging diplomatic pounces from the parking lot; two Italian women conversed in English with a Japanese couple.

There was a strange atmosphere about; every group seemed to make a conscious effort to ignore the others. This was headquarters for a vast operation whose activities I could not pinpoint. This place had not popped up like a mushroom day before yesterday. It had its own routines; its standard operating procedures. It had that certain air of self-assurance that goes with confidence in one's position. But I had the uneasy feeling that there were disparate—even conflicting—interests here; that this estate was a neutral ground where enemies were linked into some whole greater than its parts; that these enemies had arrived at a modus vivendi in which they simply failed to acknowledge the presence of one another.

Though there were people about everywhere inside, we moved through them as if we were all invisible. We walked straight into a large drawing room, closed the door, and went into a full briefing on the mission. Though I heard constant movement in the house for the several hours I was there, never did it touch us, and I was convinced it did not relate to our mission.

The people with me were in a hurry now. Maps of the Mediterranean and the Middle East were spread across an enormous marble table. All three men were nervous. They debriefed me, but there was nothing I could tell them. I had not got down yet to the nitty-gritty of pulling a team together. I had been in London for that purpose when Valner called.

"You people might as well stop quizzing me," I said, "and start telling things."

"The family you are going after is Jewish," said Valner. "The father was taken day before yesterday by the revolutionary militia. He was executed yesterday morning."

"Is there a pogrom on?"

"We're not sure. We think so. The Ayatollah is fanatically anti-Semitic. The father was very close to the Shah. One of the richest men in Iran. The charge against him was profiteering. He is survived by two sons and a nephew. They are your rabbits."

"Rabbits?"

"The operation is code-named Blue Rabbit."

"You wanted me to take Jews out of Iran and into Iraq?"

"That was one plan."

"A bloody stupid one."

"We never intended you to do it."

"That's why I make my own plans. Because people tell you one thing and expect you to do something else. So I'm going after rabbits, am I? Tell me about these rabbits."

"Two brothers, twenty-eight and twenty-two. Their cousin, twenty-one. They know you are coming."

"Why is it so important to get them out of Iran?"

"They're on two death lists. Revolutionary and PLO."

"What about the rest of the Jews in Iran?"

"We can't bring them all out."

"You've got a bloody rich humanitarian upstairs," I said, nodding toward the gilt and frescoed ceiling, "if these three are worth an operation this size. What's the rest of the story? What else should I know about them?"

"Nothing." It was the Israeli who replied.

"What happened to the father? How did he get caught? Has your network gone belly up?"

The largest unknown factor still lay outside our control; that was the current situation in Teheran. It was still drastically unstable there. The revolutionaries were already fighting among themselves, left against right, while everyone was looking for the Shah's men, Savak agents, and anyone else with the misfortune to find himself on a fugitive list.

"No. He was not with the other three. He was under house arrest in Teheran. The revolutionaries thought the boys were out of the country. The father was simply taken into custody and summarily executed. We have hard intelligence that the revolutionaries have now learned the rabbits are still in the country."

"How effective is your network in Iran?"

"It is not our network."

"I'll rephrase that. How effective is the network in Iran?"

"Bakhtiar has disappeared, hasn't he? And everyone in the country is looking for him. He'll turn up safe soon in Europe. There is an effective pipeline."

"Where are the rabbits?"

The Israeli pulled a map toward us. "Marshun," he said. "A small town near Qazvin, off the main highway to Rasht."

Qazvin was a large city a hundred kilometers north and west of Teheran. I studied the map carefully.

"They were on their way to Rasht, on the coast," I said, "and they didn't make it."

No one responded. The American handed me three photographs. The rabbits may have been in their twenties, but Valner had been right in calling them boys. Their poses, their clothes, the garden backgrounds exuded luxury, a soft life that would make them ill-equipped for what we were undertaking. I laid the photos aside.

"I won't be getting any help out of these kids. I'm of half a mind to walk out on you," I said. "You couldn't keep the old man from being arrested. What kind of security can you offer me in Iran?"

"The network is intact. Safe houses. Money. Communications. Weapons. Support."

"How do I know I can trust the people running it?"

"Can you trust Mirza?" the American said with a dry smile. "He's operations."

Mirza and I had done business together. He was a captain

in the Iranian navy and extremely well-connected. I trusted him with my life. I did not tell these people that.

"What do you propose?" I asked.

"We still like the idea of the trucks," the American said.

"To go where?"

"There are many good places. Iraq was not as bad an idea as you might think," Valner said. "There is still a Jewish network inside the country. If you can get them across the border, we can inject them into the network. Get them to Baghdad."

"Terrific," I said. "What are they going to do when they get to Baghdad? Open a stall in the bazaar? You want them out of Iraq, not in it. Are you going to take them to the airport in a limousine and put them on a plane to Europe? Turkey is another loss leader. If they are fugitive, that is where they're going to be looked for. Look at your maps. Between Teheran and Turkey you have the heaviest concentration of security forces in the country. If we use the lorries, they'll have to stay in hiding until we reach Frankfurt."

"That could take a week. You want them to stay in the back of a truck for a week?" snapped the American.

"Two weeks, maybe three if the lorry breaks down. Two weeks in a lorry is better than an hour in an Iranian prison. Your first job is to go back to your humanitarian and tell him that it's going to cost him a whole lot more money."

They thought I was getting greedy.

"I don't want a penny more for myself or for my men. But with these people fugitive, the price of everything else just went up. You're going to have to incorporate that half-million-dollar float into the budget and set up a second half-million-dollar float."

"How soon can you put it together?" asked Valner.

"I was planning on three weeks."

"You might as well make it three years. It won't make any difference to the rabbits. They'll be dead by then. Nobody can guarantee a safe house for three weeks. Can you put it together in two weeks?" Valner asked.

"Maybe. I don't start until I get confirmation of the funds on deposit," I replied.

The Israeli scribbled on a piece of paper. Pressed a buzzer. A man in a gardener's uniform entered. "Send this out at once," the Israeli told the gardener. "You're on," he said to me.

We worked over the maps for several hours. The American briefed me on the military status quo—dispersal of troops, their role in the revolution, conflict in the general command, relationship to the revolutionary militia. The Israeli led me block by block over a map of Teheran, pointing out road-blocks, our safe houses, police barracks, even cinemas and football stadiums where a sudden crowd could obstruct our passage. He briefed me on security for my men in Teheran through the Mirza organization. We arranged transportation to and from the safe houses.

"What about security for the two lorries on the trip down?" I asked.

"We've penetrated Iranian customs at the Turkish border. They'll go through without a hitch. All foreign vehicles in Iran pass from checkpoint to checkpoint only on countersigned manifests and travel permits. When the trucks get to Teheran, they have to lay up in an official truck park before they can proceed in any direction. We own the foreman there."

"I'm taking a six-man team," I said, "but I'm relying on them principally for guard duty and combat. The original premise was that the rabbits would be handed over to us. Now we have to go get them. I'm going to need a lot of support on the periphery. I don't want to divert one of the lorries off the highway to go up to Marshun to pick them up. We've got to get up there some other way."

"We'll arrange transportation," Valner promised. We batted problems back and forth all night long. At first light, a silent Mercedes swept me back to the airport. I caught a commuter flight to London.

I met Santa at a Greek café in Earl's Court. Santa was to be my liaison officer with the team. Santa is my code name for a man of many talents. Officially he is a government bureaucrat of a rank and title that would not attract the attention of an unmarried typist. Yet his name on a document has raised the eyebrows of more than one Cabinet secretary. Santa works for the Foreign and Home offices in an extra-official capacity as liaison between people like me and people within the government infrastructure. Santa knows the men in the SAS or SBS who are looking for ops. He hires them on, then uses the "old boy network" to secure their release from their units. He arranges weapons purchases that are otherwise "unavailable" or restricted. Then he walks the whole deal through Box 500.

Box 500—"the Box"—is a working committee that meets

daily to exchange information among all the intelligence organizations within Britain—MI-5, MI-6, the SAS, Special Branch, Scotland Yard. The Box is a power unto itself. Without its tacit approval, no one moves a step on a mission like ours. Should they choose to fall in on your side, you have access to the resources of a brilliant organization, bold and imaginative, as good as any in the world.

Santa and I share a long history. We have saved one another's lives. He works occasionally for my company. When we were developing a new night sight, I needed a quick-release scope mounting for Britain's SLR, or Self-Loading Rifle. Santa borrowed one for me. My company did a hasty drawing from it, and Santa had it back in the armory before it was missed. On the current job, Santa would advise me of the up-to-date availability of the men I wanted to use—where they were, what they were doing, which ones had broken legs in parachute drops in the months since I had seen them. He would talk to the men, then help me assemble the team. He would function as purchasing officer for equipment and weapons. Most important, he would protect our backs in Britain while we were gone. For this, he would receive a fee of 2,000 pounds.

I told Santa the whole story. As I outlined the plans I had been feverishly revising for several days, I saw Santa's eyes narrow into two slits.

"Something rotten here," he said.

An instinctive distrust I had harbored from the beginning of the whole affair began to surface. Your nose gets keen to these things every day you survive in this business.

"Take it from the top," Santa said.

Santa debriefed me for two hours. His job was to get everything that had been said or implied to me since the initial contact. Together, we analyzed the material to determine what was probably false or designed to set someone up.

"Is that all they told you about the family?" he asked.

"Just that they were on a death list, and they needed to be got out of the country."

"The level of interest in these three rabbits is far too high to suit me," he said. "Valner told you they would be safe in Germany? Then the German authorities must know about them. Governments do not approve the arrival of prospective refugees on someone's death list unless they have a very good reason. Repeat what Valner told you about pickup and delivery."

"After we fetch the boys from Marshun, we can't take them straight out of the country. We have to deliver them to a safe house in Teheran, to Mirza's organization. We have to guarantee them at least one day with the rabbits before we bring them out."

"What explanation did they give you?"

"None. They have to see the boys."

"And what are the possibilities you see?"

"The rabbits are on their death list as well. They need something from them, probably information. After they get that, they can be killed with impunity. They don't want to be seen doing it, so they hire an outside force to deliver the rabbits to them. Once they've done the boys, they can do us."

"How do you rate that?"

"Very low probability."

"Why?"

"If they just want delivery, they can do it a lot cheaper than us. Still the possibility has to be considered. And allowed for."

"The Israeli talked to you about false passports for the rabbits once they've reached Western Europe. Does he want us to arrange them?"

"He'll take care of that."

"Ordinary refugees don't hide under false identities. There may be a grudge against them at home, but once they've fled, they're usually left alone. Revolutionary states have more to do than engage in long-distance vendettas. The ones they go after are active enemies of the state. These rabbits have something very heavy to bargain with, just to get them out of Iran. If they can't surface under their own names in Europe, they have something equally heavy to hide. Who knows who they're threatening to embarrass. The Americans? The Israelis? The Germans? If your people give them false identities and then knock them off, they're never missed. Something tells me your rabbits are going to disappear off the face of the earth."

All this was highly imaginative projection, but it was what I paid Santa for. It had kept me alive in the past.

"Any advice?"

"Let's go to work on 'opposites,'" said Santa.

Creating "opposites" is standard procedure for Santa and me on any mission. We work out a plan of operation that will satisfy the principals. Then we construct a parallel plan to which we can divert at any time, a secret plan known only to our organization.

"I need two trucks," I said, "two big overland lorries, each with a secret compartment large enough to hold us all for two weeks."

The Iranian oil fields were being fed by overland freight from Western Europe. We would send the lorries, loaded with commercial goods, on the normal overland routes, where they would attract no attention; ours would be but two in convoys of fifty trucks that were commonplace on Iranian highways.

"Weapons?" asked Santa. "How much trouble are you anticipating?"

"The PLO want the rabbits dead as well as the Iranians."

"The PLO are thick on the ground, particularly in the south. They're virtually autonomous. They're killing Iranians with impunity. Those bastards are relentless. Expect nothing but trouble when they find out you've made off with their targets."

"The only place I anticipate a strong likelihood of problems is at the pickup."

You break an operation down into titles and subtitles, then you sub it and sub it again. The operation, in briefest description, was to pick up the rabbits in the field, bring them into a safe house in Teheran, then decide whether to take them out as a group or piecemeal and in which direction to move. The danger areas were the pickup, sitting in the safe house in Teheran, and the movement close to whatever border we chose to cross. Anywhere along that route, things can go wrong. But you anticipate it at those critical points. Next you determine what kind of protection you have. I decided we had none. This was not Vietnam, where you might be behind enemy lines, but you had field intelligence, relief from half a dozen units in your area, helicopter pickup in an emergency. Here we would be a cell inside Iran, up against everybody.

Santa and I met several times over the next three days, as he walked us through the Box. Santa showed me a top secret Box 500 report on the current situation in Iran. It was alarming. Everything I read suggested a really filthy way of operating on the part of "friends" as well as enemies. The

Mirza network was giving up its own people to claim others back from the police.

Santa was in no way cavalier about giving me classified information. He knew I would not compromise the British government. I may have even been seen as an unknowing contractor to officialdom who could be discarded if necessary. This whole thing might have been sanctioned or even originated by the British government. But this sort of operation is not talked about openly even at Box 500 levels. It is whispered privately in one-to-one conversations until a mutual silent consensus is reached. Was Santa feeding Box 500 as much about me as he was giving me from there? He had one priority, and that was loyalty to the British government. But we were also very close friends.

Santa would do nothing against the wishes of the British government. Whatever was being fed to me was filtered to such an extent that, if he decided something might compromise the British, he would clear it down first. This is an area that calls for the greatest diplomatic skills. Santa would not actually expose my operation. But conversations would take place behind the scenes at the Box that allowed him to get a level of cooperation or a turndown. When I enlisted Santa for the operation, everybody benefited. I would be warned if I was being set up. I would be waved off if the British government did not want a particular thing to happen. It was a sort of mutual-protection society that operated when everyone was in the know. He offered to put me in touch with a second network in Teheran. I declined. I wanted to keep the operation as secret as possible.

Santa had a lot of desert experience and was a good sounding board for the plan. I wanted to formulate everything with him before I met the men. With them there might be discussion on details, but there would be no debate on how the operation was to be carried out.

"How are you going into Teheran?" he asked.

"As civilians," I said. "The lorries will carry our gear. We may go in as a camera crew."

"Cameras are very unpopular in Iran right now," Santa said. "I'll get you some papers. UN. Red Cross. Something like that. Who do you want on the team?"

"Davis . . ."

"Jack?"

"Yes. Danny Swann. Dean Gill. Frew Freeman . . ."

"Who's he?"

"He's a protégé of Gill's in the SBS. The Verbruggens."

"The twins? You'll want grenades, then. They're grenade-happy."

"You think you could get us some of those stun grenades?" Santa had supplied the grenades used by the Germans in the raid on the hijacked airliner at Mogadishu Airport that deafened, blinded, and stunned the terrorists.

"Out of the question."

"What's the status on these guys?" I asked.

"The Verbruggen twins I don't know. You'll have to contact them. Davis, Swann, and Gill are all available, so far as I know. Nobody hurt."

Santa and I reached all six by telephone in one afternoon. I sent two air tickets to the Verbruggens in Antwerp. The others came into London by train. We called a conference in the Great Portland Street surgery of an SAS reservist doctor who would patch us up if anyone got hit. Before the meeting, I went around to call on each man as he arrived in town.

I met the two Verbruggens at Victoria Station. They were not identical twins, though their personalities sometimes seemed as alike as peas in a pod, and they were inseparable on a job. They had served together in the Belgian paras; they were ex-Angola, ex-Congo. Despite their Flemish name, they were Walloons. Their English was perfect, though spoken with a heavy French accent, and they bantered among themselves constantly in French. Yves was now working as an intelligence officer for the Légion Mobile under Major Pinte. Marcel was running a bar somewhere. Pinte and the Verbruggens had helped me move some goods through Belgium once on an anti-terrorist operation, and I knew them both to be excellent men.

As usual, I was surprised to see how young they looked, The twins were now approaching forty. Yves was tall and thin, with thick-rimmed glasses and stringy hair, which always looked wet, falling over his ears. Marcel was shorter and stockier, with a face like a Siamese cat. Both were quiet in the civilian world, but in a service environment they loved laughing and joking and a good rumble once in a while. Both were romancers. Yves was perhaps the more stable of the two, firmly entrenched in a solid marriage. Marcel was a happy-go-lucky bachelor.

A year earlier, we had been confronted in a Southwark pub by a horde of drunken Irish merchant seamen. When their catcalls had appeared to fall on deaf ears, Marcel rose slowly to his feet and walked over to the ringleader.

"*Allo, chérie,*" he said. "Give me a big kiss," he said, leaning forward; at the same time he flicked the Irishman's nose with an enormous index finger that resounded with a splat. All hell erupted. The Irishmen never knew they had tangled with two of Mike Hoare's "Forty Commando." Now Yves and Marcel rushed forward to embrace me. Yves still carried a scar over his right eye from that encounter.

"*Allo,* Gayle! How are you?"

"Great."

"You got something good for us?"

"Terrific. Big money."

"That means big adventure, if I know you."

"I do my best."

I left them in a private house, then sped by taxi to a rendezvous with Santa, Jack Davis, and Danny Swann.

"Rivers," Davis greeted me with a curt nod.

"Hello, Davis," I said.

We shook hands formally, with a coolness that bordered on reluctance. Davis and I had worked together before, and I had great respect for the man as a soldier. But our personalities simply did not mesh, so we kept our relations at the professional level.

Davis was a reserve officer in the SAS, a captain promoted up through the ranks. He was a handsome, dapper man. He looked a bit like Errol Flynn, he once told me in a pub: more than one woman agreed with that judgment. He showed less self-confidence in command environments, where his working-class background was an embarrassment. Though now in his late forties, he still worked as a physical-training instructor, which gave an idea of his conditioning.

"What's up?" he asked.

"You'll be getting sand in your boots," I promised.

Davis smiled. He had done ten years seconded to the Dhofari regulars of the Sultan of Oman, battling rebels, North Yemenites, and Soviet advisers. Davis was a superb desert fighter and fluent in Arabic.

He was less than magnificent on the domestic front. His private life was in a shambles; for that reason, I never trusted Davis completely until we were in a combat zone. His life was a madcap dash between a wife and family in Portsmouth, a wife and family at Henley-on-Thames, the occasional skirt and other men's wives, his clubs, the pubs, and the barracks.

Danny Swann was another matter. We greeted each other with a warm clasp.

"How are Dorothy and the children?" I asked.

"Fine," he answered. "The little one's turning into a fine helmsman."

Swann's only hobby was sailing. He had crewed some of the fastest yachts in the country. His army career began as a boy soldier at age fourteen. He had done a couple of stints as a para and was now a sergeant in the SAS. He spent several years in the Emirates and was an expert driver and navigator in the desert. A veteran of Northern Ireland, he was familiar with urban warfare, experience I could call on in Teheran. Medium height, medium build whose fitness was hidden by his clothes, with mousy brown hair and undistinguished features, he looked and talked more like a bank clerk than the superb operative he was. Good father and faithful husband, most content in his Hereford cottage, professional soldier with no ambitions to be anything else, he was a man with razor-sharp battlefield judgment because he had confidence in his own ability. Swann was stable, steady, and very tough.

"Let's make this a quick one, Gayle," he said. "I want to be back for the Fastnet race in August."

I found Gill and Freeman in the lobby of the Hyde Park Hotel. A short, stocky man with a body as trim and muscular as a wrestler, Gill greeted me with a handshake that cut the flow of blood to my fingers.

"Good to see you, Rivers," he said, digging spring-steel fingers into my shoulder in a gesture of friendship.

Dean Gill was the most experienced man on the team. Like Swann, he had enlisted as a boy soldier and by now had over thirty years' active duty as a Royal Navy Commando. He was at Poole now, training the boys of the SBS (Special Boat Section), the elite from the hallowed ranks of the Commandos. The SBS may be the best beach-landing infiltration force in the world, and they learned unarmed combat and underwater demolition from Gill. He was a tough, hard cookie. He could swim tremendous distances underwater or on the surface. He could fight better in water than the average commando on land. He was adept with small weaponry, but, incredibly enough, he was a lousy shot. He was a good soldier and a hell of a nice guy. He was happily married, with four kids and a semidetached house in Poole. He did few mercenary jobs, but he was retiring from active duty in a year, so I knew he would be looking for a big score. He was on overseas call to the regiment twenty-four hours a day, so his wife was not surprised when he left abruptly to meet me in London. She knew nothing about a private venture. I would have been an unpopular man with the families, had they known I was taking away their men to do these dirty jobs.

"Got a good one for us, Rivers?" Frew Freeman asked. "I could do with a bit of action. And cash."

His tone was cocky, almost defiant. It was obviously designed to impress the stranger he had brought along with him, a fresh-faced corporal from his unit.

Bringing the stranger was a serious breach of professional ethics. I had never worked with Freeman before. Had I not known his record, I would have thrown them both out on the spot. Freeman's career was almost a carbon copy of Gill's twenty years earlier—sergeant in the SBS, Military Medal, Distinguished Service Med . As a young soldier, Freeman had worked under a close friend of mine—Howie Hill, now retired—leading dog teams in search of guerrillas. The Alsatians pulled the guerrillas apart, and they shot what was left. These were hard men who had been at the sharp end. Howie Hill had been in the SBS what Gill was today, the "old man" of the unit. Gill had called Howie "Dad." Now Freeman called Gill "Dad." Both older men gave Freeman the highest marks as a soldier. Freeman had also been on exchange with the Royal Marine Commandos in Iran and spoke Farsi, which made him the only man on the team with the native language.

With all that, I found the man bombastic, a little bit of a loudmouth. The sort of chap who loved the pubs, whether to down his pint in one go, or crack two heads together.

"Who is he?" I asked, nodding to the stranger.

"His name is Jackson. From my unit," Freeman said. "Been in Teheran. Knows the system forwards and backwards."

"The unit's closed," I said to Jackson.

"Jackson's spent two years with the Royal Marines down there. In the Embassy. He knows the way the Iranians work. He knows the whole administrative setup."

"Good. The next time I need an administrator in Teheran, I'll call on him."

"Hey, Jackson is my man. I told him he was in on this. If he's out, I'm out."

Gill exploded. "You can bloody well fuck off with your boyfriend, sonny," he said.

Freeman cooled immediately. Jackson left without argument.

"This is not Parliament," I told Freeman calmly. "I'm the commanding officer, and I give the orders. If you don't like me or the pay or the job, go on back to Poole. If you're on, take orders and mind your own business."

There was no animosity in my voice, nor in Freeman's when he replied, "I'm on."

Late that night, we slipped in the back door at Great Portland Street in ones and twos. Introductions were made, hands shaken all around. I gave the men a skeleton briefing. I wanted a mission start date of approximately two weeks. Each man told us what equipment he had and what he needed for his own personal kit. Most had their own webbing, a favorite knife or bayonet, desert boots—no one was going into the desert with new boots. All the equipment would be gathered and sent ahead of us with the trucks into Iran. We might be civilians when we entered the country, but if fighting started, we would look like soldiers. Not uniforms and berets, that sort of thing. But by God, people would know us for what we were.

Davis asked for a pair of heavy cotton twill trousers for desert walking. Freeman wanted a lightweight desert backpack.

"Who's your radioman?" Swann asked.

"You are."

"How complicated?"

"A couple of lightweight transmitters."

"There's a French one I'm particularly fond of."

"Just give Santa the designation," I said to Swann, then turned back to the group. "Your principal weapon will be the new German MP-5." I brought out a stubby nine-millimeter submachine gun that could fit into an oversized briefcase. "Has everyone used them?"

The Marine guys had not, but the SAS boys had.

"In addition, Davis and I will be carrying two silenced MP-5's."

"I'd prefer a Sterling," Davis said. "It is quieter."

I did not like the Sterling, because it was a cumbersome weapon. The magazine jutting out from the side snagged easily in close confines. The firing mechanism clogged if it was dropped in dirt or mud. But Davis knew what he was letting himself in for, and he knew why he wanted it. You cannot tell a man of his experience what weapon to use.

"You'll get your Sterling," said Santa.

The idea was to keep weaponry to the minimum; we were not gearing up for some massive operation. If combat came, it would be short and heavy. Each man would carry "first line" ammunition—ninety rounds. Gill and I chose Sig nine-millimeter automatics for sidearms. The others opted for Belgian-made Browning .38's.

I gave the men a short reading on the rabbits and outlined the operation.

"We'll have to go out from Teheran and bring the rabbits back in. From there we play it by ear. If everything has gone according to plan, we'll all go out in one lorry to the north through Turkey to West Germany. The other lorry goes south to Dubai as a diversion. That is our alternative escape route."

"Opposites" were quickly taking shape in my mind.

"If we get back to Teheran and things aren't what they're supposed to be . . . If it's a setup, or we've been double-crossed, or things are just generally untidy, we go south, to the coast, where we can effect a beach pickup."

"You expect things to go wrong?" asked Davis.

"I expect every operation to go wrong," I said. "That's why I'll have enough alternatives to make it go right in the end."

"Are we going all the way to Iran in the back of a lorry?" asked Freeman.

"No. We fly in. Santa will secure two long-distance lorries in Germany, normal overland freight haulers. One will be loaded with oil field supplies, thirty-six-inch rubber tubing. It will be rolled in great coils and packed so that there will be a gap at the front of the trailer large enough to hold all of us. We'll be able to squeeze through, but no nosy customs official will bother with a passageway through the coils. We'll have a second lorry with a secret compartment behind a false front bulkhead carrying any ordinary palletized load we can pick up in Germany. The rubber tubing will be consigned to Dubai. The pallets will be swapped off in Teheran for a return load. Both these will be legitimate overland runs, with real documentation and authentic recipients for the goods. We'll have a legitimate reason for sending a lorry in either direction from Teheran. The lorries will travel a day apart. The one with the secret compartment will carry our gear and come first. We'll rendezvous with it outside Teheran on the Qazvin road and get our gear. Then it will continue on into Teheran and into the bonded truck park. The next day we'll pick up the rabbits and rendezvous with the second lorry. We'll come into Teheran in the second lorry, which we've arranged to have parked alongside the first when it arrives at the truck park. From there, we take the rabbits to a safe house for debriefing. After that, we'll look at the ramifications of the whole thing. If we come back to Europe overland, we might have to spend a week, possibly two, in the lorry, in the event of breakdown or delay. If we go south, we're going away from Europe, but it'll be a far shorter trip. Southern Iran is a desolate place. We can move fast down there. We'll be met on the coast."

The men warmed to the briefing. On paper, it looked like a pushover. But Gill was too experienced to accept these big figures without comment.

"This is not a 25,000-pound job, Rivers," he said. "This is a 5,000-quid one. Why the big money?"

"Because I expect it to be a tough one."

"Do you know something we don't?"

"No. Is everybody in?"

They all nodded.

"Each of you liaise separately with Santa tonight or tomorrow," I continued. "Get to him all the information he needs about your bank accounts and life insurance policy beneficiaries. You are all on call from this moment. Go back home and start gearing up for the job. I'll call you when it's time to go. Anticipate two weeks from this date."

We broke up.

"Freeman," I called out, "stay behind, please."

Freeman briefed me as best he could on street conditions in Teheran, though he knew the city in peacetime and we were going into a battle zone.

"I know your truck park," he said. "There's an army barracks less than ten minutes away. I don't like the idea of sitting around that place. Or a safe house. My experience is that safe houses are bloody unsafe places to hang about."

I had to guarantee the principals up to twenty-four hours with the rabbits before we pushed off. This was a long time in one spot for any network to maintain. We would have to set up guard at the safe house, security measures at the trailer park, protection at the rendezvous point, escape routes from every one of these places. All this would be done on the spot.

You could not make provisions for those things in a Great Portland Street surgery.

When Freeman left, Santa and I put our heads together for a long session.

"What have you done about lorries?" I asked.

"People in Germany are preparing a paper on the movement of overland lorries in Iran. They're gathering copies of the necessary border documents. Bills of lading and freight manifests. And photos of your trailer park. It may all be in your Geneva office right now. How do you plan to use the team when you start back?"

"Assuming the lorry comes north... I'm going to send the four Brits with the rabbits in the back of the lorry. The Verbruggens and I will fly out to Frankfurt. We'll pick up another lorry. We'll be in radio communication with them. We'll travel south on their route, ready to intercept them. If there's any trouble, they're going to need help outside the lorry. Even if it's only mechanical trouble. I don't want them sitting beside the road for a week or two. We'll come back to Frankfurt in convoy."

I talked all that night and most of the next day with Santa, then left him for Germany to arrange lorries and drivers. It was his job to lay on the weapons, liaise with the men and get their gear to them, and see that they got fit and sighted in. The beauty of working with professionals was that we did not need a training ground. They sharpened up in their own units. Santa promised to lay on a phony training exercise and bring the SAS and SBS together to train at Hereford. Santa was to call his man at Heckler and Koch in Germany to get us the MP-5's and to prepare the silenced weapons. Grenades and plastique he was securing in Britain, the radios in France, Bengal "lights"—flares—in Germany.

As civilians, we would attract minimal interest. Western technicians—electronics engineers, oil-field workers, Bell helicopter crews—were moving all over the country even in the midst of revolution. The lorries had never stopped rolling in from Europe. We would keep a low profile, moving about as little as possible. Once in the safe house, we would simply maintain our position until it was time to move out. But the political climate was such that we could get caught up in a turmoil not of our own making. Our sweetest dream was not to fire a shot. Everyone understood that if we had to use violence to get the rabbits out, that was the way it was. If the revolutionaries got wind of our scheme, or if the lorries were subject to an intensive search, we had a shooting war on our hands.

# 4

"Opposites" began to play their role. I decided Mirza must provide us with a standby helicopter to snatch us away if something untoward arose. And if we had to go out by chopper, the nearest place of refuge was to the north and west. In Kurdistan. If Mirza's helicopter could drop us anywhere near the extremities of Kurdish-controlled territory, Big Kevin's men could pick us up and take us into Kurdistan for protection.

Big Kevin and I had been friends for years. Only recently I supplied him with weaponry for the Kurd rebels. Big Kevin was an English ex-para, a longtime merc and arms dealer. After selling arms to the rebels for years, he became the Kurd purchasing agent in Europe, then a military adviser. Contrary to the instincts of all true mercs, Big Kevin had "turned inward," the merc expression for a man who adopted a cause. Big Kevin was fifty years old now. He had been in Kurdistan a dozen years and was as true a patriot as any man in the country.

Before leaving London, I talked with Big Kevin's girlfriend at the embassy where she worked as a secretary. I left with her a thousand pounds to buy Big Kevin a round-trip air ticket from Istanbul to Europe. I instructed her to have Big Kevin leave word with my Swiss number of his ETA in Europe.

I called Valner, and in less than a day he came back with Mirza's promise of a chopper. Our northern route, at least, was protected. It was our most vulnerable, because it moved through a highly populated area, with military garrisons at every crossroads and concentrations of PLO troops around Rasht and the Caspian Sea. I was still extemporizing on the southern escape route, but it was beginning to come together.

I called Valner back and told him to meet me at ten the following morning at the Ambassador Hotel in Geneva. He must have been on tap for the operation, because he complied without comment. I was in Geneva by two in the afternoon. I took the night off to relax and run over in my mind my outline for the operation.

I began to think it was too simplistic. I had been danced right by some very big dark areas. Teheran was the darkest. Why did we have to go to a safe house instead of leaving the country as soon as the rabbits were in our hands? Why could they not be debriefed at the other end, when they, and we, were safe? No matter how well we did our job, how carefully we moved the rabbits about, our real danger came when we holed up in Teheran. I had some hard questions for Valner.

Breakfast the next morning was not a joy. Even as I briefed Valner on the current status of the operation, I could see that his mind was somewhere else.

"I called my people last night to tell them I was meeting you," he said. "It appears that moving the rabbits out of Marshun and into Teheran is not going to be easy."

"What has happened?"

"I don't know. They didn't give me any details. Only that there are complications."

Something was going drastically wrong in Teheran, and these guys were still playing coy with me. I exploded. "I want to know specifically and in detail what the position is in Teheran every twelve hours from this moment until mission start. I want to know exactly what is going on."

"Calm down," he said. "I don't blame you. You'll have it."

He and I spent the morning with bankers, moving funds around so that the operation could go on a moment's notice. I was given documentation to show the men that the 25,000 pounds had been deposited in their accounts on escrow pending instructions from my company. This was not entirely foolproof. I could always change the instructions. But the concern of the men was the release of the money from the principals; they were the ones who might double-cross somebody. The men had faith in me; but, as paymaster, I had to make the movement of money look as smooth as possible. The best mercs panicked if they thought there was any doubt about their money. You could not have them in a battle zone worrying about whether or not they were going to get paid. That was when they started blowing banks and robbing cashboxes.

"I am very unhappy," I told Valner. "My end of the operation is running like clockwork. Yours seems to be in a shambles. It sounds to me as if we're going to have a hard time taking the rabbits anywhere. I want two helicopters from Mirza, not one. One on the north side of the city, one on the south. You can tell him we won't use them unless we get into trouble. I want confirmation of these helicopters within twenty-four hours."

"I'll take care of that," Valner said.

"Oh, Valner, one point. Should we arrive in Teheran . . . Should we get down there, and things go wrong, and I learn that the information you have been feeding me is false or misleading, my Third Party has been instructed to resolve the matter with you. Do I make myself clear?"

"Perfectly."

"I want a full briefing on everything that's happening in Teheran, and I want it within four days."

"Give me your Third Party, and I'll get it myself. Let him come to Teheran with me. Do a recce. We'll see Mirza, and you can get your assurances from your own man."

They left that night and were back in four days. I met my Third Party at a Geneva restaurant.

"You have the wrong photos," he said to me.

"What photos?"

"Of the truck park. I was confused when I got there, because it was nothing like the photos I had seen. Our people in Germany photographed the wrong truck park. I have pictures of the right one."

"Did you talk to the manager?"

"He's been well paid. Don't trust him."

"Any problems at the airport?"

"We slipped in like grease. Valner is well connected."

"What about the safe house?"

"Mirza wouldn't let me see it. He didn't want to breach security there."

"Did you believe him?"

"You know me. I believe no one."

"How do you feel about Mirza?"

"He seems to have a good organization. Very large, very efficient. Contacts at every level. It's a good thing too. The streets are filled with jokers carrying weapons. You hear guns going off all the time. Every major intersection is a roadblock. I covered your route from the truck park to the outskirts of the city. The main thoroughfares are closed. You have to take the back streets and pass a dozen checkpoints.

Take lots of cash. You have to pay someone off at every checkpoint."

I caught a plane to Frankfurt. I had done some ordinary overland business with a trucking firm there, and I knew that two of their drivers regularly did a run from Czechoslovakia—where they picked up arms from Omnipol, the East bloc arms agency—to the Belgian ports. The Verbruggens knew them as well and had assured me that the two were both good and trustworthy. We met in a beer hall. I was assured that both drivers and lorries were available on demand.

The phone was ringing in my Frankfurt hotel room as I turned the key in the door.

"Santa," the voice identified itself. "Stop all conversations with anyone you're talking to and meet me in Bonn tomorrow morning."

"Where?"

"Richthofenstrasse."

I was stunned.

Richthofenstrasse 52 was the headquarters of G-9, Germany's anti-terrorist organization.

# 5

I caught a commuter flight to Bonn early the next morning. In the arrivals lounge, I checked on incoming flights. The first of the day from London was arriving in half an hour. I watched Santa as he debarked and strolled through the terminal. He looked neither frightened nor anxious. He was approached by a uniformed G-9 officer and led to a waiting car. Inside the car sat two men in uniform. One of these I recognized as Karl Ludendorff, second-highest-ranking officer in G-9, and Werner Müller's right-hand man. Ludendorff, like G-9, was a model for Europe's new breed of anti-terrorist operatives and agencies.

G-9 was formed after the abysmal performance of Germany's Grenzschutz police units at the Munich Olympics massacre of thirteen Israeli athletes. It was decided at the very highest levels in the German government that a special agency of a paramilitary nature must be put together as an anti-terrorist organization. But paramilitary units cause a lot of soul searching in Germany, and in the end the idea was killed as being too politically sensitive.

So a special section was created within the police infra-structure—not the army—which became known as G-9. Se-lected to head G-9 was Werner Müller, a veteran of German special forces since the early 1940's, including an SS Storm Trooper battalion. Müller was a superb choice for the job—a tough character, he was smart and flexible, and politically astute. The Germans sent him to Israel, where he trained in anti-terrorist tactics against the Palestinians. He was an active "observer" on the Entebbe raid. He went to Britain and undertook the standard SAS training at Hereford. Soon after, he became the first Commander, Ninth Border Guard Group Special, or Commander G-9.

Though his men remained policemen, Müller created a force modeled closely on the SAS. Long before the world had heard of them, G-9 began to prove so effective against German terrorists that they became almost a political embar-rassment. G-9 burst upon the world scene at Mogadishu, where Müller personally led a brilliantly conceived and exe-cuted attack on the hijacked plane which resulted in no loss of life among passengers or his men.

Müller and his team were instant celebrities, and as such stirred up jealousy in the army. Since Mogadishu, G-9 had kept a low but stunningly effective profile against Baader-Meinhof, the Red Brigade, and a dozen foreign terrorist groups with Middle Eastern and Japanese ties. Like any other specialist unit, they followed developments in other countries. Santa knew them through their close contacts with Box 500.

Ludendorff and Santa were standing outside the Richthofen-strasse headquarters when I arrived by taxi. I waved Santa to one side.

"What the hell is going on?" I demanded.

"I know what you're thinking. But keep your cool. Because I've done something, and when you hear about it, I know you won't object. Don't worry. We're in good hands."

We walked over to Ludendorff, who greeted me cordially and ushered us past security into a small conference room I knew from earlier trips to Richthofenstrasse on equipment deals. Ludendorff and I made uncomfortable small talk for a minute or two. Though only nearing forty, Ludendorff was now the operational head of G-9, as Müller concentrated on politicking for the group in government circles.

In a country where titles are so important, Ludendorff was still Müller's adjutant, but he was on course to be the next commander. He was far more relaxed a man than one would expect from a German special operative. He was fit and well built, but not so finely tuned as the officers of the old school. He could have passed for a handsome university lecturer.

I repeated my question, this time to both men. "What the hell is going on? How much have you told these people?" I asked, turning to Santa.

"I haven't told them anything that compromises or endangers the mission. First, since we're operating out of Germany, I thought it would be unfortunate for us to be shut down by G-9 before the operation ever got started. Secondly, I thought they might like the experience of an operation in Iran, in exchange for which they would help us out. Let me assure you, they know no details."

"That's not quite true, but Santa wouldn't know that. Whatever we've learned has come from other sources," Ludendorff said, turning his full attention to me. "Apart from the fact that you're doing something on German soil, don't you think we'd be more comfortable if we knew exactly what's going on?"

That was, I hoped, Ludendorff's way of saying, "Don't you think it would be more comfortable if we could grease the platform for you?"

"You're not going to get us into any trouble, Gayle, are you?" he continued. "One thing I must insist upon is that the Commander is in on this."

"What the bloody hell does he know about this?"

"Good morning, gentlemen. Please come into my office." It was Müller's voice booming over an intercom on the wall above my head. He had heard just enough to satisfy himself that he wanted his unit involved. If he had not liked what was said, he would never have appeared. He would not have been personally compromised by giving an ear to the situation. Then he could quite comfortably, without a guilty thought, instruct Ludendorff to crush us.

We followed Ludendorff into a large, spare office and took three chairs facing Werner Müller across a wide metal desk. With a dog-like face and gray temples beneath a brush of military-cut brown hair, a fifty-five-year-old with the body of a thirty-year-old marathon runner, Müller looked what he was: a man who had spent a lifetime in the maximum military environment. He could have been a Legionnaire or a U.S. Marine colonel or an out-of-work Storm Trooper. He was very correct, very hard. Müller's English, like that of Ludendorff, was impeccable.

"Nice to see you again, Rivers," he said.

"And you, Commandant."

"May I offer a suggestion?"

It was, as they say, an offer I could not refuse.

"Please do."

"You would be ill-advised to use the trucking company you're talking with."

Not even Santa knew whom I was calling on. Between Santa's phone call the previous night and this morning's meeting, from a short list of trucking firms in Frankfurt, they had deduced and confirmed where I had been.

"What did you tell the two drivers?" Müller continued.

"Nothing, except that there was a job coming up, and I asked if they were available. I said I would be in touch."

"Don't be," Müller said.

"Would you qualify that last?" I asked. I showed no surprise to Müller's remarks, nor had he expected any.

"Because of the nature of the operation, I think we'd rather see things arriving on German soil in another way."

"Commandant, I've been thinking about this, and I don't see the likelihood of the goods arriving on German soil. In our hands, anyway."

"The goods? The rabbits, you mean."

I ignored that. What did he not know?

"I have information from the battle zone that the lines are not secure," I said.

"You can quit speaking in riddles," Ludendorff said.

"My people were not allowed to see the safe houses in Teheran. That makes me believe very strongly that things are untidy. I haven't come up yet with a final plan, but I'm casting around for a place to drop these people off, and I feel sure it's not going to be Germany. And I feel sure that it is going to be a long way from any of your jurisdictions."

If G-9 got directly involved, Müller's jurisdictions would cover Western Europe, with the possible exception of France.

"What are you talking about? The Mediterranean?" he asked.

"In that area, yes."

"Anywhere south of the Med, and you're being very foolish."

"What do you mean by that?"

"Santa has shown you the report from Box 500 of the present situation in Iran."

"I've been briefed on current events," I said.

I was not admitting that Santa showed me a classified document. MI-6 could have been monitoring this conversation from the next room.

"We have discussed the situation," I said.

"We have information on the Palestinians that the Box has yet to receive."

This must have come directly from Israeli intelligence. Müller continued. "Your rabbits are on two death lists. You can't be taking them into an Arab country. And the Israelis don't want them coming in there."

"What has this operation to do with the Palestinians?" I asked.

"Let's just say that one group of people is trying to push another group of people out of certain businesses."

"Are you talking about illegal arms trade?"

"That, and other things."

"Be specific, Commandant."

"You'll learn more on the ground there."

"I don't want to learn anything in Teheran that I can learn here. I don't like surprises."

"I can tell you this. The Palestinians supplied the weapons for the Ayatollah's revolution. The whole thing was designed by the Russians, using the PLO as intermediaries. The money, the weapons, the intelligence; they all came through the PLO. Now the PLO are in Iran, and they want their pound of flesh. They're maintaining a holding action on the part of the Russians, while the Ayatollah's people fight each other. The Palestinians are trying to get their hands on all classified information. They have special commandos down there whose sole responsibilities are to kill Jews and collect technology. And your rabbits are maybe the prime targets."

"How many PLO are in Iran?"

"Three or four thousand, mainly concentrated in Teheran, Rasht, and up to the Caspian Sea. There are some in Isfahan and Shiraz."

"Are they under the control of the Iranians?"

"For God's sake, man, the Iranians themselves are not under control. These Palestinians are completely autonomous. They're killing Iranians with impunity. The PLO are the clandestine Cubans of the Russian scenario."

The PLO were G-9's principal adversaries. They had infiltrated Germany, mainly through its radical student organizations, to such an extent that they were almost impossible to keep track of. Palestinian students, some of whom had been in Bavaria for years, were the operative arm of the organization that carried out the Munich massacre. The PLO worked hand in glove with indigenous extremists. Terrorism had become a primary political instrument in Germany, a fixation for the German people.

"There are German terrorists in Iran today, training with the PLO," Müller said, a breach of classified information, but he was angry and frustrated.

"Baader-Meinhof?"

"Red Brigade," he replied. "The same thing. Baader-Meinhof is one part of it. The real enemy is the Red Brigade that stretches from Italy to Scandinavia. It's built around a nucleus of Italian and German terrorists, but they work in conjunction with the IRA and the Basques and the Japanese. So as you can see, we have a mutual concern over Iran."

Müller had failed to answer the most important question. Was G-9 involved in the motivation for getting the rabbits out, or did he simply want to use our mission as a method of accomplishing something else? That would remain unclear. What was clear was that Müller intended to help us, though he had not yet said so. Now he set to pumping me about the tactical details of the mission, and I did not tell him much, so we got in a long-winded sparring match.

"What about this idea of taking these people into Iraq?"

"It wasn't my idea."

"It was in the original plan, though, was it not? It's not such a bad idea, considering the short distance. Even if your rabbits are Jewish. Do you know anybody in Iraq? If you find certain conditions obtaining in Teheran, I advise you strongly to go into Iraq, because it will mean Turkey is not safe."

In these conversations, you do not ask a lot of questions. You listen. You talk as little as possible. But you do not ask, "Why? Why can't we go into Turkey?" Müller was going to answer that question in his own time. When he told me at last, his explanation was so obtuse and arcane that it took me a moment to sort out the real meaning.

"Certain people would not like to see your rabbits in Turkey," he said. "If they are found in Turkey, you and they will go right back to Teheran."

What he was hinting was that the level of protection that one needed on a mission like this was not going to be there in Turkey. That was another way of saying that perhaps too much was already known about the mission, and the Turks might be waiting for the rabbits when they arrived. Müller's intelligence must have discovered that someone at the other end knew a mission was being mounted to take the rabbits out. Whoever that party was had interests in Turkey and might expose us for their own ends. Who could that be? Müller inferred that it was the Americans, but he could have been talking opposites. If the rabbits were discovered in Turkey, they might have gone straight to Russia.

"How are you going to work these trucks?" he asked. "Are you going to do it strictly as a private venture? I advise you not to use..." and he named the company in Frankfurt.

"How do you qualify that?"

"They might be up to other tricks you don't want touching you, even peripherally."

The subject was closed. I wrote off that company. I would not phone the two drivers to warn them they were under surveillance. My loyalty was to the mission.

"If we put a couple of men on your team, we might gain something ourselves in Iran," Müller said.

"We already have a team. Santa has certainly briefed you on that."

"Yes, but what about your drivers?"

"Well, you've now left me in a position where I have to consider them."

"Why don't we supply you the trucks and four drivers?"

I had planned to use only one driver per vehicle, but it was common for these overland lorries to carry co-drivers to relieve the driving.

"Tell me about it," I said.

"Santa approached us for some special equipment to be used on an op. Now that we know what the op is, I think it is an idea to discuss it in its entirety, so that we might become involved."

This was Müller's way of saying that they were joining our

team. I had been maneuvered into a position where if I said
no, the mission would be crushed. Or we would be set up.

I was not angry with Santa. He had been confident before
he contacted G-9 that things would go our way, and they had.
Müller's motivations were unclear. He seemed to know more
about the Bavarian operation—Valner and the others at the
Munich estate—than he admitted. And he had not been
consulted on that operation by the right people. Something
was going on there, and he wanted to know what it was.
Apart from that, this was an opportunity for him to gain
firsthand knowledge of the revolution and a reading on the
counterrevolutionary underground. This was his chance to
penetrate the Mirza network on the coattails of a strictly
private venture. For all I knew, G-9 could have had a vested
interest in the rabbits and were as anxious to get them out as
my principals were. Müller could have been doing this for
somebody else; G-9 was heavily indebted to the Israeli secret
service. One quick telephone request from Tel Aviv would
have been enough. So long as it did not compromise the
German government, Müller would comply.

My mind turned for a fleeting moment to Mossad. How did
the Israelis feel about working with an ex-Storm Trooper?
Müller never showed me a trace of anti-Semitism. I assumed
that all ex-SS troopers were anti-Semitic. But you never
knew about these things. Müller could have been Jewish
himself. He would not have been the only Jew to join the SS.
It was the best place to hide. If you put aside all the romantic
nonsense—heroism, loyalty, honor, devotion—the Second World
War was six years of living hell for most Europeans. They did
things to others, and to themselves, that appear incomprehensible to a sane man who did not live through it. They
were forced to take sides, and there was no way for them to
win. Russians and Cossacks in German uniforms fought the
Red Army on the Eastern Front. One of the strongest battal-
ions in the SS was manned by French volunteers. Another
was 100 percent Dutch. Franco's Spanish Blue Division
fought against the Allies; that was forgotten at war's end, in
exchange for U.S. naval and air bases in Spain.

"I like Munich," Müller said. "A pretty place. I'm particularly fond of the old parts of the city."

Müller teased me with bits and pieces of information. He
knew about my trips to Germany. He knew about the aborted
foray to Zurich. He wanted people on this mission, if only to

keep an eye on it. We started talking openly about G-9 involvement. Ludendorff would be our liaison officer, Müller informed me.

"We'll get you the best equipment. Brand-new trucks," said Ludendorff. "I'll take care of loads, the documentation, the secret compartment. I'll liaise with Santa on all this. You'll draw all your weapons from G-9 hardware. We don't have a Sterling, so Santa will have to arrange for that separately. You'll have to buy your explosives elsewhere as well. We can't be seen to be requisitioning plastique at this time."

Müller left. Santa and Ludendorff ran through a rough checklist of priorities and exchanged contact numbers. We broke up the meeting. Santa and I went to lunch. I was not unhappy. I had lost some autonomy, but to the best people in the business.

When I called my Geneva office, I learned that Big Kevin was due in Frankfurt in two days, so I decided to wait for him. I dialed straight through to an office in Madrid.

"Miguel?" I said when his secretary had rung me through. "It's Gayle."

"*Hombre*, how are you?"

"I'm fine. I'll be in Madrid in four days' time. I want you to arrange a meeting with the representative from Esperanza. I want to see Nano the same day."

Esperanza was a Bilbao arms manufacturer. Nano was Fernando Morell, a pilot in the Spanish Air Force, born in Mallorca and stationed there now at the Palma airport.

I flew to Frankfurt. A contact arranged delivery from France, to me in Frankfurt, of two Thompson RS-10 pack radios. After that, I had two days free to think of nothing but the mission. Müller had forced me to look to the south for our primary escape route.

# 6

I was at the airport when Big Kevin's jet touched down after a nonstop flight from Istanbul. Big Kevin was a giant of a Yorkshireman, tall and broad, with the wrinkled face and sharp eyes of a rumpled U.S. Marine drill instructor. His head was shaved straight up the sides and back; what hair remained sat on his crown like a skullcap. He was three days from a shooting war, ferocious mountain rebels, mounted cavalry, and mule trains. He took a bit of adjusting when he came out and found himself in a European environment. Though we were old friends, Big Kevin greeted me at the airport with a hello and a ceremonious handshake. He was dressed in a fifteen-year-old suit that looked as if it had not been worn five times.

Big Kevin's rough edges were not hidden by a coat and tie. He had been almost a boy when he joined the Legion; by now, a war zone was his natural habitat. He was a very bright man, very good at what he did. He had a gift for languages; he spoke half a dozen African and Middle Eastern tongues and dialects. He was ex-Congo, ex-Biafra, and had been involved in Kurdistan since the mid-sixties. A merc in his mid-forties when he went there, after adopting their cause he had given up his wages. Big Kevin fought now for bread and wine, goat's meat and freedom.

Big Kevin was tough, but he was honest and dependable. He was an excellent organizer and knew the people he worked with extremely well. He was well connected; I always suspected him of CIA ties. He managed quite successfully to arm and supply a war of national independence by overland routes that wove out of Pakistan, across northern Iran, through Turkey via mule packtrains into Iraq and Kurdistan. But the problems of logistics and supplies had become immeasurably more complicated in the past six months.

Before the Shah was overthrown, a great deal of the Kurds' equipment came from Iran. The Shah used the Kurds as a buffer between himself and the Iraqis. The Iraqis were quite capable of invading Iran. They had the most combat-experienced army in the Arab world, far better than it was given credit for in the West. Even before his downfall, the Shah had been backing away from the Kurdish cause. Now the Ayatollah was mending fences with Iraq, at the expense of the Kurdish rebellion.

I took Big Kevin from the airport to a bed-and-breakfast. He did not like posh hotels. Over coffee and rolls, I told him as much as I dared. If he were to help, he would have to be an integral part of the machinery.

"You want an escape route out of Iran," he said.

"That's right."

"If you make it to Kurdistan, where will you go from there?"

"I was hoping you could tell me."

"I can always put you on a supply train through the Iraqi lines. But that is very dicey. No guarantee you'd make it. It's by pack mule. Very slow."

"You've got better ways than that to get through the Iraqi lines."

"We're fighting a war up there. I can't compromise Kurdish connections to save three Iranians. Let me think. How will you reach us?"

"Overland. We'll be moving by lorry in your direction out of Teheran. We have chopper backup if the lorry is exposed."

"There are a lot of troops between Teheran and us. If there's an alert on, you'll never make it."

"We have an alternative route out to the south. To the Gulf."

"How will you get out of there?"

"By amphibious aircraft."

"Where will you go?"

"That's when it gets sticky. I can't sort out how to get to the Mediterranean from there. How to get across Iraq, Syria, and Jordan."

"What are you going to use?"

"A Canadair CL-215."

"What is that?"

"A water bomber. The kind they use to fight forest fires."

"What in hell do you want a water bomber for?"

"A couple of reasons. First, it's the only amphibious plane I feel I can lay my hands on. Second, the specs are good. Two twenty-one-hundred-horsepower Pratt and Whitney engines. Crew of two. Runs all day long at a hundred and eighty miles per hour. That's better than getting into some souped-up machine that you have to fly at altitude and speed to use at maximum efficiency. A range of fourteen hundred miles. The one I'm thinking about has radar with terrain-contour mode, which means we can stick it right down at treetop level."

Everybody else could think we were going out by a lorry to Dubai or by boat wherever. I had made up my mind not to trust the principals with any information or aspect of the operation I did not directly control. "The Gypsy" had been dropping hints—"the Gypsy" is officialdom, because it recognizes no loyalties—that we should proceed with extreme caution. Just because the people in Bavaria were known to Müller did not mean that he condoned their activities. There was the clear danger that we were being conned into a kidnapping rather than a pickup. Who knew wherein lay the truth? We could have been hired by Arabs or even the Iranian revolutionaries themselves to pull off something sympathetic to the PLO.

All I knew was that Müller was familiar with my principal and had given me a Gypsy warning. And he knew more about the principal than I did.

As I talked to Big Kevin, I made up my mind to fly to the south as our primary escape route, though I would still leave the principals thinking the rabbits were coming through Turkey on the overland route. My biggest problem with a Gulf pickup was that it meant several hours' flying over Arab territory any way we went to the Mediterranean.

It was good to be with Big Kevin again. He had aged a bit in the two years since I had last seen him, but he was still the same character—solid, dependable, full of good advice. He told me that his people had penetrated Iraq and had a considerable network with whom we could liaise if we had to enter Iraqi territory from Kurdistan. He and I, it turned out, knew the same Iraqis. I was already feeling better about the new plan.

"Surely you have some proposed route out of the Gulf?" he asked.

"Straight into southern Iraq. Pick up the pipeline and fly west to Jordan, then refuel in southern Lebanon. From there to southern France. We'll deliver the rabbits in France, or take them into Germany by car."

"Who is your man in the Lebanon?"

"I don't have one. It's Valner's job to find someone. Chimoum . . ."

"I know he's dependable. His Christian militia are very tough and well armed. The Israelis are backing him completely now. Do your principals know him?"

"I hope so."

"They seem to know a lot of people, don't they?"

I agreed they did. I was waiting for Big Kevin's next remarks.

"That's too far, the Gulf to Lebanon. With that kind of load and low-altitude flying, you won't have a range much in excess of a thousand miles. You might as well turn belly up in Teheran as go down in Iraq or the Lebanon."

"What alternative do I have?"

"You can refuel in Kurdistan. I might even be able to arrange a safe flight plan across Iraq."

That was the kind of guy Big Kevin was. Within half an hour, I had a safe zone into which I could retreat from north or south, an ally, a refueling facility, medical attention, and rearmament if we needed it. For this the Kurds would be paid ten thousand pounds, plus any armament we could leave behind. If we could not fly out because of weather or opposition, Big Kevin would supply us guides and guards and a mule-train trek to a safe point outside the area.

"I'll be bringing three Jews," I said. "Does that make any difference?"

"The Kurds won't like them because they're Iranians," Big Kevin replied. "They won't like them because they're the Shah's people, and the Shah double-crossed us in the last year. But they'll do what I ask. My people are fanatical freedom fighters, not fanatical Moslems."

Big Kevin had a radio network that extended from set to set four hundred miles inside Iran. Valner would inform him, I said, how to link his network with Mirza so that I could be apprised of any change of circumstances in Kurdistan. If Big Kevin could not receive us, we had no business flying up there.

"When the radio link is complete, flash me one message: Blue Fire. Mirza will relay that to Valner, and he'll get it to me. That tells me the line is open. Where am I going to refuel?" I asked.

"I'll give you coordinates of a small lake on our eastern frontier. It's in a narrow valley and well hidden from air surveillance, except by planes directly overhead. We've been stealing fuel for the past two years from an Iraqi air base just on the other side of the range. We'll have fuel there ready for you when you arrive."

"We'll be flying at ground level. How am I going to find the lake?"

"I have a beacon that will transmit about twenty miles. If you can get into the right valley, the beacon will bring you straight in. The range is honeycombed with parallel valleys. If you get into the wrong one, you'll just have to go back out and start over again. What's the wingspan of this plane?"

"Ninety-three feet, ten inches."

"The valley you want is about ninety-three feet, eleven inches wide."

"Plenty of room," I said.

"Try to arrive at dawn or dusk. We'll set up flares at the eastern end of the lake twice a day."

The longer Big Kevin talked, the less preposterous became this idea of going into Kurdistan. It allowed for the contingency of splitting the party, one group proceeding north out of Teheran directly to Kurdistan, the other traveling first south, then returning north with the plane to rendezvous on the lake. Big Kevin had people inside Iran, with this radio network, feeding supplies to the Kurds. Anyone forced north could join a packtrain and go overland into Kurdistan. Mirza would contact Big Kevin, then Mirza's people would take us to the end of the Kurdish line of communications. That was arranged for Kavosh, an entry town into the Kurdish area, but off the beaten track, with wild and desolate country all around. Mirza's people would deliver us to a certain point, then after their departure, the Kurds would come and fetch us. Under no circumstances would Big Kevin allow Mirza's network to touch directly upon his own.

We spent two hours briefing on the area. He brought out maps, but they were too large-scale to serve my purposes, so he drew proximity maps of the lake and its environs.

"When will I see you again?" Big Kevin asked.

"Twenty-first of June. Allow three days on either side."

We went to the bank together and saw a three-thousand-pound down payment deposited into his account. Outside, we shook hands.

"See you the twenty-first," I said.

"Good luck," said Big Kevin gravely.

Big Kevin left me to spend a few days in London.

I caught a flight to Geneva for a meeting early the next day with Valner and my Third Party. Valner was agitated.

"There's a lot of pressure on the network in Teheran," he said. "Mirza is having to move the rabbits around almost daily. When can you go?"

"When everything's ready," I replied.

"Can you speed it up?"

"I'll try."

"I have a bad feeling about the network down there," my Third Party said. "Something's wrong. It's not secure."

"How soon can you go?" Valner persisted.

"Don't put more pressure on the operation," I told him. "Every job has its own pace. I'm putting this together as fast as I can. If we rush it, we'll botch it, and we might as well not have gone in the first place."

I briefed him on the possibility that we might walk out through Kurdistan, omitting anything about an airplane. I instructed him to set up a direct radio link between Mirza and Big Kevin and have it operating by the tenth of June, the day I picked then as our arrival date in Teheran; no one would be pushing off until we had confirmation of that link.

"I can't have my lorries wandering all over Iran," I told Valner. "If the Marshun safe house has not been turned over by then, I want the rabbits back there for the rendezvous."

"I'll do my best," said Valner.

"Then the second lorry will rendezvous as arranged on the twelfth. That will give us two days to get the rabbits to the rendezvous point."

Security aside, this business of moving the rabbits about had just added to the mystery. I felt no note of betrayal because there had never been any clear indications of the ultimate purpose for the whole operation in the first place. I told Valner that the lorries and drivers were arranged for, omitting to say that they came from Müller. Recalling what Müller had told me, I plied Valner futilely with questions. When I told Valner about the Kurdistan connection, he was visibly relieved; he assumed the rabbits would be moving through Turkey. Turkey to me meant Americans, and the Americans meant the CIA. Who was this Valner? How many roles was he playing? We agreed that it was time to discard the idea of bringing the rabbits all the way to Germany. The length of the journey made us all too vulnerable, and his people were anxious to take delivery.

"What about the Lebanon?" I asked him. "I'll deliver them there, and you can just push them into Israel. It seems the logical thing to do."

"These people," he said firmly, "are not to go to Israel."

How many ramifications can you ask for? This was no time to argue an Israeli delivery.

"Nevertheless, I want a rendezvous in central Lebanon with safe people. We're going to the Lebanon."

He looked at me quizzically. Kurdistan to the Lebanon was a hell of a walk. I had told him central Lebanon, though in fact that was not what I wanted.

"Impossible," he said.

"Why is it impossible?"

"We could help you in the south, but our people could not infiltrate into central Lebanon in sufficient strength to protect you from the Palestinians or Syrian incursion from the north."

"What people?"

"Chimoum," he replied, just as I hoped he would.

"I'm going to fly your rabbits to southern Lebanon," I told him. "I want Chimoum to refuel us."

"Fly them!" he exclaimed. "What are you going to do, land at the bloody Beirut airport?"

"No, I'm going to land at sea," I said, "in an amphibious aircraft."

Valner's eyes lit up.

"Where are you going to get that?" he asked.

"Where indeed," I replied.

Valner's faith in me was growing by the moment. He had a vested interest in seeing that it happened, and he was beginning to believe that I could pull it off.

"I want Chimoum to meet us off the coast with aviation fuel and protection. You give us the fuel. We give you the rabbits. End of mission."

Valner left to make a telephone call or meet someone in another room. He was away for half an hour. The Third Party voiced great concern about security in Teheran.

"Valner left me sitting in the hotel half the time," the Third Party said. "He never told me where he was going. He never told me when he would come back. Teheran is in an uproar. There are more guns in the street than you can imagine."

I quickly briefed my Third Party on Big Kevin's role. The Third Party would notify me when he received the Blue Fire message from Valner. Santa would contact him with the message Blue Streak when he heard from Ludendorff that the lorries and drivers were ready to roll and the equipment was in hand. I instructed the Third Party to provide me 50,000 pounds in cash on the ninth of June, prior to the team's departure from London's Heathrow Airport.

Valner returned. He wore a long, anxious expression which he tried to hide when he entered the room. Valner and I were both tired from days of travel. Now he tried to get clever. Instead it just came out sharp.

"You're being watched," he said. "We're getting feedback on this operation from all over Europe."

I did not tell him that it was his operation that was being watched. By Müller.

Valner continued. "I tried to talk my people into letting you deliver the rabbits in Israel. But it is out of the question. No Israeli delivery under any circumstances."

"Look, Valner," I said, "I already told you that the Lebanon was the end of the line. I never said anything about taking them into Israel. The Lebanon is where the mission ends. That is where you get the rabbits. I'm reconfirming that with you here and now. Now I want to know what happens to my team after the Lebanon. If we can't leave the rabbits there, we can't stay there ourselves. And we don't want to stay in the Lebanon. I want assurances from you right now that Chimoum will be there to meet us and that we have some place to go after that."

"All right. That's on. That's acceptable."

"And don't come back telling me we can fade into Israel. If the rabbits can't go in there, neither can we. There are too many people trying to get out of the way of this one to suit me."

Now Valner and I began to work out an operational exercise which was extremely complicated, but it was the only way I could see to do it. We settled on the tenth of June as our arrival date in Teheran. Valner would advise Mirza of that date and link with Chimoum on our requirements from him. Assuming we made the pickup and reached Kurdistan, Big Kevin would flash our ETA in the Lebanon to Mirza in Teheran via radio linkup. Mirza would pass that ETA to Valner, who would in turn relay a message to Chimoum to be ready to receive us. The first indication to Valner's people that we were out of the soup with the rabbits would be our rendezvous with Chimoum. There we would swap the rabbits for fuel and guarantees of a secure reception somewhere in Europe. My flight crew would ferry us across the Mediterranean, drop the team off, then return the plane where it had come from.

"Can you do all that?" my Third Party asked Valner.

"You have my word," he promised.

I instructed my Third Party to withdraw from the organization of the operation. Thereafter he had two responsibilities. The first was to run my company in my absence; the second was to establish a central listening post and liaison for all the threads of the mission, which were quickly stretching across Europe and the Middle East. He was my coordinating link to Valner and the others—Santa, Ludendorff, Big Kevin—before the operation started. Once we were out in the cold, he was my ears to the outside world. We arranged a method, coded and completely secure, for me to pick up a message in Teheran outside Mirza's security screen. If we were in trouble, I would not be picking up messages. But I could always reach home base, even if it meant grabbing up an American oil company telephone or the telex in an airline office. So everything had to be fed through my Third Party. If I ended up in jail somewhere, he would know where I was. He would know what to do.

For the first time, I could see the operation taking shape. I briefed Valner completely, with the exception of Müller's role and the source of my plane. Valner was not as enthusiastic as I was. His organization was being buffeted by too much flak right now. Valner was not a man to crack under pressure, but I could see he was getting nervous. He was also getting excited by the way I had pulled such a complicated mission together.

After Valner departed, I called Santa in London and instructed him to telex my Third Party the coded message Blue Streak Forward when he heard from Ludendorff that the lorries were ready to roll.

I packed my bag. It was time to tie up the Spanish end. I caught the last plane to Madrid.

# 7

Miguel met me at Barracas Airport on a hot, sticky night. We went straight to his flat. I briefed him on the mission.

"You're crazy," he said. "Nobody can do what you're going to try."

His dark eyes glistened. He wished he was going.

"I have a long shopping list," I said.

Miguel took pad and pen in hand.

"I want Nano," I said. "I want a copilot."

"I can't get your copilot from the air force," said Miguel. "Two serving pilots disappearing at the same time will attract more attention than you want."

"I want a Canadair CL-215. That's the plane Nano has been using to fight fires in the pine forests on Mallorca."

"Borrowing airplanes is an awkward business," said Miguel. "How do you expect me to arrange that?"

"Do you know Nano's boss?"

"General Cardova. I know him well. We served together."

"I want him to pull a plane off the line and schedule it into maintenance. Then he's to get a surplus plane, change the registration, and shove it into maintenance in place of our plane. Scatter some spare parts around."

Here was the sticky part. In Spain, in order to put a plane on maintenance, you have to take one out. If we just jerked a plane off maintenance, it would not be ready to fly. The plane that came out of the hangar had to be written into the "on line" aircraft, but somebody had to see that it did not fly. The line would not be short a plane, but nobody would be flying an unsafe aircraft.

"It would be simpler to steal one," Miguel said, laughing.

"If everyone does his job, your government won't be compromised in any way whatsoever. Remember, Miguel, the Spanish Air Force owes me a favor."

I had furnished them equipment the air ministry was not prepared to buy.

"Cardova owes you nothing. He could be court-martialed. What's in it for him?"

"Fifty thousand pounds."

"I may be able to arrange it. What more?"

"I want Nano here tomorrow for a briefing. I want full rearmament for the team stashed in the airplane. Arms for Nano and the copilot."

"They must be Spanish arms. It's too risky to buy foreign weapons here."

"We'll take Star submachine guns, with a case of nine-millimeter ammunition. Astra .38 automatics. Two Commando sixty-millimeter mortars."

These little hand-held mortars were no longer than a man's forearm, but they fired an explosive shell over a distance of 1,170 yards. If we had to defend our beach rendezvous, they were our only feasible artillery.

"I want six IDK's aboard," I continued.

A Bilbao armaments manufacturer produced immersion demolition kits triggered by timing devices I supplied. These were water-sealed carrier bags with slabs of explosives stitched into pockets inside. The sides of the bags were stripped away to uncover suction pads which adhered to a wet surface. They could be slapped onto a boat or a bridge support in seconds. On land, they were simply laid against any solid structure. The digital timers that fused them were adjustable from one minute to thirty days.

"Add on as much hardware as our weight limitations will permit," I said.

The gear would come to us as clean as the airplane. The weapons would be extracted from an assembly line, and the serial numbers jumped forward; the IDK's written off as wastage.

"Problems?" I asked Miguel.

"All of this will take some time."

"I appreciate that. I have to get some sleep. See if you can have an answer on it by morning."

Miguel looked at his watch. It was past midnight. He hesitated, then picked up the telephone on his desk.

I awoke late the following morning, washed, and joined Miguel as he sipped his eleven o'clock coffee.

"Nano is on his way," he said, rising from the table. "He left Mallorca an hour ago."

Nano strode swiftly across the airport terminal, a flight bag swinging at his side. He flung his arms open when he saw us.

"*Amigo!*" he said, embracing me. "*Cómo estás?*"

Nano was twenty-eight, a captain in the Spanish Air Force, and an irrepressible adventurer. Small and slim, he had the good looks and athletic body of a racing driver in a Hollywood film. He had the aristocratic carriage and beautifully cut clothes of old Mallorquin nobility. Nano loved the glamor and excitement of flying, but his air force salary hardly paid for petrol and insurance on his Ferrari. For the rest—a flat in Paris, elegant ladies, the nightclubs of Europe—he had money from his family and picked up substantial sums doing odd jobs on the side. Nano and I had worked together three times, and I had the greatest confidence in him. He knew how to keep his Latin temperament muted; I had seen him remain cool under the most extreme pressure.

Two years earlier, Otto Benjamin, head of the Bank of Morocco, had called on me to fly King Hassan incognito to a secret negotiating session with the Spanish government. I used a Spanish Air Force jet, and Nano was assigned to me as copilot. It was a quick, clean job, but I had time to admire Nano's talents. Later, we moved General Spinola into Portugal from his South American hideout.

Miguel, Nano, and I made small talk until we reached my office in Madrid. Nano sat back in a big leather chair and waited.

"I spoke to your commanding officer last night," said Miguel.

"I know," replied Nano. "You woke him up."

"He cleared you for this mission."

Nano waited. He was no merc, no hardened professional. I wanted his adrenaline flowing.

"Nano," I said, "we're going to make a hell of a flight."

I thrust a map in front of him and jabbed my finger down on the Persian Gulf.

"I want you there," I said, "at dawn on the eighteenth of June. A hundred meters offshore, refueled, and ready to go. You'll be flying a Canadair CL-215. Complement of twelve, including the flight crew."

"Where are we going from there?"

"Kurdistan."

I described the flight north.

"*Tremendo,*" he said, almost bursting with excitement. "This is wonderful."

"Can you get another pilot?" I asked.

"A good one," Nano replied. "Trust me. Am I protected here at home?" he asked Miguel.

"The plane will be scheduled for maintenance, then secondment to the Greek Air Force, which can explain its being in the eastern Mediterranean. We'll write you standing orders for a delivery flight. If we hear you're in trouble, we complete the orders and write the plane off as a crash at sea. The fact that it has just come out of maintenance will lend credence to that."

"Do the Greeks know about this?" asked Nano.

"They will if you lose the plane."

"I don't care what happens then. If I lose the plane, I lose me."

It was a casual remark, without a trace of concern. Nano was a superb pilot, a man with an instinct for survival. He grabbed the maps for a closer look.

"Many miles," he said. "Far beyond the range of the aircraft."

"I can get you refueled on the way down, in the Gulf of Aqaba," I said, "but that means exposing you to my principals."

I knew Valner could arrange it if I demanded, but I wanted him to know nothing of the provenance of the aircraft.

"Not necessary," said Nano. "I can put enough refueling bags in the hopper and the cabin to get us down there. But I can't carry enough to bring us back. I'll need refueling at the rendezvous."

I took the biggest gamble of the mission.

"You'll have fuel waiting for you," I said.

That fuel would come from Mirza, but I did not intend to arrange it through Valner, because I did not want to tell him where we planned to rendezvous. This meant going to Teheran without guarantee of an escape route. My suspicious nature was beginning to create difficulties for us.

"From Kurdistan, where?" asked Nano.

"West. Iraq. Syria. The Lebanon and into the Med."

Nano looked back to the maps. He frowned.

"Not so *tremendo*," he said. "Optimum performance on that plane is one hundred eighty miles an hour at ten thousand feet. We'll be flying at ground level, no? That means less speed if we want to stretch the fuel to the Med. At ground level, it won't be easy to find this."

He jabbed his forefinger at our major landfall, an oil pipeline north of Baghdad.

I knew the region well. We had the air base at Kirkuk to worry about, more military activity on the green belt in the Tharthar basin. The Dukan Dam to the north was under constant aerial surveillance to prevent the Kurds from blowing it.

For a moment, the old scheme of infiltrating Baghdad sounded sweet again, but it was just a dream. On an operation like ours, you had to isolate yourself from the native population, because everyone down to the guy selling nuts at the corner was a spy. Being Western, you had to stay so far out of sight that it became impossible to move.

"You can do it," I said to Nano. "Low and slow."

He shook his head.

"We'll be *tiro a pichón*. A pigeon shot. Find us some help, Gayle."

"I'll do my best."

Miguel had filled the rest of my shopping list. The gear would be delivered to Nano at Son San Juan Airport in Palma. When that was confirmed, and the plane was standing by, Miguel would advise my Third Party.

"Blue Flame Forward," I told him, "means everything is go."

Nano departed. I picked up the phone and dialed Big Kevin at his contact number in London.

"Colonel Tarik," I asked Big Kevin. "Do you know him?"

"Yes," he answered warily.

"Tarik is a friend of mine," I said.

Iraqi Air Force Colonel Tarik had been the chief negotiator in London with Kurdish leaders in effecting a tenuous cease-fire in the Iraqi-Kurd war. Tarik was back in Iraq. The cease-fire was holding. Some communications link must open through the lines.

"I want you to contact Tarik," I said. "I want him to give us, for a few hours, one day, a safe one-way air corridor across Iraq."

"Will he do that for you?"

"He's my friend," I repeated. "He owes me a big favor."

"I'll try," promised Big Kevin, "but I'm not hopeful. My links with Tarik are dead slow. Overland by mule. He could say yes, and we won't have his answer before you turn up at the lake."

I returned to Geneva. My Third Party arranged escrow payments of 5,000 pounds each to Nano and his copilot. I met Valner for one final briefing.

"I've been in touch with Chimoum," Valner told me. "He'll refuel you. No problem. But he absolutely cannot accept the rabbits."

"You better be there to take them yourself."

"Out of the question."

"Then they can swim to shore and walk to Israel as far as I'm concerned. Our mission ends in the Lebanon."

"Forty-five minutes," said Valner.

"Forty-five minutes what?"

"Take the rabbits on another forty-five minutes. To Cyprus. We'll meet you off Famagusta. It's just a hop over the Med from your Chimoum rendezvous."

"And after Famagusta?"

"There'll be nothing after Famagusta. We take the rabbits from you there. Your mission is completed."

He gave me coordinates for a small bay between Larnaca and Limasol. I was furious.

"This is turning into a right world tour, isn't it, Valner?

What the hell do I know about Cyprus? Who the hell is going to meet us there?"

Beirut to Cyprus was a major smuggling route, and Limasol was a gathering point for tobacco, whiskey, drugs, Mafia, Interpol, and every secret agent who ever tried to bust a crime ring.

"I'll be there," said Valner calmly.

"You're pushing me to the limit," I told him.

"That's why you can be sure it ends there. We dare not push you any farther. Don't forget we're taking over your original responsibility of getting these people into Europe. You'll be free and clear this way before you get out of the Med."

It was apparent all argument was futile. I agreed and confirmed with Valner a starting date for the mission of June tenth. He and I talked for another hour, then came up short.

"I have nothing more to say," I told him.

"Nor do I."

"This closes down this end of the operation," I said. "It's time for me to go to England and get started."

He shook my hand, wished me well, and left. I waited fifteen minutes, then departed the hotel by another entrance.

I flew to Barcelona, spent a day with my lady, and caught a late plane the following evening to London. Santa met me at the Great Portland Street surgery.

"The team's working beautifully. They spent the week together at Hereford," he said, referring to SAS headquarters.

"The Box?" I asked.

"No hassle from Box 500 to date. We don't seem to be stepping on anyone's toes. I was in Germany yesterday. Ludendorff is doing a beautiful job. The gear is all in hand. The vehicles will be doctored, loaded, and ready to roll within a day or two."

"Good equipment?" I asked.

"Brand-new Volvos," he said. "Articulated lorries. Eighteen-wheelers. Operated by something called Trans-Asian Transport out of Frankfurt. Right proper documents. I met Müller's drivers. Very impressive. Two of them are Iranians carrying German passports."

"Loads?"

"Just as you ordered. Rubber tubes in one, and I've seen that it was set up properly. The other lorry is carrying two pallets. Kitchen hardware, as I recall, and collapsible buildings. They fill up the trailer. Nobody will be crawling over them for a nose-about."

"Notify Ludendorff," I said. "Blue Streak Forward on the third of June. That'll give the lorries over a week."

I called my Third Party in Geneva.

"Messages?"

"Two. Blue Fire."

That confirmed Valner's link through Mirza with Big Kevin.

"Second message?" I asked.

"Blue Flame."

That was Miguel's signal that all loose ends were tied in Spain; plane, crew, and equipment were ready to go.

"Return this message," I said. "Blue Flame Forward on the tenth of June."

That gave Nano a week to sort out his flight plan, take possession of the plane, get the gear on board, refuel at sea, alter the plane's colors and registration number, and fly east two days to meet us. I hung up and turned back to Santa.

"What else?" I asked.

"Your tickets," he said, handing me seven one-way air tickets to Teheran with open dates.

"Confirm seven seats on Iran Air for the ninth," I told him.

I went to Hereford and met the team in a pub. They had meshed easily. I gave them two days off to get their personal affairs in order and see their families. Gill and I left them and traveled down to Poole, where he put me through my paces for the next two days. I got the feel of weapons again and toughened my body for the job ahead with range work, physical training, swimming, gym work. Word came from my Third Party that the lorries had crossed the Bavarian border. I returned to London on the night of the eighth and joined the team in a small West Kensington hotel.

# PART II

★

# THE MISSION

# 8

That morning Santa provided everyone with travel documents. Gill and I traveled as labor representatives for the Geneva Press Council. The Verbruggens carried Red Cross papers. Freeman and Davis were certified as UN observers, which gave them diplomatic status. Swann was a sales representative for a British manufacturer of bakery supplies. We all traveled under our own names with our real passports, which we would need for the return journey.

We taxied separately to Heathrow, gathered briefly for a cup of coffee, then separated again. I saw Freeman, Swann, Davis, and Gill to the immigration gate.

"Travel separately to the Teheran Hilton," I said. "Mirza's people will recognize you. The code word is 'Rabbits.' They'll take you to a safe house. Wait there for us."

The Verbruggens and I kicked our heels at Heathrow until seven in the evening, when, to my dismay, our flight was canceled until early the next morning. Iran Air bused us to the Skyline Hotel, where we had a meal and an evening out at their expense and talked about old times.

Our flight the next morning to Teheran was uneventful. Though there were few Iranians aboard, the plane was more than half filled. War and revolution are but minor obstacles to business as usual.

We cleared immigration and customs without raising an eyebrow. We were proceeding separately to the taxi rank when a man spotted the Red Cross sticker on Yves's briefcase and approached him. Marcel joined the two in brief conversation. I stood back. When all three climbed into a waiting car, I joined them.

The driver took us on a circuitous route through the city. We wandered through a tangle of old streets and houses to the south and east of the main railway station, where the remains of three thousand years of civilization gave Teheran a typical Middle Eastern look. We traveled north and west and found the sterile order of a modern Western city. We passed the Pahlavi Hospital, drove along Elizabeth II Boulevard, swung behind the racetrack, and turned through the gates of a luxurious home.

My temper had flashed momentarily at the terminal when we were met by a Mercedes-Benz and a chauffeur. Then I realized that if we were foreigners of any note, we would have aroused suspicion climbing into some grubby little car. Just as we would have if we had entered a fallen-down shack in the bazaar.

Great wooden doors closed behind us. We were in a large cobblestone courtyard hidden from the street by high white walls. There were several guards about, carrying automatic weapons but dressed in casual street clothes. I saw two men in the uniforms of Iranian naval officers, then my four came out of the house to join us.

"How did it go?" Freeman asked.

"Fine. And you?"

"Not a hitch."

"How secure is the neighborhood?" I asked.

"Half the houses around here are empty," Gill replied. "A lot of the rich people have left."

Mirza came up behind me and greeted me warmly. I introduced him to the Verbruggens. Mirza was in high spirits. A guard took the twins and me to quarters, where we washed.

Freshened, I went into conference with Mirza while the others milled about.

"The lines to Valner are open and continuing," he told me. "We're in contact with your man in Kurdistan. Good idea, that."

"What about the rabbits?" I asked.

His expression changed so abruptly I knew that the air of relaxed amiability with which we had been welcomed was a front to hide something drastically wrong.

"One of them has been taken," he said.

"What?"

"The young one. The cousin. Yesterday."

"Yesterday I was in London," I shouted. "Why was I not notified?"

"They raided the safe house. They got him, but the other two managed to escape."

"Where are they now?"

"In another safe house."

"How did they get taken? What were your people doing?"

"The safe house was compromised. It was hit by the militia. Two of the boys got away. One was left behind. He was captured. Two of my men died."

"What do you mean, 'left behind'? How did two get away and one get left behind?"

"There was a warning. The two brothers fled. The cousin couldn't follow. He was in no condition to run."

"Why?"

"He was on drugs."

"Drugs? Jesus Christ! I'm less than an hour in Teheran, and I learn that your network has been penetrated and that one of the rabbits is captured. What else do you have to tell me?"

"Nothing."

"Who penetrated your network?"

"I don't know yet, but I'll find out. Don't worry. You're safe here. We came in here only today, and the only people who know about this house are on the premises."

"Bullshit. Where is the boy now? Is he dead?"

"He's under interrogation. He's in the police barracks in Qazvin."

A distant phone rang. Mirza left, then returned a minute later.

"The boy's alive. Still in Qazvin. Interrogation has proved useless so far, because he is still drugged. They won't bring him into Teheran until tomorrow or the next day. They want to learn as much as they can before he reaches here. The army and the police keep their prisoners away from the city as long as they can. Once in Teheran, he'll be before the courts in eight hours. The revolutionary courts are issuing orders for instant execution. What can I say? This is not my country. This is not the Iran I grew up in. People are going crazy here. We're destroying ourselves."

I looked at Mirza. He was a handsome man, his bearing proud in his navy uniform. His strength and intelligence were apparent, but distress had gouged deep lines into the sharp features of his Mediterranean face. He was from the upper reaches of Iranian aristocracy, educated in the West, a man of taste and breeding, a cosmopolite with command of half a dozen languages. He was still a serving officer in the Iranian Navy, but he devoted all his energies to running an underground railroad for enemies of the revolution—principally the rich and well-connected under the regime of the Shah.

"Can you arm us—submachine guns, grenades?" I asked Mirza.

"What for?"

"To get the kid."

"He's in the police barracks," Mirza repeated emphatically.

"And I'm being paid to take him out."

"No, we can't arm you," said Mirza.

"Then he'll have to stay there until tomorrow night. Our weapons are arriving tomorrow."

"This police barracks is a big place, with a lot of people about." Mirza stopped, then continued with resignation, "When you go after the boy, pick up the other two. They're in a village nearby."

"Then I'm going after them tonight."

All my careful planning was beginning to go awry, as events caught up with us and tumbled us downhill pell-mell. My men were growing nervous. There was constant movement in the house—phones ringing, people running around, messages whispered and shouted. To a Western merc, it could appear that things had gotten completely out of control, though I knew they were not. It was just the Iranian way of doing things, and I knew Mirza to be a good operator. My team felt naked without arms, and ours were a day away in the approaching lorry. Mirza agreed to give us a sidearm each for the night's sortie. I put the brakes on further by talking with Mirza about other matters that needed tending to.

"You obviously have a man in the prison," I said to Mirza. "I want a complete briefing. Security. Where the boy is. What's happening hour by hour."

"It's not a prison," he explained. "It's regional police headquarters. Sleeps a hundred men in normal times. A couple hundred more work out of it. But it's been turned over to the secret police arm of the militia, and the regular police want no part of that. There are fewer than fifty people—probably closer to thirty—around now. Prisoners are held in cells in the basement."

"Why have the police withdrawn?"

"Because things are happening there they don't want the world to know about. People being tortured. Being shot without trial. There's a tremendous amount of killing you never hear about going on all over the country. What the newspapers and radio report is only the tip of the iceberg."

"Who's being killed?"

"Jews mostly. They're the easiest targets. Terrible things happened here under the Shah. No question about that. But the really bad people—the Savak agents and the corrupt officials—are all fugitive. They're killing the innocent now, the ones with no reason to run and no place to hide. The old regime practiced religious tolerance. Now the country is being torn apart by religious fanatics, and the Jews are made to pay for a generation of peaceful coexistence. They're being made to atone for the sins of the real transgressors. For every Savak torturer on the run, you can multiply his chances by the size of his family. Iranian families are big and spread out and look after their own. Put them all together, and you have a hell of an underground. The revolutionaries are frustrated. So they're taking it out on the Jews."

The family cell; it was an old story. A barrier the British had faced—and failed to penetrate—so many times: Palestine, Cyprus, Aden in the fifties, today in Ulster. I guessed that Mirza's network was operating on the same principle.

I called the others in and briefed them on our dilemma. There was great consternation when they heard about the drugs. It was not a matter of breaking this kid, it was a matter of how fast he was talking, how much he knew. And how much we were compromised.

"Prison or no," said Gill, "he's part of our contract. We go after the kid."

He had saved me the trouble of saying it.

Two hours later, Mirza received another message. The boy had remained untouched all day, because his torturers were too busy.

"I want two helicopters," I told Mirza. "I want one stationed south of the city, and I want another one to the northwest, accessible from the highway."

"I can't do it," he said.

"You have to," I said. "We've been brought in here under false pretenses. Nothing is like what we were promised. We were supposed to be an escort. Now we're a commando team, scheduled to hit a military post. We're not backing out. You people have to stand behind us. I promise you I'll only call on the choppers as backup if the lorries fail us."

"I'll do what I can," he said.

Mirza got on the phone. Half an hour later, he told me he could provide only one chopper. The dilemma was where to put it. North or south? I chose the south as the more likely escape route. Anyone leaving to the north under duress would have to do it on foot all the way to Big Kevin's connection.

Mirza and I looked at the maps. I decided that if we got in trouble on the southern route, we would leave the highway near the town of Abadeh and strike southwest across the desert to the Gulf. Mirza arranged to have two Land-Rovers hidden in the desert near the highway and a chopper stationed just south of town. The Land-Rovers would have radio contact with the chopper, so that we could call on it in an emergency.

It proved harder for Mirza to lay on fuel for our plane than it had been to provide a helicopter. We were exposed to surveillance from a major airfield just south of our rendezvous, and there was a lot of Iranian naval activity in the Gulf. Mirza promised me that Nano would find the fuel drums beached at our rendezvous when he arrived, strapped to pontoons so that he could haul them out to sea.

I told Mirza my plan was to go that night to the village where Rabbits One and Two were hiding. The next morning, we would get our weapons and return to the village until nightfall. Then we would hit the barracks and bring all three rabbits into Teheran together.

"I'm going to case the barracks on the way up tonight," I told him. "I want to see what we're up against."

"You're crazy," he replied with a sigh of resignation. "You'll need fatigues."

Unlike men in Arab countries, the Iranian did not go around in long robes, which were ideal for disguise and concealing weapons. So Mirza secured us some army-issue fatigues, in the hope that they would make our Western features less noticeable. Half the men in the country were in makeshift uniforms of one kind or another; seven more should not prove conspicuous.

The fatigues were brought to the house by pickup truck, which was to be our transportation for the night. It was a claptrap old wooden-sided Ford, piled high with empty packing crates. The crates covered a false floor and a hidden compartment into which we all could squeeze.

We sat and waited for night and the city to calm. Every hour, Mirza received a call from Qazvin. The boy was being tortured periodically, but he was alive. Rabbits One and Two remained in friendly hands.

At ten o'clock, the seven of us squeezed into the cramped

compartment beneath the crates, and Mirza's driver swung out through the gates. The night was stifling, and the wet air scarcely moved in our claustrophobic quarters.

Despite the late hour, the streets were chaotic, filled with swarming men in makeshift uniforms of every hue and combination. As I watched nervously through cracks in the side walls of the truck, we turned out of a residential street onto a main thoroughfare. Within a block, we were halted by a maze of wooden barriers. As we slowed, armed men raced alongside the truck. A teen-ager beat furiously on the car door with a rifle butt. Amidst a roar of shouted commands, the driver stopped. We breeched our pistols in a futile act of defiance. If we were discovered, we could neither run nor defend ourselves with a handful of sidearms. The air about us bristled with automatic weapons.

For three minutes, our driver replied in low, calm tones to his shouting inquisitors. We were dismissed with a final rifle butt against the cab. The driver dropped the truck into low gear, and we pulled away.

Once we were rolling, Freeman squeezed back beside me from the front where he had been listening.

"The driver claims to be from Qazvin," he said. "Says he delivered a load of pottery to the city. He's on his way back home with the crates."

It took an hour to cover the five miles to the city's edge. We were stopped every ten minutes. We aroused no suspicion, but our fatigues were soaked through with sweat from the tension. When we cleared the last scattered houses beyond Teheran, the driver stopped, and we crawled up among the crates for the remainder of the journey.

Traveling with caution for ninety miles over some patches of poor road surface, we arrived at Qazvin at three in the morning.

Qazvin had none of the feel of an occupied city. There was no military presence in the streets, but to my surprise there were a few civilians moving about—late-night revelers drifting home, night workers on silent errands. Our driver took us through the center without arousing suspicion and drove straight to our target on the northwestern edge of town. He went around the building once, then parked nearby on a wide, tree-lined street.

Davis and I slipped out of the truck and walked casually back toward the barracks. We were in one of those new suburbs which sprang to life in the past twenty years and began to fall apart before they had time to mellow. The streets were paved where new buildings stood, then deteriorated into rutted dirt tracks in the open spaces. Blocks of flats hung with wash lines butted against half-finished steel-and-concrete shells alongside empty fields deep in rubble and building-site debris.

"What do you think?" I asked Davis.

"Getting in is a walkover," he said. "After that . . ."

We heard a distant scream, muffled behind the thick brown walls.

"We might work a little havoc on that place before we leave," I said.

An hour had passed by the time we rejoined the others.

The police complex sat within a ten-foot-high breeze-block wall that encircled a city block. Our approach brought us to the front of the main building, a four-story brown stucco flush to the street. The pockmarked façade and several broken windows told me it had come under fire during the revolution. On the street behind, we found a gap where fifteen feet of the wall had been blown away, then patched with boards and light timbers. This would be our entry point. We climbed to the roof of a building under construction, then sat back against the chimney while I compared our view with Mirza's hastily drawn map. Davis had a smoke.

The gap in the rear wall gave directly onto an exercise yard behind the main building, separated from it only by a shallow wadi. It was a fifty-yard dash across the exercise yard to the rear entrance of the main building. But the yard was flanked on both sides by old wooden barracks, living quarters for police and militia. We sat on our perch for half an hour. A dozen men crossed the yard, but not a single guard stood post.

Davis and I squeezed into the cab with the driver. He thought we were making our raid straightway.

"What happens now?" he asked.

"Drive on."

"Aren't you going after the rabbit?"

"Drive on."

"You've got to get him out! If he stays in there, he'll die."

"I'll lend you my pistol. You go in and get him."

We drove north for another hour to where Rabbits One and Two waited in a hamlet at the end of an unpaved road that followed a river, ten miles beyond the village of Takis... were only thirty miles from Qazvin, but the trip was agoniz... slow over hilly country scored with wadis from which shifting sands hid the edges of the road. By starlight on a clear night—it was now the early hours of the morning—we approached a hamlet so small I knew the entire population was on the take. There may have been a hundred houses, but they were jammed so close together that deception was a formality; it would be impossible to conceal the presence of strangers.

The driver turned the truck through the open door of a small warehouse; it was promptly shut behind us. We climbed out of the truck and followed the driver through a door at the back of the warehouse into a small dwelling, then straight through it and another door into a second house. These buildings had scarcely been touched by the twentieth century. The only light came from a few small lanterns that hissed steadily atop gas bottles.

Though it was obviously lived in, there was not a soul in the first house. The door through a common wall led us into the main room of the second house. There our driver was greeted perfunctorily by the only occupant of the room, an unhealthy-looking peasant who ignored us completely. The peasant's wife entered from another room and shuffled pots on the stove while watching us from the corner of her eye.

Freeman questioned the man sharply, but he showed no fear of the foreigners. Yes, we were safe. The rabbits were upstairs, sleeping. He had a question of his own. How soon were we leaving? To my surprise, he did not even react when Freeman told him we would be with him until the night of the second day. We would sortie once—to fetch our weapons— but the rabbits would not be off their hands until we went after the missing one after dark the second night.

Our hosts seemed disinclined to produce the rabbits. We needed rest and had time on our hands, so I said nothing.

I looked about. The house was less shabby than the first one we had passed through. Some decent Persian rugs were scattered on the stone floor. The furniture was simple, but not crude. The man's body and hands told me he was not a farmer. I guessed him to be a village merchant or manufacturer of rugs or leather goods, which gave him reason to go back and forth to the city regularly.

The woman fed us. She was frightened but determined to

help. They must have lost family. Her husband was afraid of nothing. He so hated the revolution, he did not give a damn what happened to him.

Our driver was no more afraid than our host. I suddenly realized these were not amateurs. They must have moved a lot of people out of Teheran. But I did not lose sight of the fact that their network had been penetrated. And it hit me that it must have been penetrated a long time. Else why had they not brought the rabbits out by their own network? Why mount a mercenary operation from outside if you have your own secure organization?

The woman brought us blankets. We each found our own corner, lay down, and slept.

I did not wake until after dawn. I rose to join Yves and Gill for coffee and bread at a long table. The others were still sleeping when I heard a commotion on the stairs above. In an instant, we were all on our feet, pistols in hand. Our host came grimly down the stairs. He was followed by two young men who were talking at him and about him at the same time in nasty, sardonic tones. I could not believe my eyes.

Our two rabbits could have been on their way to the Playboy Club.

# 9

The taller and older of the two was clad in a midnight-blue velvet suit with wide lapels and bell-bottom trousers. Beneath the jacket he wore a ruffled white shirt open to the third button. Silk-stockinged feet were slipped into patent-leather loafers with shiny square buckles. He had a gold choke collar at his throat and a gold-and-diamond ring on each hand. One thin wrist was bound by a gold rope; from the other glistened an enormous gold-and-platinum Rolex Oyster.

The younger brother was dressed similarly; his velvet suit was a rich dark brown instead of blue. Nor did the jewelry match, but it was equally expensive and abundant. Their hair was styled and their fingernails long and manicured. They looked no more rumpled than after a long weekend in a Teheran discotheque.

The two young men stopped to look at us, then grabbed

bread and two coffee cups off the stove before the woman had time to serve them. They kept up a stream of conversation as they ate. Neither the man nor his wife replied.

"By God, these two are offensive," Freeman said. "You should hear the way they're talking to this couple who're risking their lives to hide them."

"So you speak Farsi," the older one said. "Big deal."

From that moment, the rabbits had lost us. This was day one, and none of us wanted to know them. Normally, there was a strong bond between rescuers and rescued. But I had seen my men clam up the first ten seconds the rabbits were in the room. I felt a deep disappointment. Every mission is easier when the people involved care about each other.

"So these are the mercenaries who are going to save us," Rabbit Two said through a contemptuous yawn.

My mind shut off completely to these two. I thought: Right, there's the bag of shit I'm taking out of here, and that is all there is to it. You do not try to educate them. You do not try to change their way of thinking. You just say to yourself that's how it's going to be. And that is good. Because now they were bags of rubbish. And rubbish is moved around with ease.

The older one—and now I understood why Valner always referred to them as "boys"—was tall and thin, with a tremendously spoiled-looking, almost manicured face. He wore a smooth tan that continued down inside his shirt. He appeared to have a good physique, but there was nothing hard about this boy; he had the waterskiing muscles, but soft hands, tender feet. His moves were slow, deliberate, disdainful.

His younger brother, shorter and equally thin, had a cockiness about him that looked ready to spill over into finger-snapping, hand-clapping jive at any moment. He had a habit of tossing his long hair out of his face with a flick of his head. He was handsome, with a toothsome smile that might have impressed some rich young girls. Mr. Smooth. I would have expected to see him driving a red sports car or being rude to a headwaiter.

The rabbits turned from one of us to the other in hopes of eliciting some response. They had not yet figured out who was in charge.

"How are we getting out of here? Have you got a plane for us? When are we leaving?"

Both spoke perfect English with a British public school voice superimposed on the very faintest Iranian accent.

They asked a dozen questions, none of them about their cousin a few miles away in a police cell. The older brother dominated the younger, but these guys were a routine, a comedy duo feeding one another lines, playing off one another's jokes. They kept egging us on. When nothing happened, Rabbit One turned to his brother.

"They look pretty tough, don't they?" he said in English for our benefit.

"Are you guys as tough as you look?" Junior asked.

"Oh, yeah. These are the real hard cases," the older brother replied, then said something in Farsi which made them both laugh.

I caught Marcel looking at me out of the corner of his eye. He shrugged his shoulders and turned to his brother. Yves shrugged his shoulders. Both went back to thinking about something else. The Verbruggens had exhausted their interest in the rabbits.

Gill looked concerned in a fatherly way. He was a stern but very fair man who, as a sergeant, had brought a lot of boys around from this sort of foolishness. I saw him stirring. In another moment, he would be shaking this pair by the scruff of the collar. I gave him the nod to do it.

Freeman ignored the boys, too busy talking with the people in the house. I had told him to do this. Talk and learn, I had said. If you are in an alien environment, and you have someone who speaks the language, he is your best contact with the surroundings. You keep him talking.

Davis watched the boys with an incredulous expression on his face. He was the one who could not contain himself.

"Have we come for this fucking lot?" he blurted out.

We all turned to Davis.

"Did we come all this way for this fucking lot? I'm not risking my life for these sons of bitches."

"Take it easy, Davis," I said.

"Fuck!" he shouted. "Jesus Christ! Shit."

He went on effing and blinding for another two minutes, then walked to the far corner of the room to sulk. He had accepted the order, and he had accepted the responsibility. But he had let us all know that he did not like it. He would drag these two out of a swamp if they were drowning. But if he had to kick them to do it, so much the better.

To my astonishment, the rabbits laughed at Davis' out-burst. They must have known better. They must have known we were men not to be messed with. But they were oblivious to any danger. The possibility that they were on pills crossed my mind.

It was tempting to get involved in their treatment of the peasant couple. But I could not impose myself on the nature of Mirza's network. I caught the attention of my men.

"Look at it, and ignore it," I said. "We've got a job to do." I turned to the rabbits.

"Stay quiet, and stay out of the way," I ordered.

"Hey, man, it's cool," Rabbit Two replied. Like a lot of foreigners, he enjoyed showing off by using American slang.

The rabbits were seated at one end of the long table. I took a seat facing them and, never taking my eyes from the boys, spoke to Freeman.

"Tell the woman the boys can eat now."

She set two plates of hot, soupy stew before the rabbits. The older boy looked at his brother, then stared at me. Deliberately, he tipped the stew out on the table and upended his bowl. When I did nothing, Rabbit One broke into a low laugh. Rabbit Two repeated his brother's trick.

Our driver jumped up and ran across the room. He grabbed the younger boy by the hair and slapped him viciously across the face. Rabbit One leapt to his feet shouting. The driver released the boy and slunk away. It was apparent that the boys had a capital of fear with the Iranians they could call on when necessary.

Gill, pipe in mouth, stood up slowly and walked to the table. He knocked the still-burning ash from his pipe out on the table, laid his pipe down carefully, then slapped Rabbit One out of his seat and against the far wall. The boy did not move. He was out cold.

Rabbit Two jumped up but made no move. Gill rested a firm hand on the lad's shoulder and gently pushed him back down.

"Sit down, son," he said, "and behave yourself."

The boy slumped to his seat.

Our host was concealing a murderous rage. He said some-thing to his wife about Rabbit One; he was not going to dirty his hands with him. She took a liquid from the spice shelf and held it under Rabbit One's nose, then gently helped him sit up against the wall.

Gill picked up his pipe, refilled it, and sat back against the wall for a smoke. It was out of his system.

Rabbit One came back to the table, sat there for a few minutes with his head in his hands, then looked up at Gill. Gill was a million miles away, puffing absently at his pipe. Freeman was the agitated one, pacing the floor nervously. Our type normally wind themselves up when it is for real. There are a few punchy ones like Freeman who want to get stuck in if it is only a football brawl or a pub fight. Freeman was nervous. It may have meant nothing, but he wanted part of the action. When this sort of atmosphere occurred, he got nervous.

I came out of my seat to keep Freeman calm. Just for something to fiddle with, I picked up a short, heavy shepherd's crook the size and weight of a heavy walking stick. Now I laid it across the table while Rabbit One tried to collect his wits.

"Are you all right?" Rabbit Two asked his brother. "Are you hurt? Is there anything you want me to do?"

I picked up the shepherd's crook and pressed the end of it into the dimple of Rabbit Two's chin.

"We've come to take you fuckers out of here," I said; I do not swear a lot, but my mood called for it. "The easiest it is going to be is a week's walk. So get out of your stupid, fucking heads any ideas that you're going out on a champagne cruise. Either you shape up or we'll tie you up and carry you out on the back of a mule like a load of firewood."

The boy raised his hand as if to push the stick away from his face.

"Don't touch the stick, Junior," I said. "Don't say anything. Just listen to me."

He and his brother were paying close attention now. Very slowly they were beginning to recognize the enormity of what they were involved in.

"Now let's talk about your cousin," I continued. "You tell me how you were separated, and how he came to get caught, and you didn't."

Rabbit One began to talk, hesitantly at first, but with confidence when he saw that I was not going to hit him.

"We were all in this safe house," he said. "We were doing a little dope. Annabel was there with us."

"Who is Annabel?" I asked. "Is she Iranian?"

"She is Dara's girlfriend. Annabel is her nickname. We met her at Annabel's nightclub in London."

"Who is Dara?"

"Our cousin. The one who got caught. She was there with us. She lined up a couple of village girls for me and my brother. We were off with her..."

"You left the safe house to go off and screw some girls?"

"We didn't know we were doing anything wrong."

"Weren't you told to stay?"

"Yes."

"You were told to stay in the safe house, and you left with Annabel to get some girls. Is that right?"

"Yes."

"You try that with me, and I'll break your legs."

Rabbit One breathed deeply to get his voice back, then continued. "While we were gone, we heard the shooting..."

"Why wasn't your cousin with you?"

"He was too wasted."

"What does that mean?"

"He was too high to go with us. We weren't far away, in another house. We heard the shooting. We jumped in a car, and Annabel brought us here."

"It cost two lives for them to fuck some peasant girls," the driver said, his voice trembling with hatred.

"We didn't know," pleaded the young one. "We didn't get to fuck them. We didn't have time!"

This pair were worse than stupid. They were fleeing for their lives, and they found time for girls and a bubbly pipe. It made me sick to risk the men I had with me for rubbish like this.

"The police went right by our front door in a jeep," Rabbit Two said. "We had to run. What could we do?"

"Do you know what's happening to your cousin now?"

Neither could respond.

"If he's lucky, he's only having his fingernails torn out. You'll get a chance to see."

"What do you mean?"

"Tonight we're going to get your cousin. You'll be able to see for yourself what happened to him."

I saw fear in their eyes.

"Get him!" cried Rabbit Two. "He's in the police headquarters. How can you get him out of there?"

"Leave that to us. After that, we're taking all three of you back into Teheran."

"Where?" Rabbit Two's voice had a note of panic in it.

"The bazaar safe house."

Their fear grew to terror.

"No. We don't have to go there," said Rabbit One. "Get us out of here. Take us to Switzerland. Take us anywhere. We don't have to go back into Teheran."

It was not Teheran he was frightened of. It was the safe house. His fear was not for the revolutionary militia. It was whatever awaited them in the house by the bazaar.

"You don't have to be afraid of the bazaar house," I told him.

"Yes, we do. Why not?"

"My job is to take you out of here alive. That is what I intend to do. You'll have our protection."

The boy began to gibber, but his older brother snapped an imprecation at him to shut up. Suddenly Rabbit Two was desperately sober for the first time since he had entered the room. It was as if a screen had dropped between the brothers and the rest of us. Something was going on that was so compelling—terrifying?—that it reached down into the very soul of this boy. Had we touched on a Jewish—or Israeli—element? Had there been instructions from the father that this was how it was going to be? Or had he done something to put them on a third death list? Perhaps the rabbits had information that the bazaar house had been a Mossad safe house, and they feared for its security. Whatever the reasons, the rabbits did not want to go there. And their objections were fundamental to their very core.

"You should be far more afraid to go into Teheran than into a safe house," I told them. "You're on a revolutionary death list and a PLO death list."

Rabbit Two laughed.

"We are one of the richest families in Iran. We can buy anything. We're buying our way out of here. We're buying you. If we get caught in Teheran, we'll buy ourselves off that death list as well."

"Just like your father did," I said. "Just like your cousin."

I turned away. He was a typical teen-ager. One moment he made sense, the next he was an idiot. He certainly did not seem to know how big were the organizations behind this operation. Nor how interested people were in his family. Or perhaps he did, and that was why he remained so cocky. But going to the house in the bazaar was another matter. We were taking them there either for a debriefing or to be executed. Or both. It might have been even money that they would get knocked off in a safe house, but it was a sure bet that they would be killed by the PLO or the revolutionaries if they did not go with us. But whatever was going on in that house was the essence of the entire mission, and oh, how I wanted to know.

We stayed in the house from breakfast on the twelfth through that day and the following night. Truck and driver remained with us. Little was said. We rehearsed for the job ahead. The rabbits were silent with us, rude to their hosts.

"Where is this Annabel?" Davis asked Rabbit One.

"I don't know."

"Is she a looker?"

"What?"

"Is she good-looking?"

"I suppose so."

That was typical of Davis. Sitting in a safe house in enemy territory, he wanted to know about a skirt.

Through cracks in the shutters, I watched the street outside. It reminded me of a sleepy Spanish town. Peasants drifted by. A farmer drove his cart noisily over the cobblestones. We did not venture forth.

We studied Mirza's map and put our heads together to work out our plan of action. Police headquarters was a long, narrow building with front and rear entrances giving onto a central staircase to the upper floors and corridors to left and right, with offices flanking both sides of the corridors. The only staircase to the cellar prison was at the end of the corridor to our left as we approached through the rear entrance. This meant walking half the length of the building to reach the cellar staircase. It probably meant eliminating anyone occupying an office on that corridor. Our best hope was to infiltrate silently. It was insane to think we could go in, guns blazing, snatch the kid, and make a safe getaway. I decided to wait until the early hours of the morning, when there was least likelihood that anyone would be in the offices.

While the Verbruggens, Davis, and Swann went inside with me, Gill and Freeman would be busy outside laying explosive charges against the walls. Inside, Swann and Davis would stay on the ground floor to guard our backs. The

Verbruggens and I would go below, take out any guards we found there, and either locate a key or blow open the cell holding the rabbit. Once outside, we would activate the timers on the charges before leaving. Our charges would blow that building apart. Release any prisoners in condition to flee and give us time to get away. The explosion would kill a hell of a lot of our potential pursuers and disorient the remainder. Make it look like a major breakout. The survivors would be looking for everybody who was in the place, not just us and one rabbit.

I reckoned on us being at the compound two hours, which sounded long, but when you are infiltrating, time speeds by at an alarming rate. Moving in pairs across the exercise yard could be desperately slow. You had to go to ground while people fought or gambled or made love or just stood and chatted.

After we had run through the plan for the tenth time, we sat back and waited for the lorries. We all went to bed early. I slept soundly.

We were up at six and down on the highway by ten o'clock the next morning. Despite their protests, we brought the rabbits with us for their own safety. Their velvets took a beating on the floor of the pickup.

The first lorry was waiting for us at our rendezvous, simulating a breakdown. Our pickup pulled alongside, as if to help out. Our driver and the Iranian assistant on the lorry quickly transferred our weapons and battle gear from one vehicle to the other, while we remained in hiding in the pickup. In fifteen minutes, the lorry was rolling toward the Teheran truck park. I did not want to make a daylight trip into the hamlet, so we hid up in a wadi for several hours. The first driver had given us an ETA for the second lorry. We returned to the rendezvous, and within minutes it rolled into sight.

Road traffic was heavy in the late afternoon, but three of us changed a tire and we attracted no attention. We hustled the rabbits out of the pickup and through the rubber tubing into the lorry. I went forward to meet the German driver. He was an impressive guy, strong and confident.

"Hans," he said, extending his hand. "You must be Rivers. Are we ready to roll?"

He expected to drive us directly into Teheran. I quickly explained the altered circumstances.

"I can take these two with me into Teheran," he said, referring to the rabbits, "and you can bring the third one in your pickup."

"My orders were to stay with them," I explained. "I only have two of them now. I'm not going to risk losing them to get the third."

"Can you bring everyone in the pickup?"

"It's not large enough. We'll have a wounded man with us. I want you to sit on these two while we get the third one. We'll join you and travel in together."

"Where?"

"Qazvin."

"I can't take this truck into Qazvin and wait around while you blow up a prison. Look at it. Brand-new eighteen-wheeler with a German inscription on the side. Everybody in town will know it."

Our driver had been listening.

"If you take it into a garage, it won't be conspicuous," he said. "Trucks are breaking down on these roads all the time and going into Qazvin for repairs. I know just the place. Open twenty-four hours."

I knifed the spare. Following our driver's instructions, Hans left for the garage with the two rabbits. It was approaching dark now. Hans would get the tire repaired, then hang about on some pretext until we showed up with Rabbit Three.

We drove into the hills and lay up in a wadi. I was impressed with Müller's thoroughness. There were extras of everything; we had enough plastique to blow up half of Teheran. We had sent the heavy stuff—the Bergen backpacks, extra ammunition, some plastique, the radios, medical supplies—into Teheran in the first lorry. Here we strapped on our personal kits, but it was precious little. No heavy pouches or packs. No helmets. Just one webbing belt around the waist with a canteen, a knife, a small medical kit. I distributed the weapons. Everyone got grenades, though we continued to pray for a silent penetration. Marcel and I carried silenced MP-5's, and Davis had his silenced Sterling. The others were armed with MP-5's. Our driver looked on with envy. He had never seen an MP-5.

It was a matter now of getting ready. We worked our weapons over. Broke them down. Checked them out. Loaded them.

When we had double-checked our own gear, we checked each other's.

"How does it feel?"

"Is that working properly?"

"That grenade clip is loose."

It was a way to get the feel of combat again. To sharpen your mind for what lay ahead. To push everything else out of your consciousness. Families were forgotten. Pain disregarded. Death ignored.

# 10

We stayed in position while the moon rose and the stars twinkled brilliantly in the clean air. The night was chill. At eleven o'clock, the driver trundled us quietly through Qazvin to the street behind our target. He recounted with rage and sadness tales of similar places all over Iran where the innocent and guilty alike were being dragged in, tortured, and shot without their interrogators' charges being brought against them. An unknown voice rang through from Teheran with a name and a location. The local militia picked up a man or a woman or a family, dragged them in, and began a routine on them without knowing what the hell they were supposed to learn. When a man was no longer a man or a woman was too despoiled even for her captors, they called in to Teheran for instructions. The reply was always the same: "Kill them." It was happening day after day in Qazvin and every other town and city in the country.

When we reached the broken and boarded-up section of the wall, the truck slowed, and we rolled quickly out. The truck sped off, to lay up several blocks away. The driver's instructions were to pass by our entry point in one hour, then every fifteen minutes thereafter.

We had the boards torn away and were inside the wall within minutes. There we found a deep but narrow wadi we had not seen from the rooftop. We slid down one bank, scrambled up the far side and lay up silently on the edge of the exercise yard.

We were stuck there for an hour, until activity in the yard and the barracks quieted down. The guys holding this place were pretty sure of themselves. There was no security any-where that we could see. There were people moving about in the wooden barracks—we could hear the occasional shout and burst of laughter, nothing more than you would expect from a group of men quartered together. We heard faint cries from the main building; that, too, was followed sometimes by laughter.

The main building was only partly lit, but the barracks windows on either side threw a lot of light directly onto our path.

We crossed the yard quickly in pairs and dropped into a four-foot-wide concrete walkway that surrounded the base-ment wall of the main building. We regrouped under the stairs to the rear entrance. Two officers emerged to smoke a cigarette on the steps over our heads. Fifteen minutes later, they went back inside. Three soldiers returned tipsy to their barracks. Slowly the lights went out in the living quarters. The place was being closed down for the night.

I gave Freeman a thumbs-up and pointed to the door overhead. He scrambled out of the walkway and mounted the stairs in three quick strides. I sent him first because I wanted a Farsi speaker to secure the communications room, which was the second room to the left. He stepped quietly into the building, looked about, and waved me in.

I heard people in the rooms between us and the stairwell leading to the basement and also on the floors overhead. The corridors were empty. I burst into the radio room. There was no one.

The telephone rang.

Freeman dashed in behind me. He hesitated. He picked up the receiver. He spoke briefly, then hung up. He nodded an okay.

"Go," I told Freeman. "Send the others."

I watched the corridors while Freeman slipped out. He and Gill were most familiar with our plastique and the digital timers. While we were inside, they would be placing explo-sives all around the building. They would then wait for us to return from below with Rabbit Three. If we escaped discov-ery, they would activate the timers to go off two hours after our departure. If we were in trouble, they would set them to go off almost immediately to create a diversion and cover our retreat.

Marcel joined me inside. He and I slipped down the

corridor, ducked around the corner, and waited on the first step. No one stirred. With Marcel covering their route, Swann secured the radio room, and Yves and Davis joined me in the stairwell.

I led the others to the bottom of the stairs. We turned right into a corridor that ran the length of the building. There was no one in sight, but from the far end of the corridor, I heard a man scream. To our immediate right was a guardroom. Next to it were a dozen cells with solid-iron doors. Beyond the last of these—from where we had heard the screaming—was a long, open cell with a barred front.

I drew up by the door of the guardroom and looked inside. Four men in militia uniforms sat at a wooden table, talking softly and drinking coffee from metal cups. Two faced the door; two had their backs to us.

I waved Davis to my side. His Sterling was the quietest of the silenced weapons.

We stepped through the door together. We fired a round apiece into the backs of the men nearest us, killing both instantly. Davis reached across the table and grabbed the third man by the hair. He jammed his weapon against the man's chest and pulled the trigger.

These silenced weapons were amazing. It is impossible to fire a nine-millimeter round without making some noise. But the explosion was so muffled it could have been a door slamming or a chair falling over. No one stirred from the cell at the far end.

I knew the fourth man was going to start screaming, but I had half a dozen seconds to take advantage of his sheer, mute terror. I threw him against the wall and shoved the barrel of my submachine gun into his mouth.

"Where's the kid?" I said. "Where are the keys?"

The guy gagged, said something in Farsi, then shrugged and turned his palms up to show me he did not speak English. He was no hero. He was terrified. He was ready to talk to anyone who spoke his language.

"Get Freeman," I told Marcel. "Tell Swann to take his place outside. You stay at the top of the stairs. Hold the corridor."

We were unprotected at the building entrance but for Swann and Gill outside, and they were instructed to do nothing until we exited with the rabbit. They were our backup in case we got in trouble inside. If they exposed themselves to anyone coming in the building, we would all be trapped within. But we were lucky. Most people wanted to stay away from this place while these guys below were doing their dirty work.

Freeman joined us in the guardroom. I nodded toward the guard and stepped back. Freeman hit him a tremendous backhand across the face, then grabbed the man by the throat and began to squeeze the life out of him. He released his grip, leaned close into the man's face, and spoke.

The guard could not answer fast enough.

"The fourth cell," Freeman said, releasing the man.

The man rushed to a desk and rifled through a drawer. He turned to Freeman with a ring of keys in his hand and an expression of willing cooperation on his face.

We hurried the man to the cell to select the right key. As soon as he turned the key, I realized that opening this great iron door would alert someone at the far end. Davis and I waited by the door with the guard while Yves and Freeman slipped down the hall.

I took from my pocket a photo Mirza had given me of the rabbit. The guard opened the door. We pushed him into the cell ahead of us. The light from the corridor fell across a straw pallet on the floor. On it Rabbit Three lay sleeping. I drew in my breath sharply.

The boy was bound by wire, wrists to ankles. His face was beaten and swollen almost beyond recognition. Blood drained from one ear. More blood was clotted around a smashed nose. As he breathed fitfully through torn lips, I saw that some teeth were broken, others missing. His back had been shredded with a whip, and his chest was covered with the grotesque marks made by hot iron on flesh. His fingernails were torn away, and each fingertip had been smashed by a hammer or rifle butt.

I looked up from where I knelt beside the boy. Freeman clapped his hand over the guard's mouth.

The man pleaded with his eyes.

"Do him," I said. We had no alternative.

Freeman drove his knife into the side of the man's neck.

I cut the wires, then shook the boy gently. He reached for consciousness, then began to whimper. He thought he was being taken for another session. He cried out when I tried to raise him. I squeezed a nerve on the back of his neck, and he fainted in my arms. I lifted the boy gently, slung him across my shoulders, went out of the cell, and turned toward the stairs without a look backward. When I work with a team like this, I do not worry about my back.

Just as I reached the stairs, I heard someone come out of the cell at the far end of the corridor. A weapon roared once at my back. I turned to see a man fall. Yves and Freeman ran down, stood outside the open cell, and fired five rounds through the bars. Again, two of the rounds were from Freeman's unsilenced weapon. I lay the boy down and followed Davis back down the corridor.

One man lay dead outside the cell. Inside, three more lay dead or dying. Before I crossed the threshold, I was hit by that particularly nauseating interrogation odor, a mixture of shit, piss, blood, and vomit.

The room was the most primitive sort of torture chamber, littered with the usual things—hand-crank generators, car batteries with jumper cables, whips made of insulated electrical wire, rubber hoses, ax handles. A wooden rack. Huge wooden tubs filled with water. A brazier of glowing coals among which rested two pokers.

Nothing new. Nothing sophisticated. Just crude and violent.

Across the room, I spied the object of the earlier laughter. A naked man was spread-eagled to the wall. His hands were bound to hoops, his legs tied to ropes that threaded through rings at either corner of the room. The ropes doubled back to wrap about a drum. A twist of a handle tightened the ropes around the drum, tearing the man's legs apart. His arms and legs were broken, and in some places flesh had been stripped from bone. Pokers had been driven into his rectum. The flesh around the anus was seared like hamburger.

Davis cut the man down, then cradled him in his arms. He looked to me. The man was breathing, but that was all. I nodded.

Davis shot him.

"Let's go," I said. "We're going to have to shoot our way out of here."

We ran to the stairs, primed for a fire fight, but Marcel signaled us to be quiet. The amazing thing was that the entire building was silent. Everyone was apparently used to people being shot down here. The only sounds came from the cells; from the cries and whimpers, I guessed there were as many women as men.

We dragged the body from the corridor into the large cell.

We bundled the three bodies from the guardroom into another cell, so that anyone coming down would spend some time looking for them before sounding a general alarm. I hoisted the rabbit across my back.

"Ready?" I asked.

The men nodded.

There was nothing more we could do here. We could free no prisoners; they would endanger our withdrawal. We had been hired to do a job, not save humanity. But our explosives would soon rip this building apart. Anybody fit to walk could leave then.

We gathered at the bottom of the stairs. Marcel signaled us from above that the ground-floor corridor was clear. We hurried two at a time to the communications room, past the closed door of an office from which we heard men talking. Again two by two, we slipped out the rear entrance and dropped down into the trench surrounding the building. Gill and Freeman were covering for us.

"What's the situation?" I asked.

"All clear," Gill said.

There was a long burst of automatic fire.

# 11

The sound came from one of the barracks. A second passed. Then peals of laughter. It was just some guys playing games with their weapons.

"Give us fifteen minutes to reach the wall," I told Gill and Freeman. "Set the timers for two hours and drag arse out of here."

We went over the top in twos. I skirted along the barracks on my left, carrying the rabbit, with Swann beside me. We reached the end of the building and stopped. At that instant, a man came around the corner.

The man walked straight into me before he ever saw us. Swann put a knife in his stomach, grabbing his mouth at the same time. There was no cry, no struggle.

In five minutes, we were across the wadi and through the wall. I lay the rabbit down while we waited. He should have come around by now, but he was still out cold.

Gill and Freeman joined us shortly. Ten minutes later, the

truck rolled up. We were on board and hidden in ninety seconds. I joined the driver in the cab. We made our way to a garage on the far side of Qazvin.

We sorely needed a respite. It was the early hours of the morning now, and we were all feeling the strain. I would take ten minutes to brief the local people. We would pile into the big lorry. We would be an hour out of Qazvin when the charges exploded and in Teheran before dawn.

"Mirza's people," the driver said when we pulled through the gates.

They had taken over the garage in our absence. I breathed a sigh of relief.

The place looked half garage, half scrap yard, with a high wall all around. A sheet-metal gate swung closed behind us. From the cab, I saw Rabbits One and Two talking to Hans and his co-driver. With them was a striking dark girl in blue jeans and a wool jersey. They were chatting as casually as if they had been outside a pub on King's Road. I stormed over.

"What the hell is going on?" I said to Hans. "Who is she?"

"This is Annabel," Rabbit Two replied with newfound confidence.

"Shut up, Junior," I said. "You tell me, Hans."

"The girl is Rabbit Three's girlfriend. He'll never leave here without her."

"The hell he won't."

"I'm absolutely convinced," Hans insisted, "that the boy won't move a step unless she goes along."

I was dumbfounded.

"Have you been listening to these kids? They're idiots. Rabbit Three won't move a step unless he's carried. He's half dead."

The girl stifled a scream. The cockiness drained from the boys' faces.

"Where is he?" she asked in perfect English. "Take me to him."

"Shut up," I told her. "I want to know what happened here. Where did you get this girl, Hans?"

"I didn't get her. Rabbit One got her."

"What do you mean? You let him out of here? By himself?"

"No, his brother went with him."

"You let these two stupid kids wander around the streets alone? Small wonder you lost the war."

Hans did not reply.

I turned to the girl. She had long hair and soft, delicate hands, but she also had an intelligent face and a quickness in her eye.

"Do you know anything about nursing?"

"I am a nurse."

"Prepare yourself for the worst. Follow me."

When we pulled Rabbit Three from the truck, she screamed once, then took control of herself. She was a strong woman, a few years older than her boyfriend. I carried his broken body to a workbench and laid him out.

The girl said something to one of the Iranians, who shook his head.

"Do you have medicine?" she asked.

"A few things."

"Get me alcohol and bandages," she said.

"Davis," I called out, "bring us the medical kit."

Annabel was bent over Rabbit Three when Davis arrived.

"Hello! What's this?" he said. "Who are you?"

The girl did not look up. Davis grabbed her arm and spun her around.

"I said, who are you?"

"Knock it off, Davis," I told him.

"Call me Annabel," she said.

"Oh, you're the kid's girlfriend."

She pulled free and returned to bathing the boy's face. He was coming around. As he regained consciousness, he began to twitch and shudder. His teeth chattered. He sat up, clutching his stomach. I grabbed his wrists and pinned him back to the table. I started to turn away, then grabbed one arm. The inside of his forearm was pockmarked with needle holes. A dozen marks had made a pincushion of the vein in the crook of his arm. I grabbed the other arm. It was the same.

"He's having withdrawal symptoms," Annabel said.

I was still uncomprehending.

"Withdrawal from what?"

"Heroin."

I slammed my fist on top of an oil drum, then kicked it over. I grabbed the boy and would have beaten him against the bench if Davis had not restrained me.

"This kid is a fucking junky!" I shouted.

The others ran over to calm me.

"We've got a fucking junky on our hands," I shouted.

"He's got to get some junk," Annabel said calmly.. "If he doesn't, he's going to die."

I slapped her and grabbed both her wrists in my hands. I tore her shirt sleeves up her elbows and turned her arms over. They were unmarked.

"Are you a junky?" I demanded.

"Never," she said. "I don't touch drugs."

We turned back to Rabbit Three. His mouth was open. He sucked his tongue for moisture. His body twitched and shivered and his moans grew louder.

"He'll be crying out soon," Annabel said.

"We can't take this guy through a roadblock," Freeman said. "He'll never keep quiet."

"We'll stuff a sock in his mouth," I said. "Tie him up. He won't move."

"He'll die," the girl insisted.

"Is it true?" I asked no one in particular. "Can people die from drug withdrawal? Someone tell me. I don't know anything about drugs."

"In his condition?" said Swann. "Easy. His body is all broken up. That stuff is tearing him apart inside. I agree with her."

"I haven't got any damned heroin," I shouted. "Where are we supposed to get it? Gerrard Street? If he dies, he dies. We weren't hired to haul a junky around."

"If he dies, and we could have saved him, we haven't done our job," said Gill, as usual the coolest head around.

The boy opened his eyes and muttered something to Annabel. She grabbed his hand, then dropped it as he screamed in pain. She tried to talk to him, but he repeated the same words again and again.

"He's begging for heroin," Freeman told me.

"Please!" Annabel pleaded. "He's going to die!"

"What the hell am I supposed to do?" I asked.

"Let me go get some."

"Heroin? You have some heroin right here in Qazvin?"

"I can go get some. Fifteen minutes' walk. Twenty at the most."

I admitted to myself that Swann was right. If we tried to move him in this condition, Rabbit Three was going to die on our hands.

My job was to bring three rabbits out of Iran. The journey

started right here in Qazvin. And I needed to move two of them fast.

Rabbits One and Two had been hanging around during all this, but they had not spoken a word. The sight of their cousin—and what might have happened to them—had shattered them. If I did not get them into Teheran quickly, I was going to have two more basket cases on my hands.

But moving the boy was out of the question. We were to hole up in the Teheran truck park for the balance of the night, and maybe even the morrow, while the rabbits went to the safe house for interrogation. Rabbit Three could not be moved to the safe house, and he could not stay with us in the lorry, where temperatures might reach a hundred and twenty degrees when the sun hit it.

The boy's condition was fast eating at the rest of us. We could not treat his wounds here in a Qazvin garage. Ministering to him—the mere sight of his broken body—was draining energy off the entire team. I could see us all getting depressed if we had to hang around here much longer.

I was sick at heart with the entire mission. I could have killed Valner for letting me risk my life and six good men to save a heroin addict.

I went into conference with the men.

"We can leave him behind," I said, "but that's not our job."

"No, we've got to take him out," said Gill.

"But we can't hang around here long," said Swann. "Those charges will be going off, and when they do, this town is going to erupt."

"Freeman," I said, turning to him, "I want a Farsi speaker to stay here with Rabbit Three. The rest of us will take the other two into the truck park. I'll send the girl under escort to get the dope. When she brings it back, you bring him into Teheran in the pickup. The driver will take you directly to the safe house. We'll meet you there tomorrow."

"What about the girl?" asked Davis. "Is she coming with us?"

"Are you crazy? We're not paid to take her anywhere."

"I'll stay here with Freeman," Davis said. "If anything goes wrong, we need at least two men to handle an action and move the kid."

"You're right," I said. "Stay behind."

# 12

It was approaching two o'clock in the morning when we crawled into the Volvo with the two rabbits and headed for Teheran. It was a long, quiet ride for me back into the city. Things had been getting unstuck with this mission since day one. Now I had separated a seven-man team, and the stark reality of how few we were hit me like a blow to the gut. But the others must be on the road half an hour behind us, and we would see them in a few hours.

In Teheran, even in the early hours before dawn, militia were milling about everywhere in a sort of free-form night watch. We attracted no attention; though there was a curfew for civilians, lorries were allowed to roll so long as they continued to move from checkpoint to checkpoint along their route. We turned into the truck park just before dawn and squeezed into a narrow slot alongside our second lorry. Hans unhooked our trailer and departed with the rig for another corner of the yard where the drivers worked on equipment damaged on the bone-crushing journey across Eastern Europe, Turkey, and the north of Iran. We were cheek by jowl with scores of other trailers; we felt free to move between the two trailers with little risk of being observed. The occasional guard wandered by, but they had long been paid to turn a blind eye to us. We moved our gear and transferred to the other lorry, where our quarters were less cramped. Hans left to meet with Mirza. He returned within the hour.

He knocked twice, then twice again on the side of the trailer, a signal that all was well. He climbed through the pallets and joined us in the cramped compartment.

"Mirza's moved," he said, "to another safe house near the bazaar."

"Have you seen Mirza?"

"No. A contact stopped me as soon as I stepped out of the gate here."

A warning had come through that the house near the racecourse was compromised. Hans chose his words with

100

care. We could not talk in private, but he made it clear that
he was more than a driver. He had been briefed on the entire
mission, and he was here to back us up.

"We can't bring Rabbit Three into the truck park on a
stretcher," he said. The bazaar house, he told me, was only a
few minutes away. As he talked, I realized how extensively he
had been briefed. He knew the Teheran operation better
than I did, and he had not even seen it yet. This meant
Müller was dealing directly with Mirza now, not just through
us. Hans knew exactly where the bazaar safe house was,
which I did not, and he had just come off a week's drive from
Germany.

"When do we move?"

"Soon," Hans said. "They'll be along."

We sat back and waited.

The morning sun turned our trailer into an oven. By nine
o'clock, it was ninety degrees inside. At ten o'clock, there
came a loud rapping on the trailer wall. Hans opened the rear
and passed in to us mechanic's overalls, which we slipped
over our fatigues. We carried only concealed sidearms; the
automatic weaponry we left in the trailer. Hans stayed behind
with the lorry, as two of Mirza's men led us away.

We twisted and turned through acres of trailers until we
found ourselves in a quiet corner littered with broken-down
trucks, blown engines, abandoned axles and drive trains. We
stepped through a simple latch gate onto the street. The two
Iranians hurried us into a waiting delivery van.

I watched through the windscreen as we moved through
the streets of a mixed neighborhood. Run-down houses and
cheap flats abutted neighborhood shops and the occasional
better residence with a walled garden. The streets teemed
with women, their heads covered, carrying bread and grocer-
ies for the noon-time meal. Children scampered over vacant
lots and tumbledown walls.

Rabbit One tapped me on the arm.

"Will you take care of us? When we get there?" he asked,
lines of deep concern drawn around his eyes.

"That's what we're paid to do," I said.

"Stay with us," he begged. "Please!"

Near the bazaar, we turned into a side street, then into the
walled courtyard of a large house better kept than its neigh-
bors. A wooden gate closed behind us.

When we climbed out of the van, I saw that the house was

much larger than it appeared from the street. There were several apartments in the one building, but guards moving about told me the entire structure was secure. This time Mirza did not greet us. I found him busy at a desk in a small office just inside the house. One look told me something was wrong. He jumped up when he saw me.

"How many of you made it?" he asked.

"What are you talking about? All of us."

"How many got caught behind? How did you get split up? What happened up there when the trouble started?"

"Mirza, stop. I don't know what you're talking about. Tell me what has happened. And where are my men? Where are Davis and Freeman and the other boy?"

"You mean you don't know?" he asked, incredulous.

"Don't know what?"

"Two of your men are still in Qazvin. They were there when the barracks blew up. Until an hour ago, I thought you were too."

"That's impossible."

"I tell you I spoke to Qazvin. Your people are there somewhere. Your charges blew up half a city block. Killed a lot of people. There must be five hundred militia roaming the streets of Qazvin. Tearing the city apart. They traced the pickup truck to the garage. One of your men was there with the rabbits when they raided it."

"One man? Two, you mean."

"No, just one."

"Slow down," I said. "I've got to get this sorted out. My men should have been an hour out of the city before the charges went up. Are you telling me that when the barracks blew up, they were still in the city? One at the garage with Rabbit Three, and the other one somewhere else? Is that right?"

"Yes."

"What in God's name happened?"

"I don't know. I thought you would explain."

"What about my men? What happened to them? Where's the rabbit?"

"Both your men are alive. One of them is wounded. But they're separated. The wounded one is with the rabbit in a safe house. I lost six men at the garage."

"Where is my other man?"

"We haven't found him yet. We know he hasn't been taken."

"What part did the girl play in all this?"

"What girl?"

"Rabbit Three's girlfriend."

"Annabel was there?"

"Fuck me, Mirza. If you don't know anything and I don't know anything, who can tell us what's going on?"

"Your man must be with Annabel. She'll have hidden him. She knows the safe network in Qazvin."

I was on a short fuse. One more lie or evasion would put me over the top.

"I want to know who's with whom," I said. "And where. And I want to know fast."

The message came back within minutes. Freeman and Rabbit Three were in the hands of Mirza's people, in a safe house outside Qazvin. Davis and the girl had disappeared.

"Who is hurt? How badly?"

"Your man Freeman has been shot under the collarbone, but the bullet hit no bone and did not stay in him. He's all right."

"They should have been back in Teheran hours ago. Do you know what took them so long to get out of Qazvin?"

"I don't know why they stayed there in the first place," Mirza said. "Why did you leave them behind?"

"Oh, you son of a bitch," I shouted. "Because your rabbit is on heroin. They had to stay behind to get drugs for him, so that he wouldn't die. I could kill you for this."

"How could we tell you? I'm sorry. What can I say? How can I make it up to you?"

"You can't. I've got six of the best men in the business down here, risking their lives to save these spoiled, obscene little dope addicts. There's no way to justify that, Mirza. Just get us out of here. I hope these brats are important to you, because they've compromised your entire network. What condition is the rabbit in we left behind?"

"Alive. He can walk, but not much more. He and Freeman are on the northern outskirts of Qazvin. But we'll have to keep them moving constantly. We can't hold them anywhere now."

Now it was Mirza's turn for a temper tantrum. If we had not blown the prison, he said, everything would have been all right. I tried to explain the sequence of events, but he refused to listen. The scene was growing explosive when I heard the voice of Hans behind me.

"What he says is true," Hans said.

"Hello, Major," Mirza greeted him.

# 13

"Your people really stuck us in it," Hans said. "My principals don't get involved in drugs."

"There are drugs, yes. There are also the rabbits," Mirza reminded Hans. "This operation justifies that involvement."

"Before we go any further," I said, "I want my men and the two rabbits with me. They have a right to hear this."

Mirza spoke sharply to a man standing outside the door. A moment later, my team filed in, the rabbits in their wake. The past two days had taken its toll on these kids' arrogance. Now they were almost cowed. Mirza spoke to them harshly, then soothingly, like a stern headmaster dressing down the wayward sons of the rich man in town. The boys did not reply.

My men were curious but quiet. Hans and I briefed them on what had happened in Qazvin. He seemed to have a sobering effect on all of us. No one had to ask; they all knew he was someone other than a Frankfurt truck driver. I turned to Hans now, to speak on a professional level.

"You've obviously come well briefed on what's happening here. There's been a screw-up. Two of my people are still in Qazvin. Mirza lost half a dozen men at the garage."

"Was anyone captured?" Hans asked Mirza.

"No," Mirza said, not very convincingly.

"Before we even talk about doing anything else," I said, "I want my two men back. The rest of us are not going anywhere, we're not giving up the rabbits until I know my men are safe."

"I must speak to someone," Hans said, starting for the door.

"Hang on a minute, Hans. Let's not break this little party up yet. So far, I've been told virtually nothing about this mission, and what I have been told is a pack of lies. From now on, I expect to be fully briefed and fully involved in exactly what is going on here."

"Done," he said.

Hans left the room. I turned to Mirza.

"We're not giving the rabbits up," I said, "until we have some assurance our men are coming back."

As I spoke, Gill and Yves moved between Mirza and the boys. Mirza never blinked. We were not bluffing entirely, but a shootout, pistol against automatic weapon, with our only allies in Teheran would have been a desperate act indeed.

"Let's all calm down," Mirza said. "The quicker we get the boys in front of our people, the quicker you can all get out of here."

Hans left us to speak to someone with greater authority than Mirza. This house was growing more important by the minute. It was more than part of Mirza's network. Whoever was in the house knew we were here; we were the biggest thing in Teheran at the moment. But they chose not to reveal themselves. I turned back to Mirza.

"All right, Mirza, what the hell do they want the boys for?"

Rabbit One pushed his way forward and stood at my elbow.

"They're not going to get everything they want," he shouted, "unless we leave with you."

For the first time, I saw something in Mirza's eyes—was it respect or subservience?—for these boys. Rabbit One was rapidly regaining his composure. He was afraid, but not for his life. Something had to be retrieved from these boys here in Teheran. But for some reason, these people had to see that the boys arrived alive and in good shape outside Iran. And they knew it. I guessed Rabbit One would give them the key to what they were seeking here in Teheran. But the lock that fitted that key was somewhere in the West, and he had to turn the key in the lock himself.

These rabbits had something of enormous value to bargain with. Money? Knowledge? Whatever it was, it moved men to risk their lives, and Rabbit One understood that very well. Was it heroin? Was that part of a greater whole? Had his father been dealing in intelligence *and* drugs, and Rabbit Three was the victim of his uncle's venality?

There was a big, big score somewhere. People were in this one for a profit, and not just a fee for smuggling the rabbits to a safe haven. This operation was costing upward of a million dollars. What were these kids sitting on? Ten million? A hundred million? Or was it a thousand lives? I felt betrayed, dirty, and ashamed. Angry.

Hans returned.

"Mirza, you and Rivers come with me. The rest of you stay here."

"It's all right," I told the men.

Outside, I saw that the hall was now sealed off at either end by armed guards with automatic weapons. We mounted a staircase, walked along an outside balcony overlooking the courtyard, descended another staircase, and entered a large living room in another wing of the complex. Standing inside were three Iranians I recognized from the first safe house and the driver of the pickup truck. Two men were seated on a leather sofa. They rose and came forward with extended hands.

"Welcome, Rivers," the first said, grasping my hand between his.

The second man shook my hand in silence. The first waved us to chairs facing the sofa. We sat down.

"You've made a bit of a cock-up of it out in Qazvin, haven't you?" the first man said.

"I can't answer that until I get the full story."

"My associate and I are in charge here," the second man said.

I had assumed these two were Iranians, but from their accents I suspected they were Israeli. The first man was very military, erect, thin, and broad-shouldered; he had short hair, a sharp chin, and a keen expression. The second man reminded me of the editor of a newspaper who had been up every night for the past month, fretting over the early edition. He was podgy and dressed in nondescript sports clothes a size too small. His slightly bulging eyes were anything but keen; the lids appeared ready to tumble at any moment. Podgy remained silent now, while Soldier continued the conversation.

"Everything's in a bit of a mess," he said.

I did not like hearing that because I knew he was not talking about my operation, but his own.

"I want my two men brought to Teheran," I said.

"We can't give any indication of that possibility until we know what's happening in the field. The militia are on a rampage in Qazvin. The town is ripping itself apart. There is a frenzy of killing."

"Look," I said, "I'm not leaving here until my men are

safe. If you want my cooperation, you must start telling me what is going on. Do you still intend for us to take the rabbits out of here with us?"

"It is imperative," Podgy replied with a sleepy drawl, his fingertips touching just below his chin, "that you remove the rabbits from this country."

He paused for thirty seconds. We all waited.

"Our network is under extreme pressure. The safe house you were first in has been raided. Fortunately, it was empty. We lost no one there. A second house was raided. The people were not so fortunate. An entire family was killed, including a six-year-old boy."

"This is not the result of what we did in Qazvin, because it's happening too fast," I said. "What's going on up there may be a direct result of our blowing the barracks. But not here. You've been infiltrated. And long before we came on the scene."

"We have our suspicions that may be the case."

Podgy's hands never varied from their attitude of prayer beneath his chin. I began to warm up.

"You knew you had been penetrated, so you put pressure on Valner to hurry us down here. We were compromised before we ever got on a plane. Now you want to blame us for your own failure. We were hired to bring some very important people out of Iran. We come down here to find we're to play nursemaid to two disco dancers and a junky. We're professionals. We don't fight our wars for junkies."

"Two disco dancers and a junky," Soldier repeated. "They're wanted by the revolutionary government and the PLO. When their father was executed, it made the front page in every newspaper in the West. Don't be stupid, Rivers. Papa was paymaster."

Yes, but of what? A Mossad or CIA intelligence network, or a heroin ring? No one was going to tell me. I was simply expected to accept that it was all big and worthy and justified.

"The Iranians want the rabbits. And the PLO," I said. "I accept that. But why do you want them?"

"That you cannot know." It was Podgy again. "Believe me, there's a lot more at stake than drugs. Do we look like a heroin ring?"

"Do I look like a mercenary?"

"Indeed you do."

"And you could be a drug trafficker."

I did not believe my own remark. These two were bigger than Mirza's organization. They were not running an ad hoc network to run heroin or smuggle rich Jews out of Iran. They looked as if they had not been outside in five years. These were the silent operators who keep the intelligence world ticking year after year. My instincts were screaming, "Mossad operation." Mossad had its own indefinable—but still distinct—way of doing things. This operation bore that imprimatur.

What difference did it make who was operating here, or why? I wanted to shrug it off. I had only to take care of my men and get the rabbits out of here. But it was no good ignoring what was going on. These people were going to give me nothing, so for our own protection, I had to come up with some conclusions of my own.

My Bavarian principals, I decided, were most certainly not intelligence people—though I remained equally certain that Valner *was*. Neither were they an underground railroad, moving bodies for humanitarian reasons. What then but drugs could have provided the impetus for mounting a mission of this magnitude? Was the boys' father hauled into the streets and shot for political reasons, or because he was trading both drugs and intelligence?

Papa's Bavarian connection had been infiltrated by the intelligence people, because the drug traffic was compromising them. They let him go down because they could get what they needed from his sons.

Now they were going to swap the boys their freedom for information, or money, or secret documents, or whatever it was Papa had stashed away as life insurance. Before these boys left Teheran, they had to extract as much information as they could on the nature of the network there, to what point it was commingled with the drug ring.

I kept recalling Müller's warnings on the Bavarian connection. We *were* meant to get these kids out, so they could be fed into that Bavarian pipeline and expose the entire operation to German authorities. If we let that touch us, then we could go down on drug charges. Neat and simple.

Valner was the one to watch. He had to be the link man, serving two masters. He was more than a contact man for drug smugglers, else how could he have laid on Chimoum so easily? Set up a Cyprus pickup? Or used Mirza's network?

That Soldier and Podgy were Mossad was no more than an assumption, but it was one sharpened by years of experience.

They could have been CIA. Even British. Not Soviet, I told myself. This did not have the smell of a Russian job. Nor French. The French and Germans get along too poorly for coordination at this level. No, my instincts told me the efficiency and raw courage of this organization originated in Tel Aviv.

The hardest question was why Papa had entrusted these idiot kids with this information. Maybe they were not so hopeless as I had imagined. Rabbit One was not stupid. He was flash, but no fool.

I pressed again for answers and got the same vague response. The rabbits had certain knowledge essential to their own survival which these men intended to extract before the boys left Iran. Podgy even claimed they wanted to coordinate the boys' arrival in Europe. This was a blatant lie, because that was my mandate; the boys had nothing to do with it. But the longer I argued, the more Soldier and Podgy convinced me they were going to have the rabbits before we left.

We had nothing to bargain with. Certainly not sidearms. But they were not anticipating trouble from us. These men had complete confidence in me and my team. Our reputation preceded us. Mirza had briefed them on every move we made. They knew I had mounted a sophisticated operation and pulled it off, despite the way their end had botched it up. I agreed to give them the rabbits. One of the Iranians rose and left the room.

"What about my men," I said, "and Rabbit Three? Where is Davis? Can I go back and get them myself? Can you get them into Teheran?"

"It's impossible, either way. The region's under martial law. You'd be spotted in five minutes. Even bringing them into Teheran is out of the question. They'll have to find another way out."

"Where is Davis?"

"You can hear the phones ringing. We're as desperate to find him as you are."

"Do you still have a network up there?"

"Yes, and it's holding."

"Mirza has a radio link with my contact in Kurdistan. Find my missing man. I want escorts for the two of them and Rabbit Three to the northwest. I want you to arrange a pickup. To pass along all three to the Kurds."

The telephone rang. One of the Iranians answered, then

passed the receiver to Mirza. Mirza listened for over a minute, spoke a few words, and hung up.

"Rabbit Three and your man Freeman are well clear of Qazvin," he said. "My people are holding them in a house thirty kilometers north of there. Freeman's wound has been tended. It is not bad."

Within minutes, the phone rang again. This time it was Annabel herself calling. She and Davis were unhurt, but they were holed up in a safe house in the heart of Qazvin. It was riskier to stay there—some parts of the city were under house-to-house search—than to flee. Mirza ordered them to be picked up.

"I'm not responsible for that girl," I said. "We were hired to move three bodies, not four."

"Don't worry about her," Soldier said.

I felt reasonably confident I was not abandoning Davis to the hands of an amateur. The fact that she had this contact number told me Annabel was part of Mirza's organization, possibly the way intelligence had infiltrated the family.

But I could not overlook the fact that a massive manhunt for us was just over the horizon. With Qazvin in an uproar, it was only a matter of hours before the news reached Teheran.

Soldier and Podgy seemed to have no room to maneuver. If I took a tough line with them about moving my men around, or even tried to question them closely on the rabbits, I ran into a stone wall.

"How important are these rabbits that we're all hanging about, waiting for a big bust, just so you can see them?" I asked.

"Our people and yours," Soldier replied, "are determined to see these boys out of here."

I wished he had told me who "your people" were; I was fast losing track of where friends ended and enemies began in this game. Everybody but us seemed to be playing a minimum of two roles.

"I wonder," I said, "if these boys are as important to their enemies as they are to you."

There were a lot of Jews in Iran who desperately needed to flee, and here we had an entire network committed to saving these three. My remark went unanswered.

I refused to leave until I knew Freeman and Davis had been reunited, but I grew more nervous with each passing hour. The revolution was far from past history. We had heard periodic gunfire ever since we arrived. It was time to look at our alternatives squarely. The northern route was out of the question.

"I want reconfirmation that the fuel will be on the south coast as promised," I told Mirza.

Mirza thrust a map in front of me. I showed him the small beach on a headland between Hesar and Bandar-e-Deylam. I had been on this beach two years earlier; it would be as quiet as any place in southern Iran.

Mirza made a call, spoke briefly, then placed his hand over the receiver.

"The fuel will be there twelve hours ahead of your ETA. But there's no road to that beach. We'll have to bring it in by boat. Will there be someone there to take it ashore?"

"I want it left on a pontoon float," I said. "It will be that much easier to refuel our boat."

I feared they might try to stop us, if they knew we were taking a plane back into Kurdistan with their rabbits.

"You asked for aviation fuel," said Podgy. "You're not leaving in any cigarette boat. You're being met by a float plane."

Our security breached again—not through carelessness, but by necessity.

An hour later, a report came through that Freeman and Rabbit Three were reunited with Davis and the girl, and all four were en route for Kurdistan.

"I am ready to push off," I said, "as soon as you've seen the rabbits. Just give me final reconfirmation of the chopper down south."

We had arranged to meet it near the spot we had to leave the Teheran-Dubai highway to strike cross-country to our rendezvous. I figured the hour and a half flight would save us a three-day desert drive.

"The chopper's out," Mirza said evenly.

"You promised us," I shouted.

"Forget my promise. Yesterday I had you a helicopter. Now they've all been moved north, because of what happened in Qazvin. Sorry."

"The Land-Rovers?"

"In place and waiting for you. Extra fuel, food, and water on board."

My conversation with Peter Fox and his fat friend from Scotland Yard came to mind. If I had relied on the helicopter, we would have been stuck in Teheran.

Soldier and Podgy agreed to finish quickly with the rabbits. We would push off as soon as night fell.

# 14

The rabbits were gone when I returned to the team. I briefed them on Freeman and Davis and brought everyone up to date on events in Qazvin.

"We're taking one lorry south," I said. "Leaving the one with the pipe here. Somebody sooner or later will remember our lorry hanging around that garage in Qazvin. I'll guarantee you someone was looking out a window. Peeking through the shutters. Someone always is."

"Why change lorries?" Swann asked. "They're twins."

"More room. Why the hell we took two identical trucks, I do not know. But we did, and we have to live with it."

"We'll have to go through Qum and Isfahan," said Gill. "They're the heart of the revolution."

"Yes, but no one's looking for us there yet. The north is crawling with people hunting us. By the way, we have one more man on the team. Hans is carrying an MP-5 under the driver's seat. He's no truck driver. He's a G-9 major. We're leaving a radio with Mirza to set up south of the city. With luck, if they trace our lorry to Teheran, they'll find it holed up in the truck park and forget about the other one. But if anyone gets on to our lorry, Mirza will flash us a signal."

Mirza brought us army fatigues to replace the air force ones which would be more conspicuous in the desert. I advised him he would receive a message to be passed on to Valner giving our ETA in the Lebanon.

"Chimoum is ready for you," Mirza replied.

If Valner had told Mirza, how many more people knew?

After a quick round of goodbyes, we piled into the van and returned to the truck park. The pallets were gone from the rear of our lorry. Swann passed out a radio pack for Mirza's man, then we all squeezed into the cramped secret compartment. The few people about—mostly foreign truck drivers—ignored us.

There was only four feet clearance between the forward bulkhead and the false wall of our hiding place. When the rabbits crawled in two hours later, we had to press our bodies one against the next to get everyone inside.

The boys had come away from the safe house very glum. I probed them with a few questions but they were afraid to speak. These boys were now looking upon us as their saviors. They had suffered no visible knocking about, but a lot had been deflated from these guys. They were practically jumping to follow our orders now.

We made an agonizingly slow trip down to the railroad yard, where Hans supervised the loading of two new pallets—Persian carpets and bolts of cloth under plastic sheets bound by heavy rope—to leave us as much room as possible outside the hidden compartment once we were back on the road.

We returned to the truck park at three in the morning to hole up until Hans could clear our documentation. He had a new Iranian co-driver, from Mirza's organization; Müller had used our mission to insert his man in Iran.

The strain of waiting was almost unbearable. We were locked in a closed vehicle, without even a sentry to warn us of danger. If word hit the city from Qazvin about our twin truck, we were sunk. I stared out through the grill on the escape hatch but could see nothing. Yves cleaned his fingernails with a small pocketknife. Gill sucked at an unlit pipe. Swann drummed his fingers.

"We've got to get out of here," pleaded Rabbit Two.

The minutes ticked off an hour. One hour became two. Footsteps approached the truck. A hand rapped sharply on the gate.

"Hans," he identified himself.

He opened the tailgate, slipped into the trailer, then closed the gate behind him.

"Are we ready to go?" I asked.

"The yard foreman won't give us our papers," Hans said.

Rabbit Two retched noisily.

"He wants five thousand Deutschmark."

"The son of a bitch has already been paid," I said.

"He wants five thousand more."

I stripped a thousand pounds from my money belt.

"Tell him this is all he gets. If we give him what he asks for, he'll come back for more."

Fifteen minutes later, Hans fired up the engine. Just before dawn on the sixteenth, we rolled out of the truck park and headed south for the Dubai highway. It was stop and go for the first hour, past a dozen roadblocks and guard posts. Swann struggled to tune in Mirza on our radio, but the aerial was restricted in our tiny compartment.

"You can't raise the bloody dead on this thing," he complained.

Moments later, Hans took a hidden mike from his medicine kit and switched on the intercom rigged between cab and trailer. "We're clear of Teheran," he said. "Good driving conditions ahead."

At the same instant, Swann let out a whoop. "I've got Mirza!" he cried. "He says everything is okay. We're to keep rolling."

We opened the door and spread out into the space behind the wall, trying to make ourselves comfortable for the long journey. Physical conditions were not bad. It was hot and smelly in the trailer, but we had ample dry rations, plenty of water, and a plastic tub with a tight lid for relieving ourselves. We had light from electric bulbs both in the hidden compartment and in the open body of the trailer. We had all worked in worse circumstances.

The rabbits were far less happy than we were. They were not used to the monotony, the long distances, the discomfort. By the second hour, they were restless; by the third, miserable. The distance from Teheran seemed to put a bit of starch in their collars. They began to grumble between themselves, then aloud.

"Come on, you guys. Let's stop and stretch our legs," Rabbit Two said.

When no one bothered to reply, Rabbit One joined in.

"These guys are just the living shits," he said.

"Shut up, bigmouth," said Marcel in his heavy French accent.

It was the first time he had spoken to either of the boys. They sat back, slightly frightened, but with enough spirit left to go into a deep sulk. To date, the mission had not even tested our endurance. We had had adequate sleep, several hot meals, plenty of liquid, no long marches, no nerve-searing extended combat. The kids complained because they did not know better. I had too much on my mind to give them a thought. We were fast approaching Qum, the spiritual heart of the revolution.

By midmorning, we reached the outskirts of Qum. Hans pulled into a truck stop and topped up the fuel tanks. He knocked on the escape hatch and passed in several loaves of fresh bread, Cokes, and some bottled lemonade that made us all sticky but kept the boys quiet for a while.

We sat out a nervous ride through the city, with only Hans's occasional remarks to tell us what was happening: "We're going into the city." "We're approaching a roadblock." "We're clear of the last barricade." Hans downshifted, and we picked up speed steadily for two minutes. Suddenly, he braked sharply. I felt the lorry pull onto the shoulder of the highway and stop.

"Somebody's gone off the road," Hans's voice came over the intercom. "We've got to stop and help."

To keep going was a gross violation of the code of the road that would have attracted immediate attention. As Hans jockeyed the big rig, I inched forward and pressed my face to the escape vent. Fifteen huge lorries made a snake nose-to-tail and tugged furiously at a furniture van from Glasgow hub-deep in soft sand, while relief drivers dug frantically with shovels and pitched scrub grass under the wheels. The van did not budge. I turned away and sat back against the wall. Our trailer was stifling. We were in for a long stay.

"It's too hot in here," Rabbit Two said. "Can I crawl outside? Just while they're digging the truck out? Nobody will see me."

I told him to shut up. His brother pitched in and began to argue and whine as well. Gill rose and leaned over the two boys as if to hit them. They were near passing out. I felt my own head growing lighter. At that moment, we heard Hans climb back into the cab.

"It's not moving," he said. "We may be here half the day."

"Open the tailgate," I said. "We've got to get some air in here before we pass out."

We sat trapped under the blazing sun, our clothes drenched in sweat, while the men outside struggled for two hours to free their fellow trucker. Only the whisper of a breeze through tailgate and escape vent kept us conscious. At last, the lorries shook themselves free of the snake, and we pulled back on the highway.

Swann tried vainly to raise Mirza on the radio; we were out of range by now. Hans turned into the next village and called a contact number in Teheran. Through the vent, I saw him walking back to the lorry as fast as he dared without attracting attention. He spun the heavy rig back on the highway and rammed it through the gears.

"They're on to the truck," he told us. "The police found the other one in Teheran and staked it out, hoping to catch us. Mirza discovered who were the double agents in his organization. He's sent them north in the other truck with a load of drugs hidden on board. When those guys are picked up, they may be tortured to death before anybody bothers to corroborate their story. That will buy us some time. But sooner or later—and I suspect sooner—they'll be coming after the truck we're in."

"How far are we from Isfahan?" I asked.

"Almost four hundred kilometers," Hans replied.

"We must stop," I said. "Stretch our legs. Get some clean air in the trailer."

We rolled along for another twenty miles until the convoy we were riding in broke up. Hans stopped on a firm shoulder, and we climbed down on stiff legs. To our right, only a few yards away, a massive oil pipeline paralleled the highway. The sound of car and truck traffic passing in both directions rose and abated for miles in the clear desert air. We were relieving ourselves by the side of the road when I heard a more ominous sound.

"Choppers," said Gill, pointing low on the northern horizon.

There were nine of us—far too many for one lorry—standing down on the road, but it was too late to be seen hiding.

"Hold your position!" I hollered out. "Keep pissing."

Two military choppers came down the highway at seven hundred feet, one either side of the road, and shot past us traveling very fast.

"They're looking for us," Swann said.

They had never slowed to inspect us. But under the circumstances, we had to assume the worst and prepare accordingly.

"We're in a bloody shooting gallery if something starts," said Marcel.

As we scrambled back onto the gate, I grabbed the two Belgians.

"Yves, you and Marcel stay just inside the tailgate. If an action starts, you'll have to make time for the rest of us to get out."

The rest of us crawled forward to the open space. Yves and Marcel were out of our sight beyond the pallets, but we could hear one another by shouting. The rabbits began to panic; once more their lives were on the line. So were ours, but that was nothing new for the rest of us. It was three in the afternoon; the heat of the day added to our discomfort.

"Do we want to go through Isfahan in the dark?" Hans asked over the intercom.

"If we go in there, and the truck is known, we're fucking knobbled," said Swann.

"We're running out of time," I said.

"And luck," said Rabbit One.

"Shut your gob," said Swann.

"What did Mirza say about Isfahan?" Gill asked Hans.

"Not as tough as Teheran, but a lot of hot troopers about."

We lapsed into silence for a quarter of an hour, then Gill spoke.

"Why don't we stir up a little activity before we get there? Draw people away?"

He and I grabbed the maps simultaneously.

"Is there a pipeline on our right?" I hollered out to Hans.

"Still there."

"Here we are," said Gill excitedly, jabbing the map with his forefinger.

Half an hour down the highway from our estimated position, the pipeline turned sharply west-southwest away from the highway on a bearing for the Gulf.

"Hans," I shouted, "in the next few miles, the pipeline is going to turn west. When you get there, simulate a breakdown."

No more than ten minutes later, we felt the lorry roll to a stop. Hans climbed down and came to the escape hatch.

"Put your trailer legs down," I told him. "Break the hydraulics. I want your tractor unit for half an hour."

He had the legs down and the tractor unit freed in less than two minutes. The abandoned trailer would attract little attention; there was trucking debris scattered all up and down the highway.

We scrambled out the rear of the trailer, dragging our bags of plastique with us.

"*Voilà*," said Yves.

We were staring across a narrow wadi at a massive, forty-eight-inch pipeline suspended a foot off the ground on concrete stanchions. Thirty yards to the south, where the pipeline turned west, a precipitous trail led to a boulder-strewn ford across the wadi; on the far side, a rocky track followed the pipeline on its westward journey.

I ordered the rabbits back into the trailer. Gill and Swann

took up positions near the tailgate, and Hans and his assistant went to ground below the lip of the wadi at the front of the trailer.

Marcel jumped behind the wheel of the tractor, and Yves and I piled in behind him. We lurched off the road and hurtled down the bank of the wadi and up the far side at full throttle. We dropped Yves off at four hundred yards, and I jumped out four hundred yards farther on. Marcel took the tractor another mile down the pipeline before piling out himself. It took less than a minute for each of us to slap a charge of plastique to the bottom side of the pipeline. Marcel turned the tractor around and collected us, and we raced back to the wadi, where we laid a fourth charge, then hurriedly rigged the tractor back on the trailer. The entire job had taken less than fifteen minutes.

The most distant charge was set to go off in two hours. The second would explode in four hours, the third in five and a half, and the last thirty minutes later. Two hours until the first explosion would leave us still shy of Isfahan and should send every soldier in the region north to protect the pipeline. The first charge would not go up until after dark—it was near dusk now—and the subsequent ones, in the black of the night, would hopefully create the illusion that the pipeline was under attack, or that a guerrilla group was infiltrating the army lines.

The Verbruggens, Swann, Gill, and I climbed hurriedly into the trailer to join the rabbits. Hans fired the engine and shifted into low gear. The trailer lurched an inch or two. Then I heard the four great driving wheels spinning helplessly in the sand.

Hans de-clutched. He re-engaged the engine. We rolled the same distance in reverse, then stuck as before. The tires whined.

"*Merde,*" said Marcel.

"Jesus God Almighty," said Gill. "We're stuck."

"We're stuck," said Hans, far more calmly, over the intercom. The rest of us were less than serene, locked in the trailer, unable to see what was happening. I felt the hackles rise on the back of my neck. The rabbits were near hysteria. But Hans was a cool customer.

"A couple of you get out and give me a hand," he said, opening the trailer.

Gill and I pushed stones and scrub grass futilely under the

tires for half an hour, while Hans tried to rock us out, but the rig never moved. Traffic had dropped off, but now I heard the distant groan of an approaching lorry.

"Get back inside," he told us. "Leave it to me."

It was not one lorry, but one of the frequent convoys of fifty or more rigs traveling together for safety and companionship. When the lead vehicle came alongside, Hans gave him a wave and a signal for help. The leader blasted a reply on his air horns, and the last lorry dropped off the convoy to help us. While we sweated in the rear, eyes on our watches, Hans chatted amiably in German with the other driver for several minutes before he hooked his nose to our cab and with two link bars pulled us out in reverse. We were out of the sand, unhooked, and ready to roll again in ten minutes. But pulling off and rolling to beat hell was not the way it worked. No quick job and "see you, mate." The two men shared a smoke and a lemonade for another quarter of an hour, while Gill and Swann held their hands over the mouths of the rabbits, who were ready to cry out in fear. We pulled back on the highway with three quarters of an hour to go before the first explosion, then rolled in convoy with the other German for a few minutes, before dropping behind to travel alone.

We were an hour and a half north of Isfahan, rolling at seventy miles an hour across the desert landscape, when Hans braked and downshifted.

"Big roadblock," Hans informed us. "There must be forty or fifty lorries ahead of us. We're going to be here a hell of a long time."

"What the hell's happening?" I asked. "Are they looking for our truck?"

"I don't know what they're doing. It's a military roadblock, but there seems to be no panic on. They're not getting rough with anybody. Just checking. But it's all taking a long time."

"What are they checking?"

"Cabs. Loads. Papers."

"Are they searching the vehicles?"

"Just opening the backs."

"How many?"

"Twenty-five or thirty. With automatic weapons. Several military trucks about."

The waiting became excruciating, because we had no way of knowing when we might get a call to arms. I had been in tight spots before but, I promised myself, never again where

I could not see what was going on. Hans kept up a running commentary to calm us. The soldiers did not appear to be working under any special orders. The truckers were milling about, wandering from vehicle to vehicle, bantering with the security forces. The atmosphere was unstrained, but the searchers were taking about ten minutes a vehicle; at that rate, we would be camped here half the night.

We were proceeding down the queue when Gill looked at his watch.

"There goes the first one," he said.

We were too far to hear the explosion but near enough to see the glow against the night sky.

"Anything happening?" I asked Hans.

"Nothing. That one must not have ignited the oil."

Ten minutes later, pandemonium broke out among the soldiers. They ordered the drivers back in their cabs and told everybody to wait. Shortly a convoy of troop carriers sped past on their way north. Chopper traffic came over the top, sped away, then returned to land somewhere near our lorry.

We breeched our weapons and made ready for a shoot-out. I sent Gill and Swann to hide among the pallets, then turned to the rabbits. Rabbit Two was shriveled up in a corner like a frightened animal. Rabbit One shivered and blinked his eyes; he worked his jaw to rid himself of a tic.

"They're coming up the line," Hans said. "They're opening the backs of the lorries."

I yelled for Gill to come take care of the kids. Swann hid among the pallets, where he would not be found except by the most conscientious searcher. When Gill saw the condition of the boys, he grabbed Rabbit One by the collar, slapped him—not hard—and ordered him to keep his brother under control.

"Stand by us, and the worst that can happen to you is that you'll lose your life. If you start making a lot of noise and turn us over and you fall in their hands, you're a lot worse off."

The boy struggled against his fear trying to appreciate what Gill was telling him.

"I'm pulling off," Hans warned us. "Everything's suddenly speeding up. They're waving me ahead about a hundred meters. There's a big conference going on between the chopper crews and the officer in charge."

"How far are we from the roadblock?" I asked.

"We're about number ten in line. Here they come. They'll

be opening the rear of the truck in about ten minutes. My man is cracking up."

He was talking about his Iranian relief driver.

We heard the footsteps of several men on either side of the cab, then Hans in conversation with them. A minute later, he climbed back in the cab, and the footsteps started toward the rear of the trailer.

"They've cleared my papers," Hans said hurriedly. "They'll be looking in now," he said; at that moment, we heard the bolts being thrown in the tailgate.

"Keep me informed where the choppers are," I said; if we had to fight, it would be toward the choppers. "How's your man?"

"Sweating like a pig. Scared shitless. But no one's noticed. Shut up!" he snapped, and went off the air.

There was more rattling in the rear. The relief driver was having trouble with the tailgate. Hans got out of the cab. Rabbit Two made a small squeal. Swann threw him to the floor, and Marcel clapped a hand over his mouth. Gill did the same to the older boy. I released the latches that held the grill of the escape hatch in place.

"It's going to take all six of you to open the tailgate. It's very heavy," Hans said loudly to let us know what we were facing.

The soldiers opened the rear of the trailer, jumped inside, made a cursory inspection. They were gone within two minutes, and we were able to relax. We waited while they went through another ten trucks behind us. We were brought forward to the roadblock, where we sat for an hour while the other trucks were brought in line behind us.

"Five minutes to the next charge," said Gill.

A lorry engine turned over, then half a dozen more burst into life.

"They're sending us out in convoy," Hans said.

We rolled through the roadblock with two minutes to go. Hans had just settled down at the cruising speed when he came back on the air.

"Big yellow glow on the horizon. It's burning like hell."

# 15

Just before midnight, we were brought up short by gun-waving pickets at a roadblock on the outskirts of Isfahan. It appeared our diversion had worked against us; our time was running out. The last charge, by the road, would have cut off traffic from Teheran and created a vacuum between us and the pipeline. But the south was aflame with revolutionaries bent on wreaking vengeance on those who dared challenge them. These people were trigger-happy, waiting for the least word of defiance from the argumentative truckers to arrest or kill us on the spot.

Our convoy was ordered cleared to a truck park in the city. Three armored troop carriers with trained machine guns led us there. We were clustered bumper to bumper and told to wait until morning.

All around us, we heard truckers cursing in half a dozen languages. Hans left with a group searching for hot food. It would have looked odd if he had refused to mix with the others.

The Iranian brought us cold food and drinks, which he slipped through the hatch while pretending to repair hydraulic cables. They did little to lift our spirits. We had been cramped, hiding somewhere, since the mission began. Our bodies were tired, our muscles sore and stiff, we were ready to scream our heads off.

Rabbit Two fell asleep in a heap.

Rabbit One struck up a conversation in a low voice with Gill. He was the only friend they had among the lot of us. Swann had taken an immediate dislike to the older boy, which sentiment was reciprocated. The rest of us were simply not interested. I almost never spoke to the two boys. I had little patience for them. I was too occupied and bloody worried about the job at hand.

When Rabbit One turned away momentarily, I spoke to Gill quietly. "Keep him calm. Keep him talking. Learn what you can."

He told Gill about public school in England. He had been to a university in the United States, somewhere in the East, and was a graduate of a business school in France. He mentioned in passing that he had spent time in the Lebanon and made several trips to Israel. For a youth of his tender years, he had put down a lot of mileage circulating through his father's business interests. He was not the fool I had first suspected. He had been a loyal son. He had followed his father's orders, run the errands the old man commanded.

Perhaps he had not learned a lot from what he had done, but I was getting the impression he got the job done.

"What do you think happened to Davis and Freeman?" Marcel asked.

"They must have been in different parts of the house when they were raided," I postulated. "They went out in different directions and weren't able to get back together."

"Do you know anything about Annabel?" Rabbit One asked, sitting up and stretching.

"Only that she was safe the last I heard. Do you know her well?"

"I brought her into the family. Then she dropped me for my cousin. He is my cousin, you see, but he is also my brother. He lived in our home since he was one year old. My father and my brother loved him as if he were our own. But he never believed that. He felt like an outsider."

"How did he get on heroin?"

"Friends. They all used it."

"Some friends," said Gill.

"Have you ever tried it, man? You don't know. It might catch up with you, but it's the greatest high there is. I mean, I don't do heroin. I don't even chip. But I've smoked a lot of opium. Cocaine is nothing compared to that."

"I wouldn't know," said Gill.

It was beginning to sound like a conversation in university digs. I fell asleep.

There were only a dozen lorries ahead of us when we joined the queue at six the next morning to leave the truck park. But there was mass confusion at the gate, soldiers and police milling everywhere, and every trucker and his documents seemed to fall under the microscopic inspection of a man whose grasp of the pertinent language was at best rudimentary. The drivers gave as good as they got, shouting, waving papers and passports, thrusting documents under the noses of men who pushed them aside.

When Hans's turn came, he engaged in a fifteen-minute shouting match with a youth armed with an automatic weapon, then disappeared for half an hour into the supervisor's shack. It was past ten before he climbed back into the cab, threw the big truck into low gear, and pulled off. Trucks were backlogged all the way across the city. An hour passed in silence, then Hans left the last house behind. He burst into the intercom.

"They wanted to know every bloody thing," he shouted. "They wanted to know if we were in convoy before we reached Teheran. I had to say yes. They asked if there was another vehicle from our company. They're on to us."

"That's crazy," I said. "If they had been on to us, they'd never have let us out of the truck park."

"Those guys didn't have any authority," he replied. "They didn't know exactly what they were supposed to be doing. They were intimidated by all those screaming truckers. I think we got the benefit of the doubt because they wanted to clear the trucks out. But they know it's us. And they had a radio."

"We're only eighty miles from the Land-Rovers," I reminded him.

"That's three hours," he said, "in the traffic. Trucks are spacing out for ten miles in front of us."

We rolled on in silence. I could not imagine we were going to cover those eighty miles without incident. Half an hour passed. As if in answer to my thoughts, I heard the approach of helicopters from the north.

"Two choppers watching the highway," said Hans. "Up high and in a hurry. They're taking a look at everything."

I heard them disappear down the road to the south. A few minutes later, they were back. They were much lower this time.

"They're really taking a look," Hans said.

"At us?"

"We're on a straight stretch of highway. There must be fifty vehicles in sight of one another," he said. "They're not paying any more attention to us than to the others. Wait a minute. They're leaving."

Two minutes later, he came back on.

"One of them has gone. The other one has pulled way back, but he's staying in our vicinity."

"How many vehicles are behind us?" I asked.

"Four or five. We're near the end of the convoy."

"We've got to know if they're watching us. Slip to the back of the convoy," I said.

That maneuver took twenty minutes.

"The chopper's still around."

"Around us?"

"Around the end of the convoy."

"Cut your speed way back," I said. "Get a good mile between us and the end of the convoy."

Hans lifted his foot from the throttle. This move would attract no undue attention. Truckers regularly dropped off a convoy because they were having mechanical problems or because the strain of making the pace became too tiring.

In five minutes, Hans came back on the intercom. "The chopper stayed with the convoy. We're in the clear."

Hans coasted another ten minutes, then pulled off the road. He and the co-driver stood down to relieve themselves by the road and drink a cup of coffee. When the next convoy came into sight far to our north, he pulled back on the road. Now we were spaced between two convoys. There was a certain amount of security in rolling with the other lorries, but if we had to move in a hurry, we wanted an empty highway.

"Vehicle approaching very fast on the left," Hans informed us.

"From in front or behind?"

"Behind."

A truck roared past.

"A troop carrier," Hans said. "Going like hell."

Within five minutes, a second troop carrier had followed the first.

"The choppers are back," Hans said. "Standing off at a distance."

I guessed the choppers had signaled someone there was a suspect vehicle. The company name on the side of our trailer had been picked up and checked out, and the choppers had come racing back to watch us. We rolled in silence for ten minutes.

"One chopper has gone on ahead," Hans said.

"Where's the other one?"

"Right with us. Good God! The other one's parked on the side of the road. Waiting for us to go past."

I heard the rotors turning slowly as we raced by. We were jumping out of our skins in the back of the lorry, uselessly fingering weapons, turning grenades over in our hands. The kids were completely gone by now, trembling and crying uncontrollably.

"He just waited for us to go past," Hans said. "Now he's taken off again. Here comes a truckload of them going north now. We're running behind three other lorries in a mini-convoy, but we're well spaced out."

This running commentary was driving me crazy. I was having trouble keeping it all straight in my mind.

"Hans," I hollered, "what the hell do you think is happening out there?"

"The truck that just went north is setting up a roadblock behind us. There'll be another roadblock in front of us very soon. Yeah, here it comes now!"

When Hans lifted his foot from the throttle, I heard the beat of the choppers approaching from the rear. Hans's voice had been getting higher with every message. Now as combat neared, a professional coolness crept into his reports.

"We're going to be stopping," he said. "You better get someone in the back of the trailer. There's no talking our way out of this one."

"I'll stay with the boys," said Gill, placing his hand on the trembling shoulder of Rabbit Two.

Yves and Marcel looked at one another, then without a word began climbing past the pallets to the rear. Swann stayed with me near the escape hatch. We primed our weapons.

"You've got to tell us how the action is setting up," I said to Hans. "Do everything you can to keep them from opening the rear. If that tailgate goes up, we start shooting."

"If they insist on opening the truck, I'll stay in the cab and have the relief driver go with them. I'll cover you long enough to clear the trailer."

Hans saw his voice was calming us now. He kept up his commentary while we sat briefly with the engine idling.

"They're on to us for sure," he said at last. "They've just waved the other trucks through without inspecting them. They're coming toward us now."

"Where're the choppers?" I shouted desperately.

"There's only one here. It's hovering off to the side. Left rear. It's coming in closer."

Someone shouted an order at Hans in Farsi. He had only moments to talk.

"How far ahead is the roadblock?"

"Fifteen meters."

"Don't let them approach us. Drive right in the middle of the roadblock."

When Hans shifted into low and pulled forward, the guards

shouted angrily for him to stop and beat on the side of the
trailer with their weapons. He ignored them, shouting a
reply in German, and rolled forward.

"We're right in the middle of them," he said. "Two lorries
off to the left. One to the right. Fourteen, fifteen men.
Everyone in range. No one behind our lorry now."

"Where the hell is the chopper?"

"Still hovering. Left, off our rear."

Unless we brought it down, it would either gun us all down
or take off for help. Either way, we were finished. We had to
make it land.

"Marcel! Yves! Come back and hide behind the first pallet.
Don't open up until they've climbed inside!"

I was gambling that when the chopper crew saw men
climbing into the trailer, they would assume everything was
under control, and their natural curiosity would bring them
in for a closer look. In any case, if we had three or four up in
the tailgate before the action started, it would open like a
shooting gallery.

"What's the condition of your man?" I asked.

"Terrible."

Over the intercom, I heard Hans rattling around in the
cab, then a weapon being breeched. The roar of the chopper
increased.

"He's right on top of us now," he said.

The beat of the rotors was deafening. The trailer shook and
swayed.

"He's throwing up so much dust they can't see what they're
doing," Hans said. "They're waving him away. By God, he's
landing! Right behind us! On the road. Here they come!"

The chopper touched down on the road and dropped its
rotors to idling speed. I could hear at least two radios, one
from the chopper, another from in front of us, probably in
one of the lorries.

When the soldiers ordered Hans out of the cab, he played
a delaying game, at first pretending not to understand, then
setting up a big argument in English and German, demand-
ing an explanation. He did not want to leave the cab—and his
MP-5. When they started shouting and threatening, he had
no choice but to obey. He ordered the other driver to stand
down with him; that gave these guys twice as many people to
watch.

The next ninety seconds were confusing, because I had lost

my eyes when Hans left the cab, and I could hear only what came through the walls of the trailer. Four or five guards were gathered with Hans and the Iranian near the cab in a heated dispute. I heard a thump and a man falling, then Hans asking the other driver if he was hurt and telling him to stay calm. They all walked to the rear of the trailer.

"You open it," we heard Hans say.

"I don't want to," whined his assistant.

"Open the goddamn trailer," Hans snapped. "Nothing's going to happen."

The bolts were thrown, but before the gate was opened, the Iranian began to run. Two shots rang out. There was a few seconds' pause—while they trained their guns on Hans— then three soldiers threw open the tailgate and clambered aboard.

# 16

The Verbruggens let loose simultaneously, killing all three instantly. More soldiers on the road broke for the back of the truck. The Verbruggens leapt out. One threw a grenade right up under the helicopter and blew it to pieces.

"*Merde!*" cried Marcel. "I'm hit!"

I heard the Verbruggens exchanging fire with AK-47's, then the pop of Hans's sidearm. The cover on the escape hatch was stuck, and I raised one foot to kick it out just as Hans arrived to rip it away. As I squeezed out the narrow opening, Hans took a bullet in the back that slammed him up against the cab. He fell over backward and lay still. He was alive, but only barely.

I went headfirst onto the hydraulic plate, nearly knocking myself out. I was trying to untangle myself from the hydraulic lines when I saw a man drawing a bead on the prostrate Hans. I sprayed half a dozen rounds in his direction from my MP-5 and hit him with at least three of them. When he fell, I glanced around and saw another soldier dead near Hans's open cab door; apparently, Hans had hit him on the run. I rolled to the shoulder side of the trailer, opposite where I had heard the men running. Beneath the rig, I saw the legs of half a dozen men firing upright at the Verbruggens, who by this time were firing from the road. I sprayed bullets in a wide arc and brought them all down, shattering their legs but killing none of them.

Swann fell in alongside me. The odds were reducing fast. We had killed two by the cab and the Verbruggens three in the initial blast, plus the helicopter crew, at the cost of only two men hit. Marcel was on the ground but still firing and not looking all that badly hurt. That left ten men standing for the five of us.

But these guys were in a panic. They were a bunch of raw recruits, conscripts probably, who had been in total control a minute earlier, and suddenly people were blowing them away. Most of them had never fired a weapon off a range, never heard the terrible roar of a fire fight at twenty yards. The helicopter burned furiously at their backs. There was no cover anywhere. To my surprise, none of them dropped their weapons and ran. They spread out and began to drop back, still firing. Though they were unaware of it, the Iranians had far greater firepower—they were carrying AK-47's—than we did; we had to move fast to keep the fight at close range.

Swann ran around the lorry and killed three of the men I had shot beneath the rig. Two of them broke to take cover behind the burning chopper, but Marcel and Yves shot them down. The rest, firing upright in the road, began to scatter like quail.

Two of them broke into a run toward a distant lorry. I headed to cut them off—rolling, leaping, moving at a broken pace. I shot one, and Swann killed the second as he climbed into the cab.

The dice were cast now. We were far better at this game in the open than they were, and they knew it. They quit trying to fight us and set to saving their lives. I heard our tractor unit burst into flames.

I turned back to see Hans stumbling out of the cab. Somehow he had regained his feet and gone for his MP-5. He staggered across the road amidst three guys trying desperately to find some cover below the lip of the asphalt. He killed two of them, then fell dead without receiving another hit. Gill scrambled out of the rear of the trailer, dragging the rabbits with him. He hauled them fifty yards into the desert, then threw them on their faces.

"Don't move," he ordered, then ran toward the trailer.

The fuel tanks were going to explode in any second. Both boys started crawling away as fast as their hands and knees would carry them, but at least they did not stand up and run. The Verbruggens and Swann killed the last three soldiers at the rear of the trailer, then joined me to kill the final two survivors near the front. They were caught in the open and cut down by one round apiece. I saw with relief that Marcel was on his feet and moving without great difficulty, though he was bleeding profusely.

Though flames engulfed the cab and licked around the petrol tanks, Gill crawled into the trailer and emerged with one backpack and a radio. I ran to the fallen Hans and turned him over. The first bullet had pierced his lungs; he had struggled across the road as a dying gesture. Hans was a hell of a man. I hated to lose him. His Iranian driver was dead. The two or three surviving Iranian soldiers were dispatched with a knife; we could not afford the luxury of survivors. Marcel, I learned, had a bloody and painful, but superficial, wound in his side.

We stood on a field of carnage. There was nothing but desert as far as we could see in any direction. We had to move and move fast.

# 17

"Can you travel?" I asked Marcel.

"Sure," he replied.

The bullet had entered an inch or two inside his ribs and exited the same way, cracking bone in the process. I had seen similar wounds stop good men. But Marcel was in no mood to be left behind.

We policed the area quickly, double-checking that all the soldiers were dead. There was nothing on the battle scene we wanted; the Iranians carried little more than a couple of magazines and their AK-47's.

We set fire to two of their vehicles, then all piled into the third and took off like the Keystone Kops. Swann took the wheel of the open-back troop transport. I climbed in front with him. The others jumped in the rear.

We were still a long thirty miles from our rendezvous with the Land-Rovers, but the truck was new and fast, and we belted off down the road to beat hell. We caught up with our mini-convoy and blew past them in a trail of dust. We drove as fast as the truck would move for twenty miles, then took off across the desert sands on a tangent to the hidden vehicles.

"Where are the choppers?" said Gill. "They should be all over us."

"We must have cut communications with the guy who is running this operation."

There was no way to explain how we had gotten away with this last piece of action. I had seen combat on three continents, but never before had the odds been so stacked against me. Never had I looked so far down the barrel of a gun. Yet we made it. Verbruggen's grenade had frozen these guys in stop motion. Six of us mopped up fifteen people, because they were careless and overconfident and inexperienced. There was Hans, of course, and that was sad. But time was too precious now for sentiment.

Once we left the highway, we felt reasonably safe. We could have gone in any direction in the thousands of square miles of desert that surrounded us. We were a flyspeck on a brown landscape; it would take half the Iranian Air Force if they wanted to find us by aerial reconnaissance.

We drove on compass the last ten miles, having lost our maps in the burning lorry. But we had studied the area closely with Mirza, and we knew where we were going. Our tangent carried us between the highway and the village of Tarqan to our east and south; we would be shielded from the village by a low mountain. Our rendezvous was off a track that left Tarqan on the far side and wandered into the great expanse of desert to the southwest.

Dusk was chasing us, and the last five miles were a bone-shattering race to find the lorries before night fell. Swann's night driving was superb, honed by his years in the deserts of Oman. He handled the big Ford like a chariot racer; he read the sands like a Berber scout. I had little experience driving in the desert. I watched him work with increasing fascination.

But it was more by luck than skill that we hit our landmark right on the nose. We found the two Land-Rovers in a shallow wadi, buried beneath brush, loose dirt and sand obliterating their outline. One was the usual army vehicle with normal specifications; the other, the long-wheelbase model. Both were laden with food, water, weapons and ammunition, some simple maps. We drove the Ford alongside them and quickly tossed sand over the body and windscreen to deaden the color and shine. We dared not burn it.

Then we took a much-needed break. The hard desert drive had drained off the last of our adrenaline. The men's faces betrayed them. They were letting down now, physically and emotionally. The one who surprised me was Rabbit One. He appeared to be sharpening up. He was still frightened, but he was beginning to appreciate the sort of people he was with.

"Let me have a gun," he asked me. "I never want to feel again as helpless as I did at that roadblock."

I gave him nothing.

We pushed off with half an hour of dim twilight remaining. Swann took the lead vehicle. Yves the second. Swann, stopping repeatedly to lean out the driver's side, limped along at five miles an hour until the last waning light was gone. Desert driving at night, he told me, is far easier if you know the ground surface beforehand.

We followed a road of sorts which disappeared and reappeared with constant regularity. The desert ahead was part sand, part rock and shale, with outcrops of larger rock and tough desert grass. The landscape undulated, crisscrossing with dry river wadis, none too deep to traverse in our four-wheel-drive vehicles.

We were driving into the night of the seventeenth, and Nano was due to arrive with the plane on the morning of the eighteenth. We were only two hundred miles from our rendezvous, but virtually all desert driving. It quickly became evident we could do no more than thirty miles an hour at best on the good stretches. At worst, we were creeping around hamlets at walking pace, or holed up in hiding. It became a matter of how late we would be. Even so, we felt safe from discovery once in this vast expanse of desert.

When the moon rose, we took a rough bearing off Kuh-e-Alijuq, a spectacular peak that thrust three thousand meters out of the desert. The road dropped into a wadi; there, for a stretch of several miles, the hard flat surface was protected from drifting sands. We sped along at sixty miles an hour. Twenty minutes later, we pulled back up to the level of the plateau, and our speed diminished dramatically.

We were headed on a bearing for an angle in a pipeline near the desert town of Borj-e-Chin. It was a minuscule target in this wild, empty country, but we were on familiar terrain for the guys who had been down in Oman. They were at home among the drifting hills and dry salt beds.

The salt flats were our most inviting friend, or treacherous enemy. If the crust was solid, we could race across them as fast as the Land-Rovers would travel. But if we broke through the top layer of salt, we would mire helplessly to the axle. Swann was our blood and sweat here. He could spot their approach, even by moonlight, from the changing colors of the sand. He could feel the surface, he told me, from the tires right through the steering wheel.

With everything under control, I had time for my own thoughts. I was beginning to worry secretly about Nano and the plane. Knowing him, I expected him to be early. Unless he refueled quickly and went into hiding, he was extremely vulnerable because of the general alarm that must have been out for us.

We took a break for food, a quick look at the maps, and a smoke. All these guys loved to smoke on the job. So long as they were standing around smoking, everything was all right.

Yves rummaged in the back of the Land-Rover. "What about these?" he said.

He held out an armful of turbans and braided rope bands for fitting them snugly to the head. We reached for them gladly. Swept across the face, they filtered out much of the choking dust raised by the Land-Rovers. With heads covered and wearing military fatigues, we would look like any other army patrol on desert reconnaissance.

"We can take a hard-surface road," Gill said, poring over the maps with a penlight.

We demurred. Since leaving the highway for the desert, we had yet to see a human or an animal. There were clusters of houses every dozen miles or so, but these were subsistence hamlets. The inhabitants stayed alive by running a few goats, scratching the soil a bit. Subsistence farmers stay very close to home; so long as we steered clear of their isolated communities, they were not likely to see us.

We crept across country on Swann's bearings. We went fast when conditions permitted. Most of the time we crawled along.

We joined a donkey track that was worse than the desert. We rode in silence for ten minutes. Our spines were being shattered by the bumps, and knees and elbows banged with every turn of the wheel.

"Slow down," Yves shouted from the second vehicle. "Marcel can't take it."

Swann drove back into the sand without a word.

Under other circumstances, it would have been insane for us to be pushing across the desert like this in the dark, because it was crucial that we intercept the pipeline before it turned away from us to the south. If we overshot that junction, we would not know within twenty miles where we were going to pitch up on the coast. Map reading in the desert is both art and instinct, and Swann had a genius for it. The maps we had been left were large-scale, but he could read them like the inscription on a penny. When the moon fell, he did a lot of backtracking and swearing, but we stayed on course.

Just before dawn, we spotted the village of Behikhalifeh. We had covered sixty miles since sundown. It was a small village of a few hundred souls, but the countryside was so desolate that it stood to be a regional center, with maybe three or four cops or a telephone. Both were more than we were willing to meet. Just shy of the village, we turned into a dry riverbed that made a wide sweep around it, out of sight of most activity.

The river diversion was fifteen miles of hell. The hard bed was littered with boulders. The large ones, we drove around; often the smaller ones had to be moved by hand. At a deep meander, the bank had broken away and spilled loose sand and shale across our path. Swann took a run at a six-foot mound. His front wheels went over the top, then the Land-Rover sat down on dead center, its tires spinning wildly. Yves stopped behind, and we all climbed down to push. As I put my shoulder to the rear wheel, I looked back and saw the two rabbits sitting slumped over in the second vehicle.

"Get your lazy arses up here and push," I shouted.

"Fuck you," said Rabbit Two, but they both climbed out slowly and came forward.

Instead of pitching in to help, they sat down on a smooth boulder. I started to hit them, then stopped myself. These boys had been destroyed by the drive, which the rest of us made without thinking. They were too exhausted to respond to a beating. They were back to being baggage.

After forty-five minutes of exhausting digging and shoving, we put both vehicles over the top. I turned to the boys, who had neither moved nor spoken since sitting on the rock.

"Let's go, guys," I said.

Neither moved. Gill walked over, took one by each hand, and pulled them to their feet. They came aboard, and we pushed off.

The day was scorching hot. The horizon was bordered by a disorienting heat haze. I saw Swann nod twice at the wheel.

"Pull over," I said. "We'll take a break."

We halted beneath a shadow cast by the riverbank. Gill and I fueled the two Land-Rovers while the others cooled off and drank deeply from the water on board.

Miles beyond the village, we pulled out of the river and climbed back onto the road we had left earlier. The fifteen-mile detour had taken us three hours.

We met the occasional goatherd now, but these country people, thinking us soldiers, would ignore us so long as we allowed them to. We followed the road for several miles toward a major junction where the left fork would turn us toward the coast.

"Two vehicles ahead," said Swann.

The road junction was marked by a wrecked army lorry and the shell of an old Mercedes.

"How in God's name did they manage a car crash in this godforsaken spot?" asked Gill.

"They were dragged here," explained Swann, "to mark the road junction. The roads will disappear with every sandstorm. I can't see them now."

He slowed until we were just crawling, searching for our turnoff. Something caught my eye. I glanced up from the sandy waste to see a mule, then a man emerge from a wash only forty yards away that had been hidden from our view. The man stopped when he saw us. More joined him until there were six men, each with a mule. These were wild, nomadic people, dressed in a mélange of blankets, head coverings, and Western clothing. They were armed with carbines, but they made no attempt to raise them. "Militia," said Gill.

"Smugglers," said Swann.

They stopped whatever it was they had been doing and turned their eyes on us. Though we passed within twenty yards of them, no one spoke. We ignored them completely, and they made no attempt to communicate with us. We found our fork and turned southward. They stood immobile as statues until we were out of sight.

We drove a short distance, then dropped into another

riverbed. Only this river was not dry. It carried a thin stream of dirty brown water, but it was the first running water we had seen in days.

# 18

"Cool the tires," Swann explained as he drove into mid-stream, then halted.

Yves followed him in the second vehicle. We took a long break now, washing down in the river, then resting in the shade of the riverbank. The cool water seemed to wash away the strain and tension with the layers of caked red dust. Our bodies were still drained, but we were on the mend now; by nightfall, we would be back to full strength, ready to push on hard again through the night. We splashed water over the Land-Rovers before taking off again.

The trip was turning into an education for the Verbruggens and me. Desert survival was new to us, and Swann was a superb instructor.

"The next time we reach water," he said, "wet the vehicles down, but leave the dust on you. It protects against sunburn. Pull your turban close to your face. Keep your sleeves rolled down. Sunburn causes dehydration. That's the most dangerous thing you face out here. It can cripple you just as fast in the jungle, but there you know it's happening to you. Your clothes are soaked. Out here, you can be losing a pint of liquid an hour, and your shirt's not even wet under the arms."

He showed us how to take a bearing off the shadow thrown by the Land-Rovers as the sun moved west, how to recognize soft sand in bad light by its purple hue, how to cut tracks through hard sand.

He grabbed Rabbit Two's hand when the youth tried to wipe sand from his searing eyelids. Swann and Yves wore the only goggles left in the Land-Rovers. The rest of us were without even dark glasses.

"Don't rub your eyes," he cautioned. "That'll scratch the eyeball." He handed the boy his canteen. "Always wait until you can wash them clean with water."

He stopped and repeated his warning to the others in the second Land-Rover. "You can blind yourself out here in three hours. Squint your eyes like this," he said, narrowing his own to two slits. "Don't fix on the horizon or any one object for long. Look at shade every chance you get. That rests the eyes."

The next time we took a break, we all piled out to watch Swann give Yves a lesson in handling a runaway vehicle.

"If it gets away from you going downhill, don't hit the brakes. Keep the power on. Get it straight as quickly as you can. If the rear end starts coming around on you, steer into the slide, just as if you were on ice. But you must keep the nose facing the bottom of the hill. If you don't hit bottom with your front wheels straight, you'll flip."

He made it look easy, skiing down a sand dune, while we watched in wonder. He turned the Land-Rover around and made a run for the top of the same hill. The vehicle quickly ran out of momentum, stalled, then slid back to the bottom while the tires spun madly.

"Going uphill is just the opposite," he explained. "Go straight up, and you'll probably come straight back down. You can traverse twice as steep an incline as you can charge head on."

Making a series of short zigzags, the little vehicle hurried up the slope. On the top, Swann climbed out and bowed deeply to our applause.

"Time, gentlemen, please," he said.

We crossed the river and headed due west on a track we hoped would lead to the village of Borj-e-Chin. The pipeline we were seeking had to this point run south, then some ten miles east of Borj-e-Chin turned west and skirted the village. If we were on the right track, we would come upon the pipeline just where it turned from south to west. Our track then continued along the south side of the pipeline into Borj-e-Chin. To our north, radiating out of the town of Behbehan, was a considerable amount of oil exploration. Borj-e-Chin itself had a service facility for a section of the pipeline. So we were expecting to see people all along our route, possibly even militia protecting the pipeline.

We needed this pipeline to confirm our navigation. There is no landmark easier to find in the desert—you cannot miss a pipeline if it crosses your path—nor a better one if you want to avoid the towns and villages. Our plan was to follow the pipeline past Borj-e-Chin about thirty miles to the west; there, when the pipe turned northwest toward Ahwaz, we would quit it at a ninety-degree angle for the southwest on a collision course to a second pipeline some fifty miles distant.

"There it is," Swann called out as we crested a small hill.

The pipeline was dead ahead, and the bend was no more than a couple of miles south of us. Yves let out a whoop. Even the rabbits perked up a bit at the sight of it. We were just now into the heat of the day. We had little more than a hundred miles to go to the coast, so an ETA of the next morning was not unreasonable. The harder this mission got, the better we seemed to be doing things.

And this was no time for taking risks. Because of what we had done the previous day, helicopters would be patrolling the pipeline up and down its length. We left the track and went out into the sand about three miles, then paralleled it into Borj-e-Chin. Any choppers guarding the pipeline would go straight over the top at low altitude; we hoped they would not notice us. We still ran the risk of colliding with a repair party cutting across country from the nearest section house or from one of the repair stations—small sheds holding equipment but no permanent personnel—that stood alongside the taps on the pipeline every dozen miles or so.

We skirted Borj-e-Chin to the south, passing within a few hundred yards. These desert towns were very primitive—a cluster of flat-roofed, unpainted houses of stucco with doors that gave directly onto unpaved streets. A few animals milled about, but the people stayed inside during the hottest part of day.

We followed the pipeline twelve miles beyond Borj-e-Chin, then took our bearing southwest when it turned away from us. We bumped across country for a short distance, then dropped into another riverbed with a small flowing stream. Swann stopped to cool the Land-Rovers down.

"About three miles from here," he told me, "we're coming up on a large secondary road. Maybe even paved. From where we join it to Kuhgiluyeh is a stretch of about eighteen miles that's going to be very dicey. There'll be a lot of pipeline and seismographic traffic up and down this bit of road."

"We'll hole up here until dark," I decided aloud.

"There'll be more traffic when it cools off," Swann reminded me.

"Yes. But we'll be harder to recognize."

Yves and I cleaned Marcel's wound as best we could in the

brown water that coursed beneath our feet, then dressed the flesh with antibiotic cream and fresh bandages. Yves fretted over his brother like a mother hen, but there was little we could do except keep him bound. Marcel was in pain, but Christ, he had been in pain like that before. He was still a bloody good soldier.

We went into the hills and hid for five hours while we waited for dark. We took turns standing guard and sleeping in the shade cast by the Land-Rovers. The rabbits, I was glad to see, slept the entire time.

The unit was in great spirits as we prepared for our final dash to the coast. We had been through enough—days in hiding, two heavy combat scenes—to function perfectly as a team. Swann was back in his element here in the desert. The terrain was new to the rest of us, but we were too professional to let that bother us. Mission completion was a day ahead; no one doubted that Nano would be waiting for us in the morning. We were all getting along extremely well as individuals, which is relatively unimportant on a mercenary job but nevertheless makes life more pleasant. But there had never been any real attrition in morale, even in the tightest moments. These men were too professional for that.

Gill even found time to look after the boys. I think he was irritated by the paternal role into which they had inserted him, because they were looking to him for comfort and security more and more. But he must have been a little conscience-stricken, because they could have been mailbags as far as the rest of us were concerned. I was perhaps a little harder on them than the others, but they got on my nerves.

By nightfall, we were all rested and refreshed.

We dropped back down to the river, crossed, then traveled a bumpy two miles until we reached the road. Here we found ourselves among the first wheeled traffic since leaving the highway; jeeps and Land-Rovers headed for town, where another secondary road entered from the west, making it the hub of desert activity for miles around. The other vehicles looked to be carrying seismographic crews, some Iranian, some Western from their dress. We had no choice but to drive along with them, but we kept ourselves well concealed under our turbans and attracted no attention. It was unnerving at first, driving among these other vehicles, but the longer we were on the road, the more confident I grew.

"What now?" Swann asked, slowing as we spotted the first houses at the outskirts of town.

"What the hell," I said. "We've got time to make up. Let's go through."

We pulled over to let the following traffic pass. We pressed the boys to the floorboards, then rolled casually into town. I knew we had made a mistake when we approached the town proper. There was a weekly market on—vendors hawking their wares in the dust, mules laden with a dozen baskets trotting reluctantly behind their masters, children scurrying among their mothers' robes, men bartering over rugs and brasswork, women cooking hot savories on charcoal braziers. We slowed to a walking pace, then stopped completely twice, while carts made a tortuous turnabout in the narrow and crowded street.

We were in the dead center of town, just shying free of the street bazaar, when I saw two young men shouting and running toward us from our left side. Casually, I ran my hand from the stock of my MP-5, where it rested upright on my knee, down to the trigger mechanism.

# 19

The youths split, one dashing to each side of our two vehicles, beating on the fenders and doors as they went past, then waving fists overhead and cheering us wildly. More voices were raised from the older people. They thought we were revolutionary soldiers. We raised our weapons and shook them overhead, to the enthusiastic applause of the crowd. We as quickly hid the weapons afterward; there were no MP-5's to be seen in Iran, and these people were drawn like schoolboys to guns.

"Got any more good ideas?" Swann asked me when we had cleared the town.

"Jesus," I said. "That may be the worst idea I ever had in my life."

It was fortunate it had happened there, rather than at our next landfall. Behbehan was far too big to pass through in this fashion. An hour later, we knew we were approaching the town but had yet to see a single dwelling, when Gill leaned forward from the rear seat and grabbed Swann's arm.

"Stop!" he said.

Swann pulled over. The second car joined us.

"What is it?" I asked.

"There's pickets ahead," Gill replied. "There's an outpost of some kind."

"How do you know?"

He hesitated a long time before replying. "I don't know. Call it thirty years of experience. There's a wind up my nose tells me there's people camped up that road."

We waited behind while Gill and Swann crawled forward in the small Land-Rover. They were back in ten minutes. Swann switched off the engine.

"He's right," Swann said. "There are twenty, twenty-five men camped along the road. There is no way we can go through there."

Behbehan was a busy town asprawl a low hill, with rugged and broken country to the north. Our only alternative to driving right past the pickets was to circumnavigate the town to the south. We had to rejoin the road we were leaving on the far side of town to find our bearing off it to the coast. But in order to regain our east-west route, halfway through our one hundred eighty degree circumnavigation below the town, we had to cross a major north-south road.

As we turned off the road into the desert, I knew we were running out of luck. It was as instinctual to me as Gill knowing about the pickets. We had seen too many people, had too many close calls. But I did not expect us to make such a foolish and basic mistake as overlooking the possibility of pickets on the other road.

We bounced out across the desert and saw no one for twenty minutes. We reached the road and drove straight up on it without ever slowing. No more than seventy-five yards to our north, there were a bunch of these guys standing around a couple of jeeps. These blokes were typical of rural militia everywhere. They were the local guys on a sort of Friday night out, virtually without authority or a command structure. When they made up their minds to play soldier, they got their guns and tents and alcohol, set up camp, and had a good time.

They had heard us approaching across the desert. Never guessing we might be enemy—again the militia mentality—

they were waiting to see who we were. When we came into sight, they all waved and shouted greetings. We waved back and drove straight off the other side of the road. Then we put our foot down and tried to beat hell out of there, but the country was extremely rough, and we bounced along at ten or fifteen miles an hour.

A couple of shots rang out, fired into the air, then more shouting, this time with more urgency.

"Lights behind us," Gill said, turning in his seat.

One of their jeeps was rolling down the road. By the lights of a second jeep, I saw five or six guys clambering aboard, then they took out after us. No one fired in our direction. They could have been coming to see if we were something they wanted to join in with. But when they came off the road, they turned the jeep over.

And when we did not turn back to help, the guys left at the picket line knew something was wrong. They ran down to see about their pals. The jeep had done a complete flip and landed back on its wheels. When no one appeared badly hurt, a bunch of them jumped back in it and took off after us. A shadowy chase began beneath the light of a brilliant moon.

Gill and Yves could outdrive the driver of the jeep, and it was soon lost to sight. We were stretching our lead when our number two Land-Rover went high over a bump, lifted off the ground, and crashed into a shallow gully. Gill and Rabbit Two were tossed out the back like sacks of potatoes. The vehicle spun, tilted, then fell back on its wheels. Yves managed to bring it to a halt.

Swann slammed on the brakes, and I leapt out. Gill was just shaken, but the kid was out cold. We threw them back in their seats and took off.

We reached the second road, this time approaching with more caution than before. We cut our lights a hundred yards shy and crawled forward in low gear. Just as we gained the edge of the road, a Land-Rover blasted across our path without seeing us, raced a few hundred yards down the road, spun about, and sped back toward town. Word had come from the other pickets about us, and they had traveled through town and out this road faster than we had come across country. We were trapped between the jeep behind us and the Land-Rover on the road. And here they came.

"Headlights behind!" Swann called out.

They were still a mile away but closing fast. We had to take out one of the two vehicles before they joined forces. I chose the one on the road in front of us, on the off chance that only one of our vehicles had been spotted.

I jumped in the other Land-Rover, and Yves sped us down the road with lights off for a few hundred yards. We backed off the road and waited.

Just as the Iranian Land-Rover was disappearing into town, Swann pulled up on the road and threw on his headlights. The Iranians skidded to a stop, whipped a U-turn, and raced back toward him. Swann took off in our direction. First one, then the other vehicle roared past us, now only twenty seconds apart. With lights extinguished, we pulled up on the road and raced after them.

Swann slowed imperceptibly to let the Iranians gain on him. They were shouting with excitement when one turned and spotted us on their tail. Thinking we were the people who had cut across from the other road, they waved us forward to join them. I waved back, but Yves held our position.

When they closed the gap to thirty yards, they started taking aim out of the sides of their Land-Rover. Gill shouted at Swann. He slammed the brake pedal to the floor, whipped the wheel a three-quarter turn, and planed the Land-Rover sideways to a halt, blocking the road.

# 20

The Iranians slammed on their brakes and skidded sideways as well. We took our vehicle to the side of the road. They were trapped in a cross fire. These guys opened the action, but they never fired a dozen rounds. Time was more precious than ammunition. We could see the headlights of the second car approaching in the distance. We had to finish it fast, without setting their Land-Rover on fire. We let loose. Within seconds, our automatic fire ripped them apart. Swann took a frantic bearing off the moon, and we tore off across country.

Somewhere in the next half hour, we lost our pursuers and gained our original route to the west. We hit off down the road, searching desperately for our exit point. Two miles short of the next village, when our route turned vaguely northwest, we had to strike out south to meet a river at right angles. That river was the beginning of our route to the coast. But we could not know where that was without driving almost to the village itself. We were searching for a gas flare from an oil field just beyond the village. We had to take a bearing off it, then backtrack two miles to find our track. That meant unless we hurried like hell, we would be driving right back into the people who were pursuing us.

We traveled an hour down the road before spotting the flare in the distance. A quarter of an hour later, we might have missed it in the dawning light; it was silhouetted against the shade of a low hill giving way to the creeping pace of morning sun. We shot a quick bearing. Ten minutes later, we were off the road and headed south across the desert.

The light was brighter now. We were no more than a mile from the road when we saw the river in front of us. Swann sped up. We desperately wanted cover.

"Today's the nineteenth," I said.

No one replied, but they knew what I was thinking. Nano had been in the water for a day and a night now, and we were still far from the coast.

"I'm unhappy about that last bearing I took," said Swann. "We were too far away for the available light. A lot of room for error."

It seemed as if every mile we traveled compressed the problems in front of us into an ever-denser mass.

As we dropped into the river, I glanced back. Three army lorries rolled past, going away from us. I realized how much worse things could have been. Our pursuers had not had time to communicate with Teheran about us. They could not know which way we were going, because they had no idea who we were. They would have seen us as guerrillas, anti-revolutionary forces headed for any safe spot on the map. There was no reason for them to assume we were going to the coast.

We were headed for a coast road near Bandar-e-Deylam, and I was convinced it would not be safe when we got there. As soon as word reached Qum or Teheran about our action of the night before, they would soon sort out who we were and have no trouble whatsoever following the trail of rice we had conveniently left in our wake since leaving the highway two days before. A general alert would be rung throughout the entire region for us. Fortunately, we were moving again into sparsely populated territory, though it was far from being as inhospitable as what we had known before. Desert was giving way with great reluctance to savanna, and there were occasional oases with water and shade trees.

"Where the hell are the spotter aircraft?" Gill asked.

We bunched our shoulders instinctively, but none came overhead. Soon we were smelling sea marsh and salt water. We covered the last twenty miles from the river to the coast in two and a half hours.

We gained a long promontory and stopped the two Land-Rovers where the grass ended at the edge of a steep bluff, below which great dunes of white sand fell away to a blue-black sea. The coast road was directly below us, about two miles away. To our northwest, just on the horizon, I made out two offshore oil fields. Gill fished a pair of binoculars from the backpack he had salvaged from the burning lorry.

"Those must be the fields of Hendijan and Barganshar," he said, then turned back to course our maps quickly. "We're no more than ten miles off our mark."

"Not bad, if I do say so myself," said Swann.

"That'll be our rendezvous," said Gill, pointing to a headland and beach between us and the offshore fields.

I took the glasses. I had hoped to see the speck of Nano's plane off the beach, but I could not pick it up anywhere. He would be in hiding now, running in for a pickup only at dawn and dusk.

I took Yves's place at the wheel, and we came off the bluff on a roller-coaster ride to the coast road up and down a series of high dunes. Swann, in the lead car, started slowly down the last dune, which ended in a steep wadi at the edge of the road. I saw his right front wheel go high over a boulder half buried in the sand. The vehicle came down hard, bounced again off another rock, spun and slid sideways until it crashed against the hard bottom of the wadi with a sickening thump. Bodies spilled out everywhere. The Land-Rover rolled one and a half times, then settled on its back. Miraculously it had hit no one.

We skidded to a halt and jumped out.

"Who's hurt?" I asked.

Swann staggered to his feet and shook his head. Gill was winded but unhurt. Rabbit One looked sullen, but, apart from a skinned knee, he was all right. We all turned to Rabbit Two.

He sat slumped on the ground, clutching a limp left arm. It

was broken just below the elbow. The kid was whimpering and shaking and putting up a terrible racket. We had lost our splints and morphine when the lorry burned. Gill tried to straighten the fracture, but the kid howled and twisted to wake the dead. We left it as it was, strapped the upper arm to his side, and tied his wrist across his waist.

"The axle's broken," Marcel informed me with a shrug.

We piled everyone into the remaining Land-Rover and pushed off over the coast road. We had reached the coast north of the town of Bandar-e-Deylam. Our rendezvous was to our west, between the towns of Bandar-e-Deylam and Hessar, where a small but prominent peninsula divided the coast into two small bays. Nano would be waiting in the first of the two bays.

The road ran above an abrupt coastline separated from the sea by a wide expanse of dunes. A marginal green belt along the coast supported more people than we were used to seeing in the interior.

"Some farmer or fisherman is bound to spot the plane," Swann said.

"With all this oil activity," I said, "a seaplane is nothing new around here. They won't give it a second thought."

"A farmer, maybe not," said Gill. "The navy? That's another matter."

We were all acutely aware of the hornet's nest we had stirred up. There was no reason for them not to look for us along the coast. Anyone looking at a map could well have thought we were headed for the big oil port of Bandar-e-Shahpur, to try to flee aboard a Western freighter. It was an obvious ploy, and one I was holding in reserve should the need arise.

"What do we do about this," Yves said when Bandar-e-Deylam came into sight.

"Take us through," I ordered him.

Only a few hundred yards into the village, I knew I had repeated my mistake of going through population rather than around it. The place was teeming with trucks and four-wheel-drive vehicles that served the oil fields to the south, foreign geologists, drivers, and oil-field workers, and a dozen small bands of militia. Yves whipped the Land-Rover into the first side street, and we picked our way through the back streets until we broke into open countryside on the west side of town.

We stayed off the roads now, driving through rolling hills just inland from the beach; to any stranger, we would have looked like a coastal patrol.

By three o'clock we had reached our destination. The plane was nowhere in sight.

"The kid's in bad shape," Gill said. "He may go into shock if we don't set that bone."

"Don't touch me," Rabbit Two shouted, then his voice changed to pleading. "Please!"

Yves held him from behind, while I covered his mouth with my hand. Gill felt along the boy's forearm, then closed a great fist over the thin wrist and slowly pulled down and out. The boy gave out a great muffled scream. The bone slipped into place with an audible snap. Rabbit Two fainted.

I cut a splint from wild bamboo growing nearby, and Gill did quite a respectable patch-up job with the practiced eye of an old pro. We pulled the Land-Rover close against a hill, covered it with bamboo and grass, and sat down to wait for sunset.

"How do you know your guy's in hiding?" Yves asked. "How do you know he has not come and gone?"

"Because I know Nano," I said. "I count on him, just as I count on you."

Yves was worried about his brother, but I did not like this kind of conjecture. It was five o'clock now; all these questions would be answered in little more than two hours, when Nano was due on the beach. There was the occasional helicopter along the shore or a few miles inland. We lay quietly in the lee of the dunes, moving about as little as possible, until an hour before sunset. Then I decided to take us all much closer to the beach in the Land-Rover, even if it meant greater exposure. When Nano came in, we would have to clear off in a hurry.

We crept the last two miles in low gear, praying no spotter aircraft would come overhead. A strong sea breeze whipped up the sand around us. We drove along the curve of the first bay, then climbed to the spine of the headland that jutted another mile into the sea.

Leaving the others to lay up by the Land-Rover, Swann and I went forward to reconnoiter the beach. We hiked half a mile along the ridgeback of the headland, then went to ground. Behind the beach, the wind had whipped up layer upon layer of gigantic dunes, from which the tops were constantly being whisked away. We went to ground on the leading edge of the last dune, far above the beach. I scanned the shore with the binoculars for signs that Nano had already been there.

"Damn," I heard Swann say softly, tapping me on the elbow and pointing back over my shoulder.

Two air force helicopters floated above the beach behind us, then dropped out of our sight on the far side of the ridge. A minute later, one of them reappeared and flew off to the south. We hurried back to warn the others to stay out of sight, then Swann and I went forward to find out what was going on. It was nearing dark by the time we scaled the headland. The top was a small mesa covered with scrub grass. We went to ground, then crawled forward to its leading edge.

I took my breath in sharply.

The beach was crawling with soldiers erecting a large encampment. Four big tents had already been pitched. The helicopter was still disgorging arms and materiel.

Anchored a hundred yards offshore was a heavily armed navy patrol boat. A big one; sixty feet, I estimated. Its stern was turned to shore.

Moored to the bow of the patrol boat, floating serenely in the evening calm, was our plane.

# 21

"I told you Nano would be here," I said to Swann.

"What does it look like to you has happened?"

"Those guys haven't been there for long. They've still got gear scattered all over the beach. My guess is that they caught Nano this morning or sometime during the day. They're setting up camp to ambush us, and, from the pace of things, they don't expect us immediately. They don't even have anybody standing watch."

"Is your man down there?" Swann asked.

"I don't see him or anybody who looks like he could be the copilot."

I drew a brief scenario in my head. Nano would have come in the bay that morning to pick us up, been spotted, and taken by the patrol boat. He would have spun them a tale about mechanical failure, then gun running or dope smuggling, but sooner or later they would have radioed out that they had found an amphibious plane with two Spaniards aboard. We had practically drawn an arrow to the beach with our antics on the way—the blown pipeline, a roadblock obliterated south of there, the shootout at Behbehan. It would have taken an intelligence unit about three minutes to put this all on a map and realize we were going to be collected here. The only question was—why had they not waylaid us already? Nano had convinced them we were not due for a day or two.

"I know what you're thinking," said Swann.

"That plane is the only way out of here," I said.

"Let's look at the alternatives," he said. "We can try to make it to Bandar-e-Shahpur and sneak on an American ship."

"We don't have the petrol to get that far," I said. "We can get rid of our gear, go into the oil fields, and try to pass ourselves off as foreigners on a drilling rig. Try to get help from somebody. How does that sound to you?"

"It stinks," he said.

"I agree."

Finding help in the desert had a nice romantic ring to it, but it never happened. People did not want to know. They preferred to save their own skins. Bandar-e-Shahpur was equally out of the question. We were down to one vehicle for seven people with too little fuel to reach the Gulf port. We were carrying a kid with a badly broken arm. Marcel Verbruggen's wound was not critical, but it was debilitating him because of lack of rest and attention.

Swann and I looked back at the bay as our only viable escape route. Our plane, dressed in the brilliant red and yellow of the Spanish Air Force, looked like a toy on the water. The silver patrol boat alongside and the tiny figures on the beach gave the scene the eerie spectrum of a child's game.

"Do you know the boat?" I asked Swann.

"French design," he replied. "Carries a crew of twelve to fourteen. Twenty-millimeter Oerlikon gun on the stern. Heavy machine gun and rocket launcher up front."

I counted three sailors on the beach, plus three in a small rubber dinghy with an outboard motor plying between ship and shore.

"Nano must be on the ship with the captain and the rest of the crew," I said.

I counted twelve men on the beach in fatigues, whom Swann identified as marines. They were all armed with submachine guns or automatic rifles, but there were no machine-gun emplacements in sight. There was enough gear scattered about for a week's stay here.

"These Iranian marines are very good," Swann said. "But they're being careless as hell. They don't think we're within five hundred miles of here."

We crawled cautiously back to the Land-Rover.

"Is the plane there?" Rabbit Two asked anxiously; he was feeding off the dream that safety was only an hour away.

"You bet," I said.

When we told them what we had to do, Rabbit Two grabbed his broken arm and whimpered in pain. Rabbit One withdrew into his shell. The rest of us set about getting on with the job.

To keep his mind occupied, I ordered Rabbit One to help bury the Land-Rover under scrub and sand. Twenty minutes later, we grabbed all the gear we could carry and set out on the climb back to the headland high above the beach. The physical demands of the hike left my mind free to solidify a plan that had been running through my head. We gained our position with enough light left for us to watch the men on the beach below. Half of them were still milling about as if awaiting orders. They were as confident and careless as ever; there were still no forward observers. We watched, and waited for the sun to set.

The last hike had weakened Marcel considerably. While I watched, he stifled a groan and clutched his side in pain.

"You're out of this action," I told him. "You're to stay here with the boys."

There would come a time when I would have to get everyone into the aircraft in a hurry. Somebody had to stay behind with these kids, keep their heads down, and see that they did not wander off. I did not want to go looking for them.

"*Merde de merde*" was his only comment.

"How are we getting out to the plane?" Rabbit One asked nervously.

"You're going to swim," I told him.

My plan was for a couple of us to secure the plane, then the others would swim out in pairs. We would cut the moorings, then drift well clear of the boat before starting the engines.

"I'm not swimming all the way out there," he said.

"Damned right you are, sonny," I said angrily.

"You might as well kill me here. I can't swim that well."

I realized with a start how impossible my scheme was. I could drag Rabbit One out there by the hair if necessary, but we could never get Rabbit Two or Marcel to the plane without a boat. And I had forgotten Nano. If he was here—on shore or in the boat—he was going out with us. Rabbit One saw my expression change. He grabbed my arm.

"You guys are not thinking about fighting thirty people, are you? Don't be crazy," he pleaded. "We'll all be killed."

Swann turned on him in a rage.

"If you don't shut up," he said, "I'm going to stick my fist down your throat and pull your tongue out by the root."

The last thing we saw before night obscured the beach was a sailor ferrying the chopper crew out to the patrol boat. They would eat and sleep there in far greater comfort than with the marines. I looked at the plane. It floated serenely, almost forgotten it seemed, waves lapping at the pontoons.

As darkness fell around us, we primed our weapons and made ready for combat. Leaving Marcel and the two rabbits behind, we cautiously made our way down to the beach no more than a hundred yards from the marine encampment. While we took up a defensive position in the dunes, I gave Gill quick instructions.

He stripped off his boots and clothing down to his fatigues. He strapped on his sidearm and knife, then bellied like a snake across the sand into the water. His silent breaststroke never made a ripple on the calm water, but his progress was painfully slow. Soon his bobbing head was lost in the night. Twenty minutes later, we saw the plane's nose dip slightly, then rock a dozen times as he slipped on board. An hour passed.

"There he is," said Yves.

I saw him a few yards offshore, crawling in with the lapping surf. When he reached dry sand, he lay still for five minutes to catch his breath before crawling back to us. He collapsed gasping on his back.

"It's quiet as hell out there," he said finally. "There're people on board, but they're all below. There's not even a sentry on deck. I was able to get into the plane through the cargo hatch."

"What about the gear?" I asked impatiently.

The plane had been searched, but the Iranians did not know they were looking for anything. If Nano had done a good job hiding the stuff, it might have been overlooked.

"Slow down, Gayle," Gill said. "Give me a chance. The demolition bags were there, hidden in the gullies under the seats. I couldn't find the mortars."

"Where are the bags?"

"I left them in the sand. I was too tired to drag them up here."

Yves started forward to recover the demolition bags.

"Leave them," I said.

I put my head down to think, but there was no way we could do the job without the mortars.

"We've got to find the mortars," I said, stripping down. "I'll go take a look."

"Give me a few minutes," Gill said, "and I'll go back with you."

When Gill had recovered, I swam with him back to the plane. I found myself gasping for air after a hundred yards. Gill and Swann were trained for this, but I was unused to it. My fatigues dragged behind me like a sea anchor. I started to strip them off, then changed my mind. I just could not go into combat in my skivvies. I have a phobia about dying in my underwear. Most soldiers do.

Gill swam ahead and was already inside the plane when I grasped the pontoon. I rested for two minutes, then climbed one step up the rung ladder on the fuselage and swung into the cargo hold.

We watched the boat for several minutes from the cockpit, then set about systematically tearing the plane apart. For twenty minutes we were frustrated.

"Here they are," I said, ripping the back out of the pilot's seat.

Nano had strapped them carefully among the tubing in the two cockpit seats, then hidden them beneath a fabric slipcover. We searched for the mortar rounds for a half hour, but had no luck.

"They could be in the water scoop," suggested Gill.

He slipped back into the water, then disappeared beneath

the surface for sixty seconds. His lungs were bursting when he surfaced.

"Not there," he gasped.

"They're on the boat," I said.

"What do we do?"

"We're going to go look for them. First we take this stuff to shore."

We each took one of the eleven-pound mortars and started sidestroking to shore. Gill beat me to the beach by ten minutes. At last, I felt solid ground beneath my feet. I crawled back to the group, dragging the mortar behind me.

Yves's face lit up when he saw us, then fell as quickly.

"Where are the rounds for the mortars?" he asked.

"On the boat. They must be," I said.

"Did you go on board?"

"No, but we watched the boat for a long time."

"Are your Spaniards there?"

"I don't know. The boat's damned quiet. We've got to get them back, regardless. I can't fly that plane alone. Besides, I don't leave people behind."

"That means," said Swann, "that we have to take both parties."

"We must start on the boat," I said. "Even if we took the guys on the beach without mortars, which I doubt we could, the heavy guns on the boat would cut us down. Gill, you and Yves secure us a beach position here. Swann and I are going back to the boat."

Our only real hope of winning this game was to do this first job silently, but it had to be done regardless. We belted on grenades and our knives, then strapped silenced MP-5's across our backs. From the beach, we each gathered a demolition bag. We pushed out into the water for the third time. It was well past midnight when we reached our goal. We climbed into the plane to rest before boarding the boat.

I went back into the water, brought the dinghy from the stern of the boat, and tied it to the bow, out of sight of the people onshore. I climbed back into the plane with Swann.

"Everyone's settled in for the night," he said.

The only sound from on board was the low murmur of three men in conversation in the wheelhouse. The others seemed to be asleep. The wheelhouse door on our side of the boat was closed. Forward from it a few feet was an open hatch to the crew's quarters.

"How many on board?" I asked.

"I saw at least half the crew onshore. Six or eight here."

"Let's go."


# 22


We dropped into the sea and swam underwater to the stern of the boat, where we surfaced and hung on to the turbine exhausts. It was an easy climb up a rung ladder onto the deck, but we were in sight of shore, so we clambered over swiftly and lay flat. When no one stirred from boat or shore, we crept forward to the bridge.

In the wheelhouse, three officers sat talking and drinking coffee. I had wanted to take the sleeping men first, but we had no hope of slipping past the bridge without being seen. I signaled to Swann that we were going to take these out. He frowned. The wheelhouse lights were on; our action could be seen from shore. While I was trying to figure this out, one of the officers came out on deck and went below into the forward cabin.

As soon as he was out of sight, Swann and I stepped quietly into the wheelhouse. Two rounds hissed from my MP-5. Both men died instantly. Swann switched off the lights, then dashed out and pressed himself against the bulkhead beyond the open hatch.

A short silence was broken by footsteps from the forward cabin. The man who had just gone below emerged from the hatch, curious but unconcerned. Before his back foot hit the deck, Swann threw a forearm across his throat, twisted him around, and drove his knife deep into the man's kidney. The man pitched forward, and he and Swann fell up against the deck railing. They tumbled along the handrail, then tipped over the edge. I grabbed Swann's shirt, while he clung to the chest of the dead man. We teetered precariously for several seconds, then slowly regained our balance. The body went over the railing. We tugged frantically with both hands—we were completely exposed from behind—before Swann regained his footing. Slowly we hauled the dead man onto the deck and laid him out. We caught our breath. Swann shook his head in wonderment. We went below.

The lights were on in the first cabin, which was a combination of galley and mess for the sailors. The two chopper pilots were sleeping on bench seats along the walls. A door against the forward bulkhead swung to and fro. Through it, I saw the darkened sleeping quarters of the crew in the bow of the boat.

I was across the room in two silent strides. I clapped one hand over the mouth of the sleeping man, his chin in the palm, my fingers sealing his lips. I took his head in the crook of my arm and pulled him upright. He kicked and opened his mouth, and I jammed my fingers to the back of his throat. With my free hand, I drove my knife in the side of his neck and, with a backhand motion, tore his throat open and severed his windpipe.

Swann killed his man in much the same fashion. Both men thrashed violently in the throes of death.

A voice called out from the sleeping quarters. With one motion, Swann holstered his knife and grabbed up his MP-5 from the table where he had laid it. A young sailor, half asleep and dressed only in his skivvies, stepped into the room. He was still rubbing his eyes and blinking when Swann jammed the barrel of his MP-5 against the man's chest and pulled the trigger.

The weapon jammed.

He brought the stock up into the man's chin, knocking him over backward through the open door into the forward cabin. He dropped the MP-5, grabbed his knife from his belt, and charged through the open door. Swann's foot caught on the doorjamb, and he tumbled into the darkness on top of the sailor. Both men fell into a well between the bunks and were lost to sight. Two sailors, still groggy with sleep, jumped from the bunks onto the pair below. The door, kicked in the struggle, swung shut.

I tore the door open and sprayed bullets at waist level across the cabin. I killed one man and shattered the arm of the second. While he screamed in agony, I ran in and killed him with my knife. Swann had not done a very good job on the man on the floor. I put my knife in his stomach. We staggered back into the galley, grabbed our weapons, and waited.

There was only silence, throughout the boat, and from the shore.

We split and raced over the boat. We had killed the entire ship's complement, but they were not my principal concern.

"Nano's not here," I told Swann.

"I found the mortar rounds," he replied. "They were piled on deck at the stern."

Swann set the fuses on the demolition bags to go off in thirty minutes, then went over the side and fixed them to the hull beneath the waterline. He brought the dinghy around to the blind side of the boat. Meanwhile, I propped one of the dead officers in a chair at the boat's wheel and switched the lights back on.

I passed the six mortar rounds over the side to Swann, cast off the line that secured the plane to the boat, and climbed down into the dinghy with him. A dozen swift strokes brought us alongside the plane. We tried to push it away from the boat with our paddles. The plane turned on its tail a hundred and eighty degrees, then stopped. We had forgotten the tail anchor, which kept it from crashing into the boat.

"The damn thing's anchored," said Swann; he pulled his knife and began sawing at the rope.

"Stop!" I hissed. "If you cut that one, we've got no way to keep it from drifting away."

I scrambled into the plane and grabbed a spare anchor off the wall. Swann handed me the bow line we had cast off the boat. I tied the anchor to that and lowered it into the dinghy. We paddled to the tail, and Swann sawed furiously at the heavy anchor rope. As it separated and trailed away into the water, a gust of wind tore the plane from my grasp. Noiselessly, it drifted out to sea.

We grabbed our paddles and tore off after it. The wind changed direction; the plane heeled and turned and went right past our outstretched hands, this time drifting in to shore. I tossed the bow anchor over the side and let the line go. The anchor caught bottom in four seconds. The plane dragged another twenty yards, then hung fast. The plane was still anchored too close to the boat, but there was nothing we could do. We turned the dinghy toward the beach and brought it to shore as fast as caution permitted.

We ran the dinghy up onto the sand, then scrambled to join Gill and Yves. To my annoyance, I found Marcel with them as well.

"Sorry," he said. "I wasn't going to miss this."

He had directly disobeyed my orders, but I would take that up with him later.

"Take these," I said, handing Marcel and Gill each a mortar and three rounds.

They would have welcomed three or four rounds to zero the mortars in, but we simply did not have them. I planned to move them in so close they could not miss.

"Gill, you and Marcel stay here with the mortars. The rest of us will circle the camp and come in on the other side. Give us ten minutes to get in position. Then let loose with the mortars. Now listen carefully to what I'm going to say. Nano and his copilot were not on the boat. That means they're in that camp somewhere. Probably in one of the tents. We have to risk hitting them with the mortar rounds. There's no other way to do this job. But when the shooting starts, if you see two guys not in navy or marine uniforms, for God's sake, don't shoot them. We estimate eighteen targets in there. Six sailors, plus about a dozen marines. We have to get every one of them."

Swann grabbed a replacement for the MP-5 he had left on board, and the three of us pushed off. We made a wide circumnavigation of the camp, behind the first row of dunes. We dropped Yves halfway along, then Swann and I took cover behind the helicopter at the far end of the beach. We waited.

The distant crump of the mortars as they were fired was almost inaudible. Five seconds later, all six hit the ground almost simultaneously with an earsplitting roar that shook the earth beneath me. Five of the six had landed directly on target, devastating the camp. Bodies were tossed like dolls into the air. One tent was shredded. Another burst into flame. Most of the sleeping men had been killed in the initial blast. The survivors were now in pandemonium. Guys were running with bits of burning tents draped over them. Three guys ran out of the flames with their clothes on fire. I shot two, then recognized Nano. He fell into the sand, then rolled to extinguish the burning garments.

"Nano!" I shouted as the five of us moved in, firing. "Over here!"

His head came off the sand. He looked bewildered, then spotted me. He jumped up and ran, then fell down beside me.

"Are you all right?" I asked.

"Am I all right?" he asked. "You saved my life!"

His clothes were only singed, but beneath torn fatigues, I saw that he had taken some shrapnel in the legs. His face too I thought was burned until I looked closely. It was disfigured from a ferocious beating.

By now the few surviving Iranians had grabbed weapons and were returning fire, but my men were cutting them down in a cross fire.

"Stay here," I told Nano, then dashed forward.

There were six or seven of them still on their feet, only three now firing back. Yves was right in the midst of them. When combat started, he liked to go in close and mix it up. He would outrun any man on the battlefield to do it. This time, he ended up in hand-to-hand combat with one guy, but he enjoyed that sort of thing. He took the guy to the ground, then killed him with a knife thrust.

I saw Gill exchange fire with a guy standing waist-deep in the water. He must have been trying to swim to safety. Gill opened his chest with a round from the MP-5; at the same instant, he cried out from a returning bullet.

"Look out!" Gill shouted.

I whirled around. A marine was running full tilt at me, his Armalite pointed at my chest. I moved. He fired and missed. I fired and killed him.

Only two marines survived now. They ran for the dunes, with Yves and Swann at their heels. There was an exchange of fire, then my men walked casually back into camp.

"That's it," said Swann.

"We got them all," said Yves.

Rose-pink shades of dawn were seeping into the sand as the battle ended.

I broke into a run for Gill at the far end of the beach, but he waved that he was all right. I turned back to Nano. There was no bone broken in his legs, and the bleeding had almost stopped, as the wounds closed over the metal fragments.

"Are you all right?" I repeated.

"*Este machote? Sí, señor!*"

He tried to smile, squinting through eyelids swollen like hen's eggs. He had been up against a bully, not a skilled torturer.

"Goddamnit, I'm serious."

"I think so," he said. "They just beat hell out of me."

Suddenly Nano staggered to his feet and ran stumbling into the camp.

"Emiliano!" he screamed.

He tossed aside the flaming canvas of what had once been a tent. Our copilot lay dead, his head and chest riddled by fragments from the mortars.

Gill came forward to join me. He was clutching his arm.

"Nothing fatal," he said to relieve my concern. "A bullet through my hand."

He had managed a halfhearted bandage with the other hand, but blood was pouring through the gauze.

"I think it broke my thumb," he said.

He was in far more pain than he was willing to admit. Yves and I did a quick patch-up job on him, then I gathered the team about me to see how much damage had been done. Marcel had opened his wound in the scuffle and was bleeding heavily, but we stopped that with a change of wraps. The rest of us were in one piece. A few skinned elbows, a bruise or two, but we were whole. Swann had a small gash in his cheek, where he had caught something—a rock chip or a splinter, not a bullet. I was completely untouched.

We bandaged Nano's legs—it was no good trying to take the fragments out here—and he regained his feet.

"The plane!" Swann shouted.

He and I broke simultaneously for the dinghy. I had deliberately had the charges set on a short fuse, so that if things went wrong on the beach, the explosion would create a diversion. In the aftermath of combat, I had forgotten about the plane, still floating dangerously near the boat. I glanced at my watch. We were down to minutes now.

We ran the dinghy into the surf, jumped in, and rowed frantically. It was hopeless. The plane was at least five minutes away, and that might be too late.

Swann dropped his paddle, grabbed the starter cable on the motor, and gave it a wild tug. We almost capsized as the engine roared into life. Swann quickly gained control and had me scrambling into the plane thirty seconds later. While he hacked at the anchor line with his knife, I jumped into the pilot's seat, threw a dozen switches, and hit the ignition. The engine turned over once. Twice. Five times. And it failed to catch.

The bow line was severed. Swann waved both arms over his head to attract my attention.

"Come on!" he shouted. "Get out of there! The boat's going up!"

I shook my head and waved. He opened the throttle and raced the dinghy toward shore. I hit engine number two. It coughed and sputtered. Then it roared into life. I opened the throttle and raced out to sea with the tachometer swinging wildly in the red.

A volcano erupted behind me. Debris flew past the cockpit and fell like giant hailstones into the calm water around me. A huge wave lifted us on its crest. We skated backward into its wake. The plane spun like a top, one wing slicing through white water. A second wave picked us up and hurled us before it. We were completely out of control, like a runaway train on a slalom. I fought the controls, but they flapped wildly in the wind. The engine raced unchecked, tried to tear itself from the wing.

Then, suddenly, it was over. Three or four more waves followed, but they scarcely rocked us. I slowed the engine down and turned toward shore.

Gill was in the water with Swann, righting the upturned dinghy. Yves scrambled ashore with the paddles under his arm. The three beached the little rubber raft, and Swann set to work trying to start the motor.

The two rabbits came tearing down the beach from their hideout on the bluff. The way they ran, they must have thought we were leaving them. The whole group gathered impatiently while Swann tugged repeatedly at the starter cable on the little outboard motor. The full light of dawn was upon us now, and we were desperate to get out of here before more people showed up. If nothing else, somebody was going to be looking for that chopper bloody quick, when they failed to raise it on the radio.

Swann gave up on the motor. He and Yves grabbed paddles and pushed the dinghy into the water. Gill, Nano, and Rabbit One climbed aboard, and the two brought them out with paddles flying. The three jumped aboard, and Nano scrambled forward into the copilot's seat.

"Bring the mortars and as many weapons as you can carry," I shouted down to Swann as he turned back to the beach.

Rabbit Two and Marcel waited in the boat while Swann and Yves scavenged the battle site quickly for the mortars, Armalites, and any other automatic weapons they could find. They threw them in the dinghy and raced to meet us.

"Can you fly?" I asked Nano.

Without an anchor, I was having a hell of a time trying to start the cold engine while maintaining our position, because the plane kept turning on me. Finally, I let it drift with the running engine on the shore side of the aircraft. When we came too close, I gunned the engine, ran us back out a hundred yards, and started drifting again.

"I'll manage," Nano said. His legs were bleeding again, and he was in pain, but Nano was a tough cookie. He was alive and glad to be getting out of this place.

Somehow we maneuvered the dinghy alongside. Swann and Yves threw the gear on board. Everyone climbed into the cargo hold, and Yves slammed the hatch closed.

I gave them the thumbs-up and turned back to the stick. Two big Bell 212 helicopters were heading over the horizon, straight for us.

# 23

These were not scouts or battle craft; they were heavy transport choppers, bringing men in to reinforce the beach-head. They were flying low, but they must have seen the explosion over the horizon. They were getting close now, running along the shoreline. In a few seconds they would be over the battle scene.

"Number one engine!" I shouted at Nano. "Get it started!"

The engine exploded, sputtered briefly, exploded again, then roared into life. I gave both engines full throttle.

"The flight plan to the north," Nano shouted. "Under the dashboard."

I scrambled for the maps.

The Bells were flitting over the beach like flies on carrion. They hovered over the carnage we left behind, but neither dared to touch down. All they could see was one tiny red-and-yellow plane turning in spirals in the bay. A contingent from that plane could not possibly have done this much damage. There must be more of us around somewhere.

While one chopper hovered above the beach, the other swept out to sea over our heads and turned back toward us. These transport choppers were unarmed, so he was approaching for a look. He came in close. Too close for Yves, who threw open the cargo door and rounded off at him with his MP-5. The chopper pulled out of range and scurried back to the beach, where the first craft was still hovering. The first chopper came after us, and the second one, blowing up a sandstorm, spilled out a platoon of marines. A beach retreat—flight in the Land-Rover—was now a closed door.

"Why did they switch?" Nano asked.

"That'd be the command chopper coming now. Not carrying troops. More maneuverable."

We were taxiing in a wide circle less than a hundred yards offshore. The chopper cut across our nose. A voice shouted at us in Farsi over a loudspeaker. When we failed to slow, he dropped back and hovered directly over us, a few feet above our fuselage. He could stop us by touching down on us, but if he got his ski caught in our superstructure, we all went to the bottom. I held steady.

Our speed was picking up as our arc increased. We hit sixty-five, then seventy. At eighty miles an hour, the plane would lift up on the "step"—the pontoons would clear the water, and we would be planing only on the last few inches of the hull—and within a few seconds, we would be airborne.

The chopper pilot realized we were approaching lift-off speed. He pulled back and away a hundred yards, then swept directly in front of us like a yo-yo on the end of a string, so low and fast we looked down on the top of his rotor. I refused to cut my speed. Rounds began to whistle at us from the beach. He came by again, this time closer than before.

"We're going to be killed," shouted Rabbit Two. "Let's go back into the beach."

"Look at the beach, meathead," Swann said.

A dozen men, standing and prone, fired at us with automatic weapons. Two more were setting up a machine gun, while a third knelt beside them, belt in hand, to feed it. I glanced back out to sea. The chopper had come around and was bounding toward us again. At that instant, we rose up on the step.

"Open the scoop," I shouted to Nano.

He threw the switch without hesitation. The plane shuddered violently. We dropped twenty miles an hour in two seconds as water poured into the twelve-thousand-gallon tank beneath us.

"Keep it on the step!" he shouted.

I ran the engines until the rev counter was banging against the top of the red. With the aircraft straining every muscle, we gained speed and went back up on the step. We ran for five or six seconds, then I felt a sudden ebb in our power. Picking up water at this speed, we could never stay on the step.

"Close it!" I shouted.

Nano closed the scoop. The engines regained their torque.

I turned into a wide arc parallel to the beach, up on the step, just below takeoff speed.

Here came the chopper again, with a hot jockey at the stick. He was fifteen feet off the water, on a collision course. I pushed the engines to full throttle and hauled back on the stick as hard as I could. We lifted off.

We hovered at eighty miles an hour, a foot off the water. The chopper came tearing in from our right, no more than twenty feet in front of us. I jerked the stick back with all my strength. The plane stood on its tail like a puppy begging for his supper.

"Hit the gate!" I shouted.

Nano slapped the scoop release with the palm of his hand. Six thousand gallons of water cascaded from our underbelly. It smashed into the chopper like a fist. The rotors snapped like twigs; bits and pieces fluttered harmlessly into the sea. The huge transport hit the water flat, snapped in two, poised momentarily, and began to sink.

The tail of our plane kicked straight up in the air behind us and we nosed over. Through the cockpit, I looked straight down onto the remains of the chopper. In another second, we would drive in on top of it. Our engines screamed, biting futilely at the air as we stalled.

Nano grabbed his stick, and I gave a third ferocious tug at mine. The nose lifted a few degrees. We came crashing down on the sea, but the pontoons were beneath us now. We hit hard, bounced, stalled again, and fell. We bounced about six more times under full power. The wings unstalled. As bullets piled into the fuselage with unnerving regularity, we regained the step and lifted off. We burst into a spontaneous chorus of cheers and catcalls, shouting and handclapping. I looked at Nano. He was grinning from ear to ear.

"Hey, man," he said. "That's some flying."

I made a right-hand bank away from the shore. As we climbed, we saw the remains of the rotors still floating on the surface and the outline of the fuselage as it sank beneath the waves.

It was the luckiest bit of impromptu flying I had ever done. Our plane should have broken up when it hit the water that first time. But we had made it, and that was all that mattered.

The second helicopter was not chasing us, because it had no way to put us down. The knowledge gave me absolutely no comfort whatsoever, because by now the entire Iranian Air

Force must be looking for us. We struck due west out over the Gulf, flying so low our propellers were catching the spray from the waves below. The flying was made even trickier because, with the others crowded into the compartment close behind Nano and me, our center of gravity was too far forward. We had to fly with the trim all the way back. We might as well have been a boat, except that we were traveling a hell of a lot faster. We came down quickly and scooped up four thousand pounds of water to set the center of gravity back a bit.

We went about fifty miles west in the Gulf, praying the Iranians would think we were headed for Kuwait or the Emirates, anywhere but back into Iran.

"If you go much farther, we'll never get back on course," said Nano, leaning close over the maps.

"I don't want to run into the air force," I said. "By the time we get back, we'll have been gone an hour. Those boys will have finished their glory runs up and down the coast."

I turned north. We flew for forty-five minutes, then Nano tapped me on the shoulder and pointed below. "See the island? That's the Dara Inlet."

A few minutes later, he pointed again. "The Barganshar field," he said, indicating a vast offshore complex.

We joined the coast between the island of Dara and the peninsula town of Kaparha. That put us forty miles west of our intended route, much too close to the Iraqi border for comfort.

"This course will take us straight up the Karun River delta," Nano said.

The delta, a hundred-mile-wide strip between a string of mountains to our east and the Iraqi border to the west, was heavily populated, with a military base at Ahwaz; we were facing maximum exposure here. We were flying under the Iranian radar shield, but that did not protect us from spotter aircraft.

"Give me a heading for the mountains," I said. I glanced over at Nano.

For the first time, I realized what terrible shape he was in. The excitement of battle and the elation at being freed were wearing thin; only pain remained as a reminder. He touched his legs gingerly where the tiny shell fragments had raised the flesh in angry black knots. The beating had disfigured his

face to an appalling extent. Every word was an effort, through
cracked and swollen lips.

"You've got to hold yourself together," I said. "I can't make
this flight alone. You've got to concentrate on that flight plan
every minute we're in the air."

Nano was no boy. He knew that if someone else could take
his place, he would be in the back sleeping or being tended
to by Yves and Swann. There was no one else.

"I'll do the job," he said.

We bore northeast and headed for the mountains at an
oblique angle. We were map reading like crazy now. Landmarks went by like telephone poles past a speeding car. We
wanted to intercept our original track at a village called Deh
Molla. That would carry us past an air base to our west at
Ahwaz and another farther north near Sulaiman. This was
risky flying, but the terrain had a lot of natural contours I
intended hiding in. If we stayed low enough, the Iranians did
not have too much to shoot us down with. It was hard to hit a
CL-215 flying at treetop level in and out of steep valleys in a
sophisticated jet with a stall speed in excess of two hundred
miles an hour unless the pilot was a lot better than good.
Once we reached the hills, I felt much safer.

We never saw Deh Molla, nor a river we wanted to use as a
reference point.

"Where are we?" I asked Nano.

"I'm not quite sure, but we're headed in the right direction. We've got two pipelines coming up soon. They'll tell us
where we are."

If we did not miss them. As we were flying at one hundred
seventy miles per hour at ground level, that would not be
difficult to do. I put the guys in back to watching out the
cabin windows.

"There's the first one," said Nano, pointing below. It
disappeared as quickly as it had risen in front of us. If we
crossed a second pipeline ten miles from the first and running
parallel to it, we were on track. If we came upon it sooner
than ten miles, we were west of track, because these two
pipes converged before entering Bandar-e-Shahpur.

"Second pipeline coming up," said Yves.

It rolled beneath us. Nano hit his stopwatch and scribbled
a few notations on a piece of paper.

"Damned near dead on course," he said.

# 24

"Contrails. Way up above us, on the left," Marcel said.

The jet vapor trails were up around thirty thousand feet. Nobody was going to spot us from there, but we were much too exposed for anything flying lower. When we intercepted our original intended route, we would turn northwest and follow the north-northwest Iraqi-Iranian border into Kurdistan. But we needed to get into the hills first.

We were flying on track all the way. I did not give a damn what our heading was at any given moment. We might lay off for wind, go around a mountain, skirt an air base. But at some point, Nano had to find our way back to our mean track, which was our orientation into Kurdistan.

I was desperate to get our navigation right early on.

"Try to find some Iranian Air Force frequencies," I told Nano. "We can at least find out who's chasing us."

He fiddled with the radio for fifteen minutes before switching it off in disgust. He went back to his maps and charts.

"The base at Ahwaz has a TACAN beacon," he said excitedly.

He quickly tuned our VOR/DME.

"We've lost the flags," he said.

"TO" and "FROM" flashed up where the flags had dropped. Nano centered the instrument on the VOR. We got a bearing indicated on the northern nosepin of the aircraft.

"No audio indent," Nano said.

We wanted a Morse code signal to confirm we were not picking up a ghost beacon. We flew for another ten minutes. The beacon continued clear and strong.

"We'll take a chance that the audio's turned off. Use the beacon," I told Nano.

"Ground speed a hundred twenty-five miles an hour," he said.

This was far below our air speed and indicated strong head winds off our westerly quarter. We turned down the "FROM" bearing and flew away from the station. By working backward from the DME and studying the maps, Nano got us on a safe bearing to Lake Shah Pahlavi, which skirted the air base at Dizful.

To confirm our navigation, we had to find a T-junction in a pipeline—it was the same pipeline we had followed in the Land-Rover two days earlier—that should have come up some distance off our port wing. We came straight over the top of the T-junction. Nano studied his charts, scribbled a bit.

"I make us fifty miles east of Ahwaz," he said. "Three miles west of track."

We had done all right. It was instinct, some luck, and just damned good flying.

We were two hours inland from the coast now. We had done the first hour under great pressure—trying to sort out our navigation, skirting the two southern airfields, reading the ground, studying unfamiliar maps, scanning the skies for enemy aircraft.

In the delta we had the luxury of following north-south rivers. We roared along, counting off pipelines as we went. We aimed to scrape the side of the last river between us and the foothills to our right.

After forty-five miles, we lost the DME from Ahwaz. I suspected we had not done too well with it because of our low altitude, but Lake Shah Pahlavi was so enormous we could be a couple of degrees off and still hit it.

"River to our right," said Nano.

That indicated we were approaching the air base near Sulaiman. I dropped so low into the wide river canyon that at times we saw the banks on both sides of our plane. We passed a pipeline and railway bridge that led into Sulaiman but failed to spot any of the military activity I anticipated around this oil center.

We blasted past within a hundred yards of the clifftop village of Shushtar, with some of the houses above our wing tips. We must have scared the pants off the villagers, but I was not worried about a reported sighting. They were used to seeing hot pilots out of the desert oil camps.

Past Shushtar, I stayed with the river until it swung hard east near the town of Gatvand in the foothills of the mountain range ahead. We ducked into the hills, even though that took us slightly northeast of our track.

I was beginning to enjoy myself. This flight was turning into a real roller-coaster ride. I had a good plane, a superb copilot. We were on track and on schedule. Nano and I had done so many supply missions that we were used to tactical map reading at much higher speeds than the one hundred fifty miles an hour we cut back to in the mountains.

We had several hours' flying ahead of us. We both needed to let off some tension. I sat back and relaxed with a visible sigh. Nano was looking stronger, his flagging spirits lifted.

"Now tell me what happened to you," I said to him.

"We arrived at the rendezvous on the morning of the eighteenth, right on schedule," Nano said. "We carried false delivery papers to an oil company in Dubai. Emiliano came out with me, as copilot. *Pobrecito*, he was a good friend. He didn't know what he was getting into. He was just a Spantax pilot. He needed the money. We landed in the Med on the way down and changed registration numbers. There was a small problem in Cairo with flight plans, but a little baksheesh took care of that."

"How much?" I asked.

"A thousand pounds."

This was why I had hired Nano and given him plenty of money. He was not afraid to use his initiative.

"There was a landing craft in the bay when we arrived, off-loading fuel drums onto a raft. We spent a couple of hours flying up and down the coast, then came in to get the fuel. We had just finished refueling—we were puncturing the drums so they'd sink—when the patrol boat spotted us. We had no chance to get away, so I jumped in the plane and hid as much as I could.

"These guys came on board, armed to the teeth, and boy, they were angry. They knocked us all over the plane before they said anything. Emiliano was really scared. I tried to tell them our plane had broken down, but that made them twice as angry; I thought they were going to beat us to death, so I said we were smugglers. That calmed them a little. They took us to the boat. The captain was a decent man. He wanted answers, but he wasn't going to kill us. They questioned us for hours. Emiliano and I couldn't get our story together, and they didn't know which one of us to believe. The captain gave up and got on the radio.

"A helicopter brought those marines. The captain tried to protect us, but the marines took us away from the navy, onto the beach. And they proceeded to beat hell out of us.

"They put my head in a bucket of water. I thought I was dead. They weren't getting much out of me, because I never stopped talking. Poor Emiliano didn't know how to spin a tale, get them to waste time on it. He refused to talk, and they doubled up on him. They didn't have much to torture us with, so they said they were taking us to some prison. Emiliano went to pieces."

Nano paused.

"Don't write off Emiliano," he said earnestly. "He was a tough guy. They didn't crack him easily.

"Fortunately, I hadn't told him much. All he knew was that we were waiting to pick somebody up. I told them you weren't due for two days. They didn't believe me. They really worked on me, put a gun to my head. But I knew it was the only chance we had, so I stuck to it. I must have convinced them. They were very excited about capturing you. They were going to execute us all together.

"They put me in a tent with two guys who tried to fuck me, and when they gave up on that, they beat me until I passed out. The next thing I knew, I was running on the beach with my clothes on fire."

I turned to look at Nano. It took guts for him to be sitting up, much less poling a plane. We were lucky they had not worked on his hands, else he could not have helped with the flying. He had a couple of broken ribs, but most of the damage was superficial. He would recover. He seemed to be reading my thoughts.

"I'll be all right," he said quietly.

# 25

The flying was spectacular now. Often we were below the hilltops, threading our way through a labyrinth of rocky crags. This was empty, desolate country, with roads miles apart. We picked up one going in our direction. Using it as a landmark, we wove in and out of the hills, catching sight of it from time to time. Our forward progress was slow, but until we passed Lake Shah Pahlavi, I was worried about discovery by aircraft.

"Lake ahead," Nano said.

Lake Shah Pahlavi huddled at the edge of the mountains, spilling its waters onto the delta below. We cut the lake at its northeastern tip, the brilliant blue waters an inviting reminder that we were well clear of Dizful and its air base. I was feeling pretty cocky.

"Let's fly right over the top of the next air base," I said.

Rabbit Two let out a scream from the back.

"Don't worry, kid," I said. "I was only joking."

Rabbit One seemed to be enjoying the flying. It beat the hell out of anything else he had done in a while. Rabbit Two slept most of the time. He had been so scared for the past few days that his adrenals were exhausted.

We were terrain-flying all the way now—down around three hundred feet and using a lot of fuel—cutting out the smaller hills, detouring around the large ones. We tilted down the radar in the nose and read off the pipelines as we flew over them. We sighted one pipeline we should not have seen; that told us we were too close to Shahabad. We adjusted our heading and flew between Shahabad and Kermanshah, two large cities only forty miles apart, but we just bombed through there, and we were lucky.

"Aircraft off our port wing," Gill said.

I saw two propeller craft flying reasonably low but almost out of sight. They never spotted us.

Midafternoon, as we neared the Iraqi border, we ran under some low-lying invection cloud hanging over the hills of the frontier. Thunderstorms rolled down the higher peaks, and the weather came clagging in on us. We had a lot of daylight left for flying, but we were losing that light to drizzle and cloud.

Suddenly I felt exhaustion setting in. Nano and I had been flying for hours without a break. It took total concentration from both of us to keep on course and to avoid making a fatal error with the plane. I realized we had been running on nervous energy for the past hour or two, but the flying was riveting. I hitched up my trousers and took the stick with renewed vigor. We were on the home stretch now. It was no time to falter.

We drew a track from a low-frequency beacon at Kermanshah to the Iraqi border, cross-referencing it with a beacon from a place called Kifri inside Iraq. But both beacons were too intermittent and unreliable for us to trust to our calculations.

We wanted to cross into Iraq over the eastern tip of Lake Halabja, a massive lake with a hydroelectric and irrigation dam at its western end. Our maps told us we had crossed the border, but we had not seen the lake because of our low altitude.

"There it is," hollered Nano as we snaked between two low mountains, suddenly to find ourselves in a vast mountain-ringed bowl.

"Jesus God!" Swann shouted.

Directly in front of us, no more than a thousand feet away, was the Darbandikan Dam, one of the most sensitive military targets in the Middle East.

I heeled the plane over and took off in the opposite direction.

We were in Kurdistan now, but where? We took a frantic bearing off a road that ran by the lake, a second from Baneh, an airfield on the Iranian side of the border. We lost the second beacon too quickly and flew over what must have been the town of Halabja. We had done pretty well to stay on course this far; that mattered little if we lost it so near the end.

"We're lost," Nano said, his head bobbing between the map and the landscape below.

We passed over a major road.

"Go up and down that road until you find a crossroad," he said.

I circled in ever-increasing spirals until we found a second road. One way led to Sulaimaniyah, a frontier town from which the Iraqis have launched many battles against the Kurds. We turned and flew the road in the opposite direction, toward the border town of Penjwin. Beyond Penjwin lay the river that would lead us to the lake high in the Kurdish ranges where Big Kevin awaited us. I looked at my watch.

"Big Kevin's beacon will be on now," I said. "See if you can pick it up."

We got nothing for several minutes. Then, north of Penjwin, we got an NDB—non-directional beacon—indicated on our ADF off to the west, but it was moving through thirty degrees, which made it useless to us.

"If that's Big Kevin's beacon, the river's somewhere near here," I said, "but where?"

We flew northwest until our instruments put the beacon behind us. Cloud was closing in, and light was fading fast now. Winds began to toss the plane about. We had precious little time before night and a high mountain storm forced us down. And we could not find the river.

We were flying valleys now, hunting desperately on north-south headings. The needle on the ADF was swinging wildly; now the beacon was ahead of us, now behind. Nano grabbed his pad again.

"I'm working the time it takes the needle to go across two-seven-zero degrees off to our port wing," he explained.

We forgot the vacillating needle, turned on Nano's heading, and took off up the first valley we saw.

"There it is!" I shouted, pointing to a white-water river racing along the valley floor.

"How do you know that's our river?" asked Nano.

"Because it's the only one we've got. We'll give it ten miles," I said.

I dropped the flaps and slowed our speed to ninety miles an hour. The valley narrowed dramatically ahead; I had to be prepared for a sharp bank if it closed up completely. Lightning speared the sky, thunder roared, huge raindrops drove against the cockpit window. We were committed to this valley. Nano read the second hand on his watch with a penlight.

"Three miles," he said. "Four . . . five . . ."

At six miles, he let out a whoop.

"The needle's zeroing!" he shouted.

Cheers from behind.

The river climbed gently for another five miles. The valley walls opened into a wide vee. The clouds parted. The lake lay dead ahead.

# 26

It was a long and narrow lake, perhaps five miles long, two miles across at its widest point. But for the occasional natural shelf at lake's edge, steep mountain slopes plunged into the water everywhere. We made a quick run down the lake, banked, and came back again. There had been no flare, no signal fires.

"If this is not the right lake, we're going to have to come down here for the night anyway," I said.

I made another tight turn, and we went up the lake for the second time.

"There it is," shouted Marcel.

At the far northwest end of the lake, from a large shelf covered with glacial scree, a flare arced across the sky for a few brief and brilliant seconds. Two great bonfires sprang to life along the shoreline. We made an easy approach up the full length of the lake. We touched down and taxied between the two fires. A score of people waited patiently on the rocky shore. Fifty feet offshore, Big Kevin stood upright at the stern of an enormous hide-covered boat manned by two oarsmen.

He waved for us to stop and anchor a few feet off his boat. I shut down both engines. Big Kevin came up under my cockpit window.

"Everything all right?" he shouted.

"We're carrying wounded," I replied. "Otherwise all right."

Big Kevin turned and yelled something at the people on the shoreline. Two trotted away to fetch medical supplies. Big Kevin climbed aboard and joined me in the cockpit.

"Did my party make it?" I asked.

"Two of them did."

"Who did I lose?"

"The Iranian kid."

Rabbit One grabbed Big Kevin's arm.

"Is he alive?" he begged.

"No."

Both boys began to cry. Despite their bizarre behavior, they loved their cousin. I looked back onshore. This time, I spotted Freeman and Davis dressed in Kurdish garb but standing slightly apart from the others. Neither was carrying visible wounds. They waved and shouted.

We piled into Big Kevin's boat. When we came ashore, we got the usual stony stares from most of the people but a warm welcome from a few of their leaders and exuberant greetings from Davis and Freeman when they saw we were whole and more or less intact.

The shelf on which we stood was larger than it had appeared from the air. There were a dozen big tents standing and a couple of hundred people milling about. Half the complement were women, sharing the burden with their men in the front lines of this forgotten war. I turned my eyes back down the lake and the mountains beyond. We appeared as alone as explorers on an empty continent. There was not a fisherman in sight, not a goatherd or a shepherd. Yet I knew those slopes were crawling with Big Kevin's scouts and pickets. The weather closed in completely above, shielding us from the prying eyes of spotter aircraft. I felt very secure here.

The Kurds were as hard and lean as saddle leather, their faces lined from a lifetime in the open air. The men wore baggy trousers tucked into cloth-and-fur boots. A shift hung from shoulder to thigh, belted often as not with a leather ammunition belt or canvas webbing. Their heads were covered with turbans that looked more Indian than Arabian. Every man carried at least two rifles, plus an assortment of jeweled daggers, grenades, and bandoliers.

The women moved about with a freedom denied them elsewhere in the Moslem world. They wore long Arab dresses, but their faces were uncovered, and they were unafraid to stare at a man. Both sexes wore bangles and bracelets, rings and necklaces. Gold glistened from their teeth.

These fearless mountain rebels were harder than anything we had seen on the entire journey. Their eyes were as sharp as their knives; piercing, penetrating. Their faces never wavered from an expression of controlled ferocity. The Kurds were the Cossacks of Iran.

Old rifles, carbines, and AK-47's were scattered about the camp everywhere. There were horses and mules, carts loaded with food and ammunition. The children were elsewhere, so that told me this unit was in the front line of Kurdish resistance.

Once ashore, we earned no special treatment. The people ignored us or watched us suspiciously, but they were quick to carry out Big Kevin's commands.

"Just stay out of the way," Big Kevin ordered us. "Act normal. The two kids go into a tent until you leave."

The rabbits were led away.

"What happened to the kid and the girl?" I asked Big Kevin while we had a moment alone.

"I don't know anything about a girl," he replied. "Your men arrived here alone. I'll brief you on all that later."

Davis and Freeman joined us. Davis handed me a leather flask which one of the older men had been passing among my crew. I tilted it above my head and shot a stream of blood-red wine into my mouth. It was foul stuff, but I managed to swallow it without gagging.

Ceremonies dispensed with, few of the Kurds made any attempt to talk to us after that. Three old men who appeared to be tribe councilors stayed close at Big Kevin's side. I noticed that Big Kevin kept his voice moderate when giving orders. These people were quick to obey, but not out of fear of authority.

Black storm clouds blocked out the last gray light of day. Night came on with a rush, cold and damp. Fires sprang up throughout the camp. Two women led our wounded away for treatment.

Once alone, Davis and Freeman greeted us like long-lost cousins.

"Great to see you, boys," said Freeman. "We've been worried about you."

"Great job, Rivers," said Davis.

I was almost too shattered to respond.

"Good to see you blokes," I said. "We'll have a debriefing in an hour."

Big Kevin led us to a U.S. Army tent. Skins were stretched over the canvas sides to ward off icy mountain winds. Inside, more skins covered straw pallets on the ground. It was snug and cozy and very inviting. But I suspected it would be hours before I could fall in here to sleep. I left the men and went back outside with Big Kevin.

"My tent is next to yours," he said.

"We've brought a lot of hardware with us," I told him. "Our own and some Iranian gear. We don't need much now—a couple of MP-5's and our sidearms. I want to leave the rest with you."

"Keep it all with you until later," he said.

"I want to bring the things in now, before it gets any darker."

"All right," said Big Kevin, "but let me give you something to wrap it in."

Big Kevin sent a man to bring us a sheet of canvas tenting. Half an hour later, Yves and Swann brought the gear, wrapped and tied like a mummy, into our tent.

Big Kevin took me into his tent.

"You'll be staying here all of tomorrow. This stuff," he said, indicating the low cloud outside, "won't lift for at least twenty-four hours. So just take it easy and try to relax. We'll get your men well, get you some decent food and talk about old times."

"I have to debrief my men," I insisted.

"Let that wait an hour," he said. "First come out and sit

around the fire with some of the men. Bring the rest of your crew with you."

I got the guys together. Gill's hand had been patched. Marcel was stripped to the waist. His wound was clean, and someone had done a professional job on him with gauze and tape.

Mats had been placed for us by the fire, amidst a group of twenty men. We chatted among ourselves and exchanged incomprehensible salutations with our hosts. Wine and a bubbly pipe were passed around. I managed the first but had to fake it on the pipe. It was foul-smelling stuff. I could taste it before it touched my lips. I pretended to inhale and passed it on.

Beyond the nucleus around the fire, there was constant milling about, people carrying on their daily chores unrelated to our arrival. The women hovered in the background to watch us for a while, then left to prepare a feast. They were not armed, but they shared the battlefield, they carried the burdens, they tended the wounds. And they died like the men.

When half an hour passed, Big Kevin leaned over and gave me whispered instructions for presenting our weapons and the money we had brought for the Kurds.

Swann and I brought the gear, still wrapped, from our tent and made a tour of the circle by the fire, then laid the bundle down before the three oldest men. Big Kevin stripped away the canvas. There was a murmur of appreciation. The men stirred and talked among themselves as Big Kevin picked up each item and introduced it. Two or three men pointed to the mortars. Big Kevin placed one on the ground, propped it with his arm, and pretended to drop in a round. He counted off five seconds, then made a great exploding noise and raised his hands to indicate a ball of dust. The men applauded and cheered. Then Big Kevin picked up an MP-5, breeched it as he talked, and raised it over his head. He nodded to me.

I took my own MP-5 from my lap, stepped in front of the senior chieftain, bowed, and handed it to him. His eyes lit up; he splashed a golden grin that nearly blinded me. He fumbled briefly with the weapon, then, to my astonishment, handed it back to me. This old man knew almost nothing about weapons.

With a wave of his bony hand, he indicated that I was to demonstrate it for him. The circle opened toward the lake, and I fired round after round—at first single-shot, then on automatic—into the air. The old man rose and took the weapon from my hands. He thrust it skyward in one hand. The crowd cheered him wildly. Still grinning, he clasped the weapon firmly in both hands, leaned back, half closed his eyes, and sprayed the night sky with bullets. The men whooped again. A few leapt to their feet and fired their own weapons skyward.

When everyone had grown quiet again, Big Kevin made a brief speech about what I was bringing to their cause. I had decided to give everything I was carrying, minus 10,000 pounds for expenses, to the Kurds. That came to something near 40,000 pounds. It was a cash penalty to Valner, Mirza, and the rest of that lot for all the lies and deception. I stripped my money belt from beneath my shirt, laid it on the ground in front of the old man, opened the pouches, and brought out the cash by the handful. When Big Kevin translated the sum into local currency, the crowd was ecstatic. The grim reserve fell away, and they became a merry band feasting by firelight.

I had seen animals roasting two to a spit all around the camp. Now they were rushed in, fifteen or twenty goats for the multitude, half a dozen sheep for the privileged and the guests. Great wooden bowls of fresh green vegetables and steamy potatoes were set before us by the women. We sliced the barbecued meat from the carcass and ate it with the vegetables or with a heavy bread that crumbled in the mouth. I tried to refuse the thick wine, but Big Kevin reproached me.

"Don't turn it away," he said. "That would be insulting."

I forced down another mouthful.

"I don't want to get drunk," I said.

"You won't," said Big Kevin. "It's half blood."

The women had joined in the feasting now. They were high-spirited and enjoyed fussing over us. They rushed forward and dropped a new dish in front of us, then hung back—but not very far away—while they ate with their fingers from their own bowls. A lot of Islamic tradition went by the board when you are a fugitive nation.

Gill got a little drunk and began to nod. He was showing his age. Marcel's spirits were restored by the attention to his wounds. Now he and his brother laughed and drank deeply of the blood wine, roared and sang in French.

The meal ended with sweetmeats and a huge pastry like a rum baba sweetened with honey and filled with a yellow custard. It stuck to my hands when I tried to eat a bit. The sticky pastry brought the rabbits to mind, and I realized with a start that they were not present.

"Where are the kids?" I asked Big Kevin.

"They stay out of sight until you leave. They've been washed. The young boy's arm has been reset. They'll be fed. But they don't show their faces in this camp."

Big Kevin offered no explanation, nor did I ask for one. I had seen fear in the boys' faces when we came ashore. Kurds and Iranians have been killing one another for a long time. These people had no time for rich dilettantes from Teheran.

A few people had followed the Verbruggens' lead and broken into song of their own. Others leapt to their feet in wild and graceful dances. Even as the crowd grew more lively, I could feel my exhaustion setting in.

"We'll debrief in the morning," I told Davis and Freeman. "It can wait another twelve hours."

Gill was by now passed out face down on the mat beside me. Two men helped him to his tent.

Big Kevin sat at my right hand and talked quietly to me about the Kurds.

"The Iranian revolution can't afford to let us survive. The Kurds are Moslems, so the revolutionaries feel dissension should have ceased with the rise of the Islamic republic. But Kurds are not Iraqis. They are not Iranians.

"We're fighting skirmishes every day with the Iranians. The Iranian Army is sending patrols into villages that have been ours for ten years. There'll be a full-scale war here soon.

"These people," he said, pointing to the revelers around the campfire, "will die. Maybe every one of them. And their children and their children's children, but the Kurds will never give up. In five years or ten or fifteen, there will be a Kurdish republic.

"They're not asking anybody for anything. They're not resorting to terrorism. All they're doing is fighting a war for freedom and independence."

"You have a cease-fire with the Iraqis, don't you?" I asked.

"Not a cease-fire. An understanding. Every now and then, almost without malice—sort of a reminder, I suppose—the Iraqi Air Force comes over and blows one of our villages apart. The old people and the children die in an exercise for the Iraqi fighter pilots. Apart from that, we have a modus vivendi with the Iraqis right now.

"But the Iranians will be here soon. So long as we're here with our cause their Islamic republic can never feel secure. But they'll never defeat the Kurds. We can retreat into these mountains and fight them for fifty years. Eat grass, bark off the trees, like Tito's guerrillas did. But we will never give up. And we can never reach a settlement with Khomeini. He will accept nothing less than the total disappearance of the Kurdish people."

# 27

When the food was at last cleared away, the people broke into groups, some playing games, others singing and dancing by the light of the campfire. Two men stood shoulder to shoulder with knees bent and their hands cupped in front of them. One by one, the youngest men ran at them, jumped into their cupped hands, and were flung head over heels in a back flip. The man who could do the most somersaults before hitting the ground was the winner. The crowd roared with approval and even cheered a few who landed on their heads and knocked themselves out.

There were a couple of mock knife fights and some good-spirited wrestling. Big Kevin joined in and tackled a huge man with the hands and arms of a blacksmith. They rolled along the grass for several minutes, then slapped one another on the back in a happy truce.

Big Kevin was a different man from the ill-at-ease stranger I had seen in Europe; there he was out of place and time with his surroundings. I realized I had never seen him smile before. Here his face was broken into a wide grin for love of these people, as he went among them joking, hugging them to his chest, slapping the younger men on the back, teasing the women. He was a giant figure here, loved and respected by all. He came laughing back to my side.

"Have you been in touch with Tarik?" I asked.

"In the morning."

"Any trouble with your linkup with Mirza?"

"For God's sakes, relax and enjoy yourself for once in your life," Big Kevin said with a touch of good-natured exasperation.

He and I were both fading from the wine and the long day. I tried one last time.

"Did my men have any problem reaching you?"

"No. I was surprised when they turned up, just the two of them. When Mirza contacted me, I assumed you were all coming out of the north. The boy died in the company of my men. I'll leave Freeman and Davis to brief you on that."

I gave up and went to our tent. I fell beneath the skins of hide and fur and sank into a deep sleep.

As the light of dawn waxed red across the lake, I grabbed a chunk of bread and a bowl of strong black coffee by the fire. Big Kevin was out in the camp, moving quietly but purposefully among his men. Swann stood at water's edge, his hands thrust in his pockets against the chill dawn air. I joined him.

"Get the men together for a briefing in thirty minutes," I said.

Big Kevin and I woke the rabbits from a sound sleep. Rabbit Two was recovering remarkably well from the broken arm; he could even grumble a bit now.

"Most likely, we'll be here today and tonight," I told them. "Don't try to leave this tent. In no way are you to compromise the hospitality of the people here. If you are in desperate need of anything, there'll be somebody outside the tent."

"What happened to Dara?" asked Rabbit Two of his cousin.

"Is Annabel here?" asked Rabbit One.

"You'll be filled in later," I said, "after I've briefed my men."

Big Kevin followed me to the briefing. All the men were dressed and lounging about the tent when we came in. They sat up. I turned to Freeman and Davis.

"Let's hear what happened," I said.

Freeman took the lead. "The bloody bastards hit the safe house," he said. "We had to fight our way out. We got away with the kid. He was in terrible shape."

"Wounded?"

"No, not in the fire fight. From prison. The beatings." He paused, then continued. "Mirza's network got us as far as Big Kevin's people. They brought us in here on horseback. The kid died on the way."

Freeman waited for me to comment. When I did not, Davis interrupted. "The trip was too hard for him."

"Is that all there is to it?" I asked.

"That's it. What else could there be?" said Davis.

I turned to the rest of the men. "We're going to be here for another twenty-four hours. Do what you want. Rest. Go fishing. Be courteous, but stay out of the Kurds' way as much as possible. It may not look like it, but we're sitting in the middle of a battle zone here. These people saved our lives, so please treat them accordingly, with that in mind. Dismissed."

All six started out of the tent.

"Jack," I said to Davis, "you and Freeman stay behind. Big Kevin, I'd like you to stay as well. . . . All right," I said to the two men, "I want you to tell me again what happened in Qazvin."

"Look, old boy," Davis said, his tone cocky, "we briefed you. We had a bloody hard trip up here. We made it, and that's all there is to it."

"You're lying," I said.

Davis was not used to people talking to him that way. His face filled with a black rage, but he said nothing.

"Let me tell you what I know about it," I continued. "You, Davis, were not in the safe house when it was hit. The two of you were separated for the better part of a day—you with the girl, Freeman with Rabbit Three—until Mirza could get you back together. Whatever you're hiding, I'm going to have it right now."

It was Freeman who replied. "Gayle," he said, "I had no control over Captain Davis leaving my presence. I want that registered and acknowledged right now."

This was Freeman's way of registering an official complaint, letting me know that Davis had pulled rank on him so he could get away with something he knew was wrong. Davis held no rank over Freeman on this mission, but he damned sure did back in London, and there was no way Freeman could ignore it.

"Explain yourself," I said to Freeman.

"As soon as the rest of you left in the van for Teheran, Captain Davis ordered the girl's Iranian escort to stay behind with us. He told me he was going off with the girl. I argued with him, but he wouldn't stand for it. He finally ordered me to shut up. He told me he had an affection for the girl, and this was the reason the separation would be affected."

Freeman was not an articulate man; he was searching now for words to make his statement as formal and precise as possible.

Davis jumped between us. "That's absolutely rubbish," he shouted, his clenched fists red and trembling. "That's a lie from beginning to end. I never went off with that girl. I was there with them when the house was hit. We got separated in the fire fight afterward."

"This man's negligence," interrupted Big Kevin, "cost the life of the lad and damned near cost your lives as well."

This last woke Davis up. Fooling around with a woman and lying about it was one thing, but jeopardizing the rest of us was another. His professional aptitude and ethics were on the line. He was up against us all, and he knew it.

"So what if the bird wanted to screw me? How the hell did I know this was going to happen? She said we could pick up the heroin and be back in fifteen minutes."

"Fifteen minutes? You weren't back in two hours. You knew what the timetable was. You simply didn't give a fuck about the job or the rest of the men. Let's hear the story again, from the beginning."

"Right. The girl and I were diddling. We lost track of time. The whole fucking town blew up around our ears. We took off. She put us up in a flat above a bakery. Mirza's people collected us there and took us to meet Freeman and the rabbit. They put us in a Land-Rover and sent us to meet Big Kevin's people."

"What happened to the girl?" I asked.

"She stayed behind when we started north."

I almost believed Davis' story this second time around, until I realized how preposterous it was. Here was a girl whose boyfriend had just been brought in half dead from torture and drug withdrawal. Now Davis was telling me the girl went out to get some lifesaving heroin but did not care enough to come straight back because she had fallen for a stranger in dirty clothes she had known for a total of fifteen minutes. Davis had a way with women, but this was too much. He may have attacked her, and they were fighting all the while. He may have raped her. That was no concern of mine, so the point lay moot. But I resented the small-minded way he had to save face even while betraying the rest of us. I turned to Freeman.

"This guy's cock nearly got us all killed. You're responsible for relieving an officer in the field when he's unfit to command. Davis was obviously unfit."

I paused for effect. From the corner of my eye, I saw Davis seething with rage, but I ignored it.

"I repeat, sir," said Freeman, "I had no influence on the departure of Captain Davis."

"Dismissed," I said.

Freeman left the tent. I felt no resentment from him. I turned back to Davis.

"You're one fucking lousy soldier, aren't you, Davis?" I said. "You pulled rank on Freeman. You forgot what we were down here for. You jeopardized the operation and cost people's lives."

"Can we talk alone?" Davis asked.

"This will be done in the presence of the commanding officer here. This is Big Kevin's jurisdiction."

I turned to Big Kevin.

"Did you lose any men bringing them up here? Tell me what you know about the boy's death."

"I didn't lose anybody," Big Kevin said. "My men say the boy was in no condition to walk or ride. He needed to be carried, but we had nothing to carry him with. They say he was shaking like a man with palsy, trembling from head to foot."

Suddenly it all came clear.

"The kid didn't get his heroin, did he?" I shouted to Davis. "That's why the girl stayed behind. You had abused her, and then she saw you were going to let the boy die. She couldn't go with you, even if it cost her life."

Davis hung his head, but did not reply.

"He rode for a while," Kevin continued. "Then they tied him to the horse's back. They were riding along, and he fell off, dead. His heart stopped."

In my business, you do not court-martial a man and shoot him for an incident like this. But neither do you let it pass. It is a matter of professional ethics.

"We'll mark the boy's death up to you," I told Davis.

I called Gill into the tent.

"Sergeant Gill," I said, "as senior NCO, I want you to witness what is taking place here. Captain Davis, stand at attention."

Davis was a toughie, a senior officer with lots of experience. But he knew I had carried superior rank in more than one army, and he knew there was a code of conduct among mercenaries. He had no choice but to obey. He stood at attention.

"Your per diem allowance and twenty-five-thousand-pound bonus are hereby reduced by one half. The balance will be distributed among the rest of the team."

Davis exploded.

# 28

"You fucking cunt," he screamed.

He lunged at me, but Big Kevin and Gill wrestled him to the ground. He calmed immediately. They turned him loose. He stood up, but made no effort to attack me again.

"I'll kill you," he said quietly. "You try that, you're a dead man. I've done this mission, and I get full pay."

"I'm telling you now, witnessed by Sergeant Gill, that you are going to suffer a fifty percent loss of earnings. That is all there is to it. Case closed. Dismissed."

Davis wanted to argue, but Big Kevin led him out of the tent. Outside, I heard him speaking in quite a normal voice to Swann. He had regained his composure. I had brought him in for the sake of propriety and military justice, nothing more. I had not humiliated him by holding the hearing in front of the other men. Our grudge was private. As far as I was concerned, the others would never know about it.

We spent the day milling about the camp. Nano, who had collapsed in the tent after medical treatment the night before, surfaced again. His wounds were clean and closing— most of the shell fragments had been removed—and, coming off fifteen hours' sleep, he was beginning to act like his old self again.

Big Kevin brought me a flat leather pouch containing navigational maps of our route through Iraqi airspace and a letter for me from Colonel Tarik. It had come through the lines at great personal risk to Tarik.

"Can I trust Tarik?" I asked Big Kevin.

"As much as you can any man," he said. "I've fought against him for five years, and he's as honorable as any soldier in this part of the world. Since things have gotten hot on the Iranian side, Tarik and I have a sort of fragile liaison. He's using us to put agents into Iran."

Tarik's flight plan was dead simple. It took us straight across the northern regions of Iraq and Syria. But a page of accompanying instructions stressed it was imperative we stay on course. There was no indication whether we had his protection in Syria. If it was not secured internally, I prayed he would scramble some aircraft elsewhere to create a diversion. But Syria was a big place. Most of their planes were concentrated on the southwestern and western borders of the Lebanon and Israel.

I turned to the personal note. It was warm and brief, wishing us good fortune and emphasizing that we stay on course. Tarik had paid his debt in full.

My mind turned back a few weeks to the plane hopping between Geneva and London, Zurich and Frankfurt, Munich and Madrid. What might have seemed an unnecessarily Byzantine scheme had in fact been the preamble—the architect's renderings, so to speak—to the construction of a reliable piece of machinery which was now paying dividends. This was not to invest our mission with undue importance. Big Kevin had been called on to convince Tarik that a certain mission commanded by me was going to take place, and its successful conclusion was not counterproductive for the Iraqis. Big Kevin had his reasons for doing this that transcended our mission, Tarik his own for cooperating. Money may have changed hands. Mirza had an operation that was functioning before we were ever thought of and, presumably, was still functioning in our absence. I had tipped Box 500, and they had given no gypsy warning. Müller used us to put four men into Teheran. Everyone had his own interests to serve. These interests had meshed like gears on a Swiss watch. The machine had been so well constructed from the beginning that, despite a week of the most horrendous misadventures, all seven of us and two of the rabbits were sitting snug and dry by a lake in Kurdistan, a day's journey from mission complete.

I set Gill to supervising the refueling of the plane, with Davis and Freeman to help. The Kurds had brought the drums in over the mountains, on the backs of mules. Marcel, I gave the day off; Nano as well. They both needed time to recover their strength. I did nothing. I was tired. I had done my share bringing the plane in here, and I had hours more of the same on the morrow.

Big Kevin and I chatted for an hour by the fire. I questioned him closely about what he was doing; not many people choose to be stuck up in the mountains for several years with the Kurds. We did a little business, talked about my company supplying him arms through a contact in Antwerp.

I told him about our operation. There was no point in having secrets from a guy like Big Kevin. He could throw no new light on the mission; he understood as little as I did. He left me by the fire to look after his people. I called on the rabbits.

Rabbit Two's arm was well enough for him to be full of misery and complaints, just like his brother. They had been cooped up in safe houses, lorries, Land-Rovers, an airplane, and now a tent for the past week. I felt no sympathy. People had died fighting over them. They were not going to compromise our position with the Kurds so they could look at a lake and a mountain. I was dressing them down when I heard shouts from the beach.

I recognized Davis' voice, yelling angrily first in English, then in Arabic. He was answered in equally vociferous tones by a couple of Kurds. I dashed out of the tent. Davis and two Kurds were at the pushing-and-shoving stage of a fight, yelling at the top of their voices. Freeman tried to break it up, but when he came between the three men, the Kurds thought he was joining in on Davis' side.

It went off like a flash. The four men were on the ground, with fifty more gathered around them shouting. Big Kevin beat me to the fight. He reached down and pulled Davis and Freeman off their smaller opponents. A curved knife flashed from a belt. Big Kevin shouted a command. It was over as fast as it had started.

I asked Big Kevin what had happened. He questioned the bystanders.

"Your man Davis doesn't like the way we run our camp," he said.

"Any apologies due?" I asked.

"Never apologize to these people."

We had a quiet meal around the fire that night and turned in early.

I took a second look at Tarik's letter. "I know that what you are doing is for the good of all of us," he had written. Tarik was a friend, I realized, not a debtor repaying his due. Friendships are strange in my business. I might not see the man for twenty years, yet there lived a bond between us that would not be broken by time or distance. When next we met, our greetings would be warm and genuine.

The sky cleared.

By morning, cloud had descended again into the upper peaks and high valleys, though not low enough to hinder our departure. I sought out Big Kevin.

"We're leaving," I said. "Radio Mirza an ETA off the Lebanese coast of nineteen hundred hours."

The message, relayed from Big Kevin to Mirza to Valner, would hopefully reach Chimoum ahead of us.

"That gives us an hour's leeway for time lost en route," I said.

"What will you do if you're early?" asked Big Kevin.

"Sit off the coast."

"That's Israeli gunboat territory," he said.

"I know. And they're as likely to blow us out of the water as ask who we are."

Our rendezvous was three miles off the coast, on a bearing of two-five-zero degrees from the beacon at the Beirut airport. I had anticipated Tarik would give us a route across southern Iraq. When it came through to the north, I decided to fly directly across Syria to the Mediterranean, then come back down the coast at wave-top level, without violating Lebanese airspace.

I also gave Big Kevin a coded message for my Third Party in Geneva, ordering him to freeze Davis' funds pending further instructions.

On the rocky shore we said our goodbyes to Big Kevin and a few of the people who had helped us. We shuffled the rabbits out of their tent, into the boat, and onto the plane as quickly as possible. We boarded with full fuel tanks, a little ballast in the water tank, some weapons, food, water, and high spirits.

We had arrived so spectacularly two days earlier at the eastern end of the lake. Our departure now was to the west. The bearing to our first landfall, the Little Zab River, was almost a direct line out of the valley. We ran up and down the lake twice to check for debris, then made a circling takeoff, whipping over the waves in ever-increasing spirals until we came up on the step and lifted off.

As I nosed the plane to the west, I saw Big Kevin on the shore below. He raised one arm and waved it in a slow goodbye.

# 29

We passed over the end of the lake just after ten o'clock. We went straight up the valley, and the mountains rapidly fell away beneath us. The clouds lifted. Fifty miles from takeoff, we broke into beautifully clear skies.

We came out of Kurdistan on a heading of two-seven-five. We passed south of the town of Taqtaq, still roaring along only three hundred feet off the ground. We skirted the Dukan dam to the south by a score of miles, flying too low to see it. We hit our landfall on the Little Zab, and when it widened abruptly thirty miles on, I dropped us right down on the starboard bank of the river. When the river branched left and right, we split the vee, crossed a railroad line and a major road, and found ourselves in a wild scrub-grass desert that seemed to go on forever. It was flat, monotonous country, devoid of natural landmarks or any sign man had ever set foot there. Somewhere in this empty landscape, we had to intercept the Wadi Tharthar.

"Keep your eyes out for the river," I told the guys in back.

With two more passengers, the rear compartment was very cramped. But everyone had relaxed visibly once we were clear of the mountains. We were on the last leg and feeling it.

"Aircraft closing on the starboard side," Nano shouted to me.

"What altitude?"

Instead of answering, Nano turned toward the rear. The guys in the back had not heard his warning over the roar of the engines.

"Hold on to your hats, boys," he said calmly.

A Suchov SU-7 blasted across our nose at five hundred miles an hour, shaking the plane like a child's rattle and nearly deafening us. Four seconds later, a second plane repeated the stunt. I was startled, and I had been warned. The guys in back damn near had heart failure.

The two fighters went straight up to five thousand feet,

then began a series of rolling circles to keep pace with our slow forward progress.

"They must have come out of Kirkuk," I said, referring to the air base just south of our track.

"What the hell do they want?" asked Nano.

"A little reminder to stay on course and not mess around with Tarik's instructions. They don't want us wandering off the track to the south, violating Baghdad airspace. There's the river," I said, pointing to the Wadi Tharthar.

The small river was prominent as the only landmark for miles around. We turned off our western track on a south-westerly bearing for Syria. The two fighters turned slowly with us, watched us a few minutes, then peeled away.

From the river, we had a hundred thirty-five miles to fly across the Al-Jazira Desert. The Al-Jazira was a wild, empty desert with only salt marshes to define its perimeters. We saw salt on either side of our plane while we were still over sand; that meant we were flying an indentation the sand made into the salt and put us within two or three miles of track. We turned on a heading of two-five-zero degrees and struck for the Syrian border.

We picked up a radio beacon which kept us on line for an oil pipeline that crossed the Iraqi-Syrian border. Tarik's instructions were to cross the border at the town of Abu Kemal, but not to join the pipeline before we reached a point known as T-2. T-2 was in Syria—Tarik's note made it clear that even he could not protect us if we flew Iraqi pipeline.

We crossed a river near the border, spotted and circumnavigated Abu Kemal, and changed heading ten degrees to the south. We intercepted the pipeline a bit too soon and had to duck back away and fly along its northern side a few miles until we saw T-2 below. T-2 was a service facility for the pipeline, a cluster of sheds surrounding an administration building, atop which "T-2" was boldly painted. We were in Syria, clear of Iraqi airspace and possibly beyond the reach of Tarik's protective hand. We had nothing to do but follow the pipeline another two hundred miles to the Lebanese border.

Nano and I limited our conversation to cockpit chatter. The men in back talked quietly, a note of unease in their voices. No one felt relieved, even though we were closing fast on our destination. Head winds slowed us a few knots. We flew over T-3 and T-4. We passed our halfway mark near Palmyra. The men in the back were cramped and uncomfortable. It was early afternoon now, and scorching hot inside the cabin.

"How much farther?" asked Rabbit Two.

"Not a lot," I replied.

"Today? Tomorrow? When?"

These boys did not know if the mission's conclusion was an hour or a month away.

"Not much longer."

"Where are we going? Tel Aviv? Haifa?"

"You'll see."

"Are we going to make it?"

"You're not going to make it if you don't shut up."

The boy withdrew into grim silence. Swann gibed Davis about the girl, but the joke fell flat. That was a can of worms none of us wanted opened.

"Buy you two a drink tonight," said Gill, leaning forward to slap Nano and me on the shoulder.

We were all hiding our anxiety about a last-minute Syrian interception. Syria was the last place any of us wanted to be caught; they are real sinister bastards, the Syrians. I dropped the nose of the plane down. Two hundred feet. One hundred. Eighty. I leveled off at seventy feet. Even Nano was impressed.

"*Coño!*" he said.

"Jesus!" came a voice from the rear.

Davis began to talk and laugh nervously now, putting on a brave face for the others. When no one responded, he climbed to the rear of the cargo hold and sat back there in the semidarkness, not speaking to anyone.

Gill mentioned his wife; he was anxious to get back to family and home. The Verbruggens compared the mission to others we had done together. "Remember in Biafra . . . ?" one would say, or "This reminds me of that day in the Congo . . ." We were all winding down, perhaps too soon, but it was something you could not prevent.

"We're closing on Homs pretty quick," Nano warned me.

I was anxious to avoid the last Syrian city, which I knew had a lot of air traffic. The city had spilled out into the desert; the pipeline, which once had skirted it, now ran through the suburbs. We had to go right over the top if we were to keep to our prescribed course.

"Twenty miles," Nano said.

I turned off on a tangent of two-three-zero degrees, toward a point where the Lebanese border bulged into Syria. Once in the Lebanon, I would feel relatively safe. The Lebanese Air Force was virtually grounded because of the civil war. The Syrian involvement in the Lebanon was in the south, far from our intended route.

"Becharre," I said to Nano, pointing off our port wing to a prominent peak I knew to be just inside the Lebanese border. I turned to the men in back.

"We're over the Lebanon."

Cheers.

We flew straight across the country, with Becharre to our south and Tripoli to our north. Within minutes, the blue coastal waters of the Mediterranean broke beneath us.

# 30

I headed out to sea at wave-top level. I counted us safe, but there was no taking chances. These were busy air routes. There were contrails all over the sky, but way up above us. By now we were two hours ahead of schedule for our rendez-vous with Chimoum.

"Let's go swimming," I said.

I came down on the water ten miles off the coast of Tripoli. This part of the Mediterranean did not see too much traffic, so it was a reasonable risk. Down south, closer to Beirut, it was a bit naughty.

I was occupied with bringing the plane in, so I did not hear the argument start. When I cut the engines down, I heard heated words from the rear cabin.

"You could have got me killed," Freeman said, his voice trembling with rage.

"Knock it off, Sergeant," said Davis. "Nobody got hurt."

"Yeah, Gill got hurt," Freeman shouted. "Marcel is shot up. And the kid died. All because you're a third-rate soldier. Don't ever pull rank on me again, Davis, or it'll be the last time."

I came out of my seat just as the others restrained the pair from tearing into one another.

"Hold it, chaps," I said. "We're almost home. This is no time for dissension in the unit."

"Fuck you, Rivers," Davis said. "I'm not taking any more

orders from you. I'm taking care of myself from now on. You can all fuck off."

I was too busy stripping out of sweaty fatigues to reply.

"Come on," I said to Swann. "Let's hit the water."

Two by two, we swam and frolicked around the plane. It was fantastic, as if the water and the sun were ours alone. The days of strain seemed to wash away as the men's eyes laughed for the first time. Even Gill jumped in and paddled about with his one good hand. Rabbit One dunked himself a few times, hugging the pontoons tightly.

"*Tiburón*," said Nano quietly, pointing to the water a few feet behind the boy.

"What is that?" he asked.

"Shark."

The boy scrambled back onto the pontoon and, despite our laughter, refused to venture forth again.

An hour and a half later, clean and refreshed, we pulled back into the air. This time I climbed to three thousand feet. I took a bearing off a Beirut beacon, stabilized my heading, then dropped back down to water level. We decreased the bearing on this beacon until we were on our radial. We flew the radial just above stall speed.

"Boat dead ahead," said Nano, "carrying the flag."

A big, fast motor launch—once a yacht; now painted gray, with a fifty-caliber machine gun mounted on the stern—lay idling on calm seas. From the mast flew a green flag with a yellow half-moon, our signal for recognition. We touched down and motored alongside. Half a dozen men patrolled the decks carrying automatic weapons, and two more sat idly behind the machine gun, but none made any menacing gestures toward us. Chimoum hailed me from the bridge through a megaphone.

"Come aboard, Rivers," he hollered out.

I had dealt with Chimoum from a distance, and I was looking forward to meeting him. He was a guy who had things under control. From the strife of civil war, he had carved a mini-nation out of the Lebanon, backed by the bared teeth of the Israeli Army.

He snapped a quick order. A dinghy ferried me to the boat, then hauled the fuel drums back to Nano, who supervised refueling with Yves's help. The rest of my crew crawled out on the wings to watch and sunbathe. Following my orders, the rabbits remained in hiding.

Chimoum greeted me with a warm smile and a strong handshake. He was a tall, slim man in his late thirties, handsome and flamboyant in tailored fatigues. A Swiss-made Sig submachine gun was slung beneath his arm; his hip boasted a chrome forty-five automatic.

We made small talk about a few things from the past.

"I know your credentials, Rivers," Chimoum said. "I hope we can do business in the future."

We talked weapons for a while, then he began to touch on the perimeters of this mission. He did not know exactly what we were doing, but he knew it was a major operation and complicated. Because of the Valner connection, he knew some big European organization was behind us. He gave up pumping me after the third discreet question was turned aside with a wave of the hand.

"All fuel aboard," Nano shouted to me.

I looked at Chimoum. There was a short pause.

"That will be eight thousand pounds," he said.

"Five thousand," I said. "That's all I have for this fuel."

He took the five thousand without a word. Valner would have already paid him a small fortune in advance.

"You're going from here to Cyprus," Chimoum said.

I made no reply.

"I have a message for you from Valner. Your plans have been changed. You are to disregard your previous coordinates. Three miles south of your original destination, you are to meet a boat carrying the same flag as ours."

My stomach knotted, but I remained calm on the surface.

"Is anything wrong?" I asked.

"I'm just relaying Valner's message," Chimoum replied. "They're waiting for you now."

We said our goodbyes. The men and I piled back into the plane and we took off. I said nothing about the change in plans, just passing the revised coordinates to Nano without comment. We had a short hop ahead of us, then it would all be over.

This was a beautiful way to end a mission. Our western horizon burned with a brilliant orange flame from the setting sun. The Mediterranean lay black beneath us. The coast of Asia pressed against our backs. Europe waited an hour ahead.

I brought the plane up to a thousand feet on this final leg. We were in one of the busiest air routes in the Mediterranean now. At that altitude and at our speed, the Turkish Air

Force would write us off as a smuggling run at worst. So long as we did not violate Cypriot airspace, we did not have a worry in the world.

My mind wandered over the events of the last ten days. I had to count the mission a success, despite the loss of the youth. I had brought all my men out. If Rabbit Three had been in friendly hands when we arrived, he would be sitting in the back of the plane right now.

Five miles shy of Cyprus, flying a reciprocal of our bearing, we spotted a large boat in the diminishing light. I came in low and circled once. The green flag with the yellow half-moon fluttered from the mast. Valner stood on deck, waving his arms slowly overhead.

I wiggled our wings in reply, then pulled back to make my approach.

Because of a following sea, I touched down in the same direction as the boat was traveling. I held the plane steady while the boat drew alongside. It was an old wooden trawler with three men on deck who looked so much like Cypriot fishermen they may well have been. Valner stood alone by the bridge, dressed, even here, in his impeccable dark business suit.

I had anticipated an eruption of cheers when we found the boat, but everyone had remained quiet. I smelled caution, uneasiness in the air. We taxied for a mooring rope at the stern. Behind me, I heard a weapon being cocked.

"I'll keep the engines turning over," Nano said.

# 31

Valner came aft to meet me. There was no sign of deceit in his welcoming face.

"The rest of you stay here," I said.

I climbed down the nose of the plane and jumped onto the stern of the trawler.

"How did you do?" Valner asked, smiling and extending his hand before I could reply.

"We lost the cousin," I said.

Valner frowned.

"Your fault. He was half dead when we got there. A junky."

"Let's not go into that right now," Valner said. "Are the other two boys all right?"

"They're all right. Hardly worth saving. The little one has a broken arm. My men are all right as well, by the way."

"Oh, good. Good," said Valner absently.

"I'll bring everyone on board."

"No, leave them in the plane for now."

Valner was being far too abrupt. Something was happening I did not like.

"Look," I said, "if we take too long about this, the guys are going to start getting nervous."

Valner finally came out with it.

"We can't take the rabbits off you here."

I exploded. I began to shout at Valner.

"What are you talking about!"

"It just can't happen in Cyprus."

"This is our deal, and this is where you get them."

"The deal has changed."

"What's the bloody alternative? Heave them overboard?"

"We've made arrangements for you to drop them off in Tunisia."

"Fucking hell!" I was seething. "That's over a thousand miles from here."

Valner spoke slowly and firmly.

"That's the only situation we can give you."

"I want to know why we can't put them off here."

"Because we cannot accept them."

"Then we'll dump them in Israel. We can pop them over there in an hour."

"You know that story already," Valner said.

"I don't know that story at all."

"If you take the rabbits into Israel, you're goners."

"That's great. First we were going to take them to Turkey. Then Germany. Iraq. You wanted them to go to Iraq at one point. Now Cyprus is out. We can't take them into Israel. I'm bringing those kids off that plane and putting them on board this boat right now."

I started toward the plane.

"Gayle," Valner said quietly, "if that happens, nobody is going anywhere. You'll never get back where you came from."

I whirled and put my hand on my pistol.

"Don't threaten me, Valner. I'm in no mood for it. All I

have to do is wave my hand, and this boat will be ripped apart in two minutes."

"I assure you, Gayle, I'm threatening no one. This is a warning. And it does not emanate from me. The rabbits must be put to bed in Tunisia."

I threw up my hands in frustration.

"You know what's going on inside Iran," I said. "You must know the trip we've done. The lengths people were willing to go to help us. When we got to Kurdistan, we had to hide the boys. The Kurds didn't want to know about them. What the hell are these guys all about?"

"You know everything you need to know. I'll add this. The acceptance of the rabbits has been taken out of my hands."

All I could imagine from that remark was that the Bavarian connection had gone belly up. Intelligence had moved in to take over the exercise.

"You put together a hell of an operation, Gayle," Valner said. "We've only managed to piece it together today. You cut us a jigsaw puzzle with your Spanish plane that kept us occupied until two hours ago. It would be a shame for you to blow it now."

Valner was clearly not talking about Bavarians now. Only a major intelligence network could have sorted out what I had been up to for the past month.

"I promise you," Valner implored, "take these boys to Tunisia, and it's finished."

When I did not reply, he took another tack.

"You have maximum exposure in Spain, Rivers. A lot of people have gone out on a limb. Put their names on documents. Moved men and equipment around. You don't want your friends to go down. They will, if you don't follow orders."

If I had thought this was Valner threatening me, I would have killed him. But what he said was true. I could take a lot of friends down with me. Santa, Miguel, Nano, Nano's boss. Who knows? Maybe Valner. My Third Party in Geneva. Mirza. Even Big Kevin. Certainly Tarik. The operation had created an untidy ending. By now, a German agent would have been found shot to pieces in Iran. Mirza's network was hung out on the line, partly because of what Davis had done. And that had been under my command. I could hear people closing doors behind us. Müller would have shut down the trucking company. Written off two Volvos and one operative.

Mirza must have gone to ground. Now a power higher than any of us was trying to tie the loose ends back together again.

Valner, at least, was offering us a way out through the other end of the tunnel; that exit could not be closed until the rabbits were delivered, and we had them.

"The Cypriots," said Valner reflectively, "are sick to death with being caught between East and West. They have their own war to fight here. They don't want to see any more PLO hijackers, Egyptian paratroopers, American spies, or rabbits from Teheran. You don't want to go to shore here."

"What you're asking is insane," I told him. "It would be stretching the range of the plane to the absolute limit."

"Gayle," said Valner patiently, as if he were speaking to a six-year-old boy, "we know you can fly the plane to Tunisia."

"So what if I do?" I asked. "What do we do when we get there? We'll have to be refueled, or we can't leave. Somebody has to take the rabbits off our hands."

"You'll be met."

"Goddamnit, one more vague answer like that, and I swear I'll shoot you."

He gave me instructions, coordinates, recognition. I had been on board twenty minutes now. The guys back in the plane must have been jumping out of their skins by now.

"Okay, Valner," I said, "I'm bringing everybody on board, so they can hear it from you."

I said this to make Valner uncomfortable, and I succeeded.

"That's not necessary," he said. "No need to waste the men's time."

"We're in no hurry," I said. "You sweat awhile. We've been sweating for days."

I brought everyone on board, and we advanced to the foredeck. The rabbits were agitated; they knew something was wrong. I looked for a sign of recognition between them and Valner, but there was none. The team remained composed, asked no questions, waited for answers.

A sailor brought us bottles of cold beer in an ice chest. Valner ducked below and instructed someone to fry up omelettes for us all. At last, he could put it off no longer. He came and stood alongside me, and I saw he did not know where to start. I took the bit in my teeth and told everyone what I knew.

The rabbits did a double flip.

"What's going to happen to us?" the little one cried.

"Please take care of us," Rabbit One begged.

Now he was near tears for the first time. He thought rescue was at hand, and suddenly it was a thousand miles away.

"I don't want to go to Tunisia," he said.

"Sonny," said Swann, "you go where we take you."

"Please! Please!" Rabbit Two pleaded with Valner.

"How do we know the same thing is not going to happen in Tunisia?" Nano asked. "Where will we get fuel?"

"You'll be met," Valner told him with the same irritating vagueness.

"Met? Met by whom?" asked Rabbit One. "I want to know what's going on."

Valner turned to Rabbit One with anger in his voice.

"Look"—and he called the boy by a pet name I did not catch—"you know what this is all about. Shut your mouth. Because these men are not going to take it."

I looked at Valner. "Don't do us any favors. We can take care of ourselves."

"You know you're going to be looked after," Valner said to the boy.

Both youths appeared slightly mollified. My men were far calmer about this turn of events than I was. Davis was the one who had to register a complaint.

"Something's funny," he said. "I want to be sure we're getting more money for this."

"Let's just get it done," said Gill, speaking what seemed to be the consensus; there was no real drama.

The Verbruggens did not care where it ended. "Will we still be dropped off in Málaga?" asked Yves, not knowing to whom to direct the question.

"We'll put you into Melilla or Almería. You have my promise on that," I said.

"Repaint your plane before you get there," Valner instructed us. "Put the Spanish registration back on."

What else could we do but get on with the job?

# 32

Valner called me paranoid when I debated taking the plane up to altitude to lean out the fuel.

"This is the Med, Gayle. There's no war out here. You could be anybody going anywhere."

Then he warned me to stay clear of Malta.

"Nobody moves on the Med," he reminded me, "without the RAF knowing about it."

Our instructions were to stand off the port of Kelibia, on the cape. We would be met by boat.

As night closed in, we lifted off the Cypriot coast. I took the plane up to eight thousand feet, leaned off on single magneto, and got an honest one hundred eighty miles an hour. I sat back. Our destination lay twelve hundred miles dead ahead of us, straight up the Mediterranean.

It was all routine. The guys slept fitfully in the back, while Nano and I took turns at the stick. We tuned into the area frequencies. There was a lot of chatter, but none of it about us. We got weather out of Malta. We told them we were a ferry flight and identified ourselves with the American delivery registration.

As we neared the Tunisian coast, Nano took the stick and I climbed in the back. Valner was right. We were going to make it with a teaspoon or two of fuel to spare.

"Everybody all right?" I asked.

"What the hell do you think is going on?" Marcel asked.

"Your guess is as good as mine. But Tunisia's where we stop taking orders. If they start any funny stuff on the boat, we blast them. Beach the plane and take off. Any objections?"

"Yeah," said Gill. "I don't want to go down in an Arab country. Sicily's only eighty miles. Let's go up there and take what comes."

We all agreed. We should have just the fuel to make it.

"What about us?" piped up Rabbit Two.

"We've hauled you far enough," I said. "You can make it on your own for a while."

We ducked down into the water south of the Italian island of Pantelleria, only twenty miles off the Tunisian coast at Kelibia. While Nano got out the inflatable dinghy, I looked around for paints and stencils.

"Just get in the boat, Gayle," he told me.

While I kept the dinghy alongside the plane, Nano scraped his fingernails along the fuselage, then peeled away an enormous sheet of adhesive plastic painted to match the plane. Beneath it, the Spanish rondel appeared, fresh and untouched. The cross on the tail and the original registration were covered in the same manner. In two minutes, the plane was Spanish again.

"An old smuggling trick," Nano said with a smile.

We went back up, and fifteen minutes later we set down a few hundred yards off the coast just outside the harbor at Kelibia. It was insane. We sat there for over an hour in broad daylight with fishing boats moving all around us, the occasional sailboat drifting by. Sooner or later, the port authorities must send a cutter to see what we were about.

Instead a yacht came out from a marina on the better side of the port. The harbor was filled with pleasure craft; Kelibia must have been a summer resort.

The yacht stood off us by thirty yards. It was an Italian job, an expensive motor cruiser, big and fast. Yves and Swann dropped into the dinghy and sat by the sponson, with an MP-5 and the Sterling at their feet. They made a lackluster pretense at maintenance on the sponson. They were not fooling anyone, nor did they intend to. They were underscoring our mood.

"Hello, Mr. Rivers. Would you like to come aboard?" a voice boomed across the water.

# 33

It was a friendly hailing through a loudspeaker from the bridge in very upper-crust, public school, English. Whoever was on board waited until it became apparent I was not joining them in our dinghy, then lowered their tender. A sailor motored to pick me up.

The sailor was Tunisian, as were the other five milling about the deck, from all appearances unaware that a twin-engined plane was hove to fifty feet off their starboard bow. He and I did not speak until we reached the yacht.

"Please go to the wheelhouse," he said with a heavy accent.

I climbed aboard, conspicuously adjusted the forty-five on my hip, and walked to the bridge. I guessed the boat as a fifty- or fifty-five-footer, which gave it triple the complement of seamen a pleasure craft needed. I stepped into a cabin, beautifully appointed in soft leather, polished teak, and stainless steel, more suited to a cocktail party than an unshaven mercenary in bloody fatigues. The cabin was empty. I went through a hatch at the forward end and climbed two steps into the wheelhouse.

The two men who greeted me were so much what I had anticipated it was almost unnerving. Their yachting attire consisted of Savile Row suits, black lace shoes, white shirts, school ties, and sallow complexions. Their manners, if one overlooked the fact that they did not introduce themselves, were as faultless as their dress.

I could live with the oversight. The game was getting dirty. People think you say, "Ah, British! Safe hands!" That is a load of crap. They play as treacherous a game as anyone.

The first man smiled first. He would be the Man from the Embassy. An undersecretary no doubt, in his fifties, waiting for retirement, hating these nasty chores. The second man was much younger, in his thirties. Reeking of British intelligence. More subtle, you see. When I did not smile, neither did he.

"Could you accompany us to the lounge below, please?" said Undersecretary.

We took seats around a polished wooden table.

"You have the rabbits with you?" Undersecretary asked.

"Rabbits One and Two. The cousin died."

Neither man seemed perturbed by that news.

"Right. This is what you have to do," he continued.

"I beg your pardon?"

Intelligence could speak after all. "Mr. Rivers," he said, "don't make any problems. There are quite enough problems from this little affair already. Now we're going to tell you what you have to do."

I sat back to listen. We could have been at Whitehall for all this meeting differed from a hundred others I had sat in on there. Undersecretary took out several pages of printed instructions from the typical Whitehall soft-leather briefcase, minus the Crown imprint. He read the instructions through, then turned to me.

"Mr. Rivers, I assume your intention is to fly back to Mallorca with the aircraft, after dropping your men off elsewhere. It's not going to be quite like that."

He turned back to the instructions, read them to himself, then to me.

"You are to hand over the rabbits to our representatives"— he paused to let me know he and Intelligence were the "representatives"—"on this boat. You will return to your aircraft and proceed with your people around the cape, to the Gulf of Tunis, where you will be refueled as a Spanish

aircraft. Shortly thereafter, you will be met by a second
tender. All of you, with the exception of the pilot, will leave
in the tender..."

I interrupted. "If you expect my pilot to get that plane
back to Mallorca alone, you are mistaken. He's in a hell of a
shape. He was tortured for two days. Blown up. He's wounded. He's been flying for three days now. He can't do it."

"Mr. Rivers," Intelligence said, "you can hardly turn up in
a Spanish Air Force plane as a crew member at Son San Juan
Airport in Palma."

"That's not the point," I said. "The man is simply not going
to make it. I know you're not interested in this flight, but I
am. He's my man, and I'm going to look after him. I'll make
it easy for you. Are your principals more comfortable if he
goes down at sea or if we get the plane safely back to
Mallorca?"

The two looked at one another.

"All right, Mr. Rivers, you take the plane back. All your
men have their passports, do they not?... Good. Then the
rest of it is quite simple."

He took a handful of air tickets from the briefcase.

"They'll be put on board a Tunis Air flight to London."

"You seem to have overlooked the fact that they're wearing
fatigues," I said. "Are you going to have them roll up at
Heathrow looking like they've just come back from the
Russian front?"

"We have a change of clothes on board for each man. In the
correct sizes."

"Let's have it straight. Are my men in trouble?"

If there is one thing on this earth that will scare a hardened
mercenary, it is to be in trouble with his own government.

"Mr. Rivers, all they have to do is act sensibly and return
to London," said Intelligence with patience and transparent
exasperation. "We're not going to have them running around
in Spain. We're not going to have anybody running around
anywhere. We want to put a lid on this thing so we can all go
back home quietly and peaceably."

His words were interrupted by a commotion on deck.
Swann shouted out my name. In an instant, my forty-five was
in my hand and cocked.

"Don't try a bloody thing," I said. "I'll blow your heads
off."

# 34

"Don't be dramatic, Mr. Rivers," Intelligence said with a sneer; he thought he could embarrass me.

"There's no drama here," I said. "Do exactly what I say, and you'll go home to see the kiddies tonight. If you think I'm joking, read my dossier. You'll have it right there in your little leather bag."

I edged toward the door, then called them forward. I sent Undersecretary up the stairs ahead of us, then jammed the forty-five against the base of Intelligence's neck and followed him up the stairs, one step at a time.

Swann was on deck with the Sterling in his hands. Yves was bringing the crew forward under his MP-5, their hands thrust as high as they could reach.

"What's going on?" I asked.

"While you were below," Swann explained, "they sent the tender over to pick up the rabbits. We weren't going to give them shit until we heard from you. They started arguing, so we decided to take the boat."

The tender was tied up to our plane, the two sailors in it under gunpoint. The crew relaxed when I surfaced with the Englishmen. One dropped his hands to his sides.

"Put them up!" shouted Swann, slamming the barrel of the Sterling into the man's stomach; we were on the point of blowing this lot away out of sheer frustration.

"Don't shoot anybody just yet," I said. "Just hold the boat."

The rest of my guys were hanging out of the plane.

"Nano," I yelled out, "stay in the cockpit. Be ready to go."

"No one comes on board the plane," I instructed the others. "If anything goes wrong, blow this boat apart."

I marched the two Englishmen to the wheelhouse.

"Sit," I said. "If anybody moves, I'll blow your head off."

Okay, we were enjoying a bit of power, but we had been kicked around by these people long enough. I had to admit the two were pretty calm about it all. But they knew I meant every word I said. The crew, outside with Yves and Swann, were more frightened. But they were not learners. They were not here for their seamanship.

"You guys better realize now that we mean business. We have alternatives to that bullshit list of instructions of yours. You're going to have to convince my guys they are not in trouble back home, or we start doing things our way. If we do things our way, nobody is going to win."

We certainly were not going to kill the boys, but they had no way to know that.

"These rabbits talk a lot," I said; let them worry, I thought, about how much we knew. "Now you tell me," I said, "just what all the hassle is about. Why are we having so damned many problems?"

Intelligence took the lead now. "Frankly," he said, "the operation you put together was too concealed. A lot of people were left in the dark. You, it seems, were the only one who knew exactly what was going on. That, in a way, made it difficult for us to keep the mission sealed in. We didn't know where to protect our own flanks."

"We've been trying to fill in the unknowns for days now," said Undersecretary. "When we realized you'd used your Spanish connection, we drew a blank there. Nobody gave us any feedback. Your man in Geneva has been misleading us."

My Third Party. That was what he was there for.

"You left a man behind in Iran," he continued, talking about Hans. "His body was identified. We're all catching hell now for violating the integrity of Iranian sovereignty. Then there's the matter of the pipeline. That will take weeks to repair."

"What pipeline?" I asked.

"Our American friends are rather put out about that. You put a penny a gallon on petrol in the U.S. The CIA would like to have someone to blame for that. Then the incident in the Gulf . . ."

"What is that?"

"I don't have a full report yet, but I'm quite sure I'll be most unhappy when I read it."

"We're not going to get anywhere until you answer my question," I said. "Are my men in trouble if they follow your instructions?"

"No. That's why we're here. All we want is to get the British contingent back into Britain without attracting attention."

"What about my Belgians?" I asked.

"They can fly to Heathrow and transit to Antwerp."

Their plan was better than mine, though they would never know that from me. I was not keen on turning my men loose in Málaga. Coming off a hard mission like this, there was no telling what kind of trouble some of them could get in. Mercs are not hard to spot. The Tripoli Hilton Assignment group got swept up in Italy in one go. And Freddie Forsythe's crew had been grabbed just outside Málaga.

I nodded agreement.

"I'll bring everybody on board. For God's sake, let me dictate the moves to my men. I've got guys out there in the SAS and the SBS, and if they think they're in trouble at home, they're going to panic. They won't understand your end of the operation. Let me do all the talking."

I went back outside and told Swann and Yves that everything was all right, they could lower their weapons. I told them what the score was; they accepted the new arrangements without comment. They left me their weapons and went below to change.

"The best thing," Intelligence said, "would be to leave all your weapons with us. We'll get rid of them for you."

"The best thing," I replied, "would be for us to keep them." I turned to the others on the plane. "Everything is in hand," I hollered.

I slung a line to Nano, and we tied the plane, which had been drifting without an anchor, to the bow of the boat. Swann and Yves returned from below in civilian clothes. They made a conspicuous job of slinging their weapons under their arms without directly threatening anyone. I took the dinghy back to the plane, climbed into the rear compartment, and briefed everyone.

Gill, Marcel, and Freeman shrugged off the change in plans. Davis was still sulking in a corner. The rabbits were frightened, afraid to leave us, unsure of what lay ahead. When Gill and Marcel climbed down into the dinghy to row over to the boat and change, Davis suddenly came alive.

"I'm not going back on a scheduled flight," he said, jumping to his feet.

"What are you talking about?" I said. "That's how you were going all the time. What's the complaint?"

"You said we would be dropped off in the south of Spain."

Gill and Marcel, who had pushed away from the plane, now turned back to listen.

"Well, you're not going to now," I said. "You've got a free ticket home from here."

I was genuinely puzzled by Davis' response.

"You can take your airline ticket and stuff it," he shouted. "I'm staying on this plane."

Rabbit Two had been leaning against the bulkhead during this exchange. Now he sat up.

"Mr. Rivers," he said softly, "why don't you ask him what he's got?"

"What are you talking about?" I asked.

Davis' face had swelled with anger, tendons popping at his neck.

"What's the matter, Davis?" I asked.

"There's not a goddamn thing the matter. Pull that dinghy over here. I'll go change my bloody clothes."

"Mr. Rivers," Rabbit Two repeated, "why don't you ask him what he's got?"

"Shut up, you little wog!" Davis shouted, then slapped the boy hard across the face.

He was reaching for the still-defiant youth when I pulled my pistol.

"Okay, Davis," I said. "Just hold it right there. Now tell me what's going on."

"Nothing's going on," Davis replied, edging away from me toward the darkened rear of the cargo hold.

We went back and forth that way for a few seconds, and I lost my temper.

"Come out of there," I said, and pointed my forty-five directly at Davis' stomach.

"What is this all about, Gayle?" he said, coming forward. "Don't point your gun at me. I don't know why you're reacting like this. I just don't want to go back on a scheduled flight."

"Give me your pistol," I said.

"No."

I heard Nano cock his automatic behind me.

"Slow down, chaps," said Gill from the dinghy below.

When I turned to speak to Gill, Davis drove his fist into the side of my head. I blacked out.

# 35

I came around before I hit face down in the belly of the aircraft. My pistol was clattering beneath the seat in front of me. I looked up to see Nano thrust his automatic two inches from Davis' face.

"Stop," Nano shouted.

"You fucking spic," Davis said as he calmly twisted Nano's arm until the pistol fell to the floor. "I'll break your fucking arm."

Gill had his pistol out by this time. He laid it on the sill, pointing at Davis.

"Sit your arse down, or I'll blow your head off," he said quietly.

Davis sat down. Rabbit Two scurried back in the corner of the plane where Davis had been huddled. He came forward to me with his arm outthrust.

"Mr. Rivers, this is what it's all about."

He handed me a leather pouch the size of my palm, drawn tightly at the top with two thongs.

"I don't know what that is," screamed Davis. "It has nothing to do with me. It must belong to the kid."

I opened the pouch. From it I pulled a thick plastic bag sealed tightly with sticky tape. I cut the tape. Inside was about a quarter pound of a brown granular substance, looking much like unrefined sugar crystals. As I turned back one corner of the plastic bag for a better look, a spoonful of crystals fell to the floor. Rabbit Two scooped them up, rubbed them between his fingers, studied them closely, then licked his fingertips.

"That's real high-class junk, Mr. Rivers," the boy said. "There's enough there to make Davis a rich man. If he'd spared just a little of it to my cousin, he might still be alive."

"Keep your gun on him," I told Gill.

I was hurting from the blow I had received. I sat down in the pilot's seat. I looked at the bag in my hands, then at

Davis. I turned to the boy. "Are you sure this is heroin?" I asked.

"The best, Mr. Rivers. The best."

"What the hell game are you playing?" I said, turning back to Davis.

"I've got no comment to make," he said. "What the hell are you going to do about it?"

"Do you realize what you've done to every one of us?" I said. "If they wanted a setup, you've done it for them. Whose side are you on? If we'd turned up in Spain with you, we'd all have gone down for twenty years. The double cross, it came down to you, Davis. You're the guy who was going to put a noose around all our necks. I may blow your fucking head off."

The thought crossed my mind that the girl might have saved us, might have sent word out of what Davis had done. That was why the British were not letting us loose in Spain.

I picked up Nano's pistol and smashed it into Davis' face. He went down. I knelt beside him, cocked the hammer, and stuck the barrel of the forty-five under his chin.

"Save it, Gayle," Marcel said. "He's not worth it."

"Shut up," I replied, but he had saved Davis' life.

"Just stay calm," Gill said.

Davis was looking down his nose at the pistol in my hand. I drew back and smashed the heavy weapon into his chin with a vicious uppercut. He went out.

I body-searched Davis, then went over the plane quickly, but the one bag was apparently all he was carrying. I sat down beside the unconscious man, breathed deeply, and slowly regained my composure. I picked up the bag of heroin, resealed the sticky tape, and put it back into the leather pouch. I tossed that out the cargo door. It sank without a murmur.

"I want you to forget Jack Davis did this. There is to be no word of it to anyone, ever."

It was not Davis I was protecting, but all of us. He would certainly not mention it. None of us wanted to be tarred by the brush of a drug smuggler. That is anathema in our business.

Davis had come around in time to see his heroin disappear beneath the waves. He pulled himself up on his elbows, leaned back against the bulkhead, and stared at me in silence. As much as I might have liked to get long in the tooth and think Davis would never harm me, I knew that from that day forward, if he and I ever came up on opposite sides, one of us would have to kill the other. Davis was a professional soldier, and he had shamed and degraded himself, sold out the men with him for money. It was probably the first time he had done something like that, and he would carry the stigma to the grave. He had to even the score. That was how you made enemies in this game. People like Davis and me have memories like elephants.

I sent Gill and Rabbit Two over in the dinghy. Swann brought it back to pick up Rabbit One, Freeman, and Davis. Davis was still groggy from the beating, and I dumped him unceremoniously out of the plane.

"When you get to the other side," I said, "tell them he slipped and cut his face on the plane door."

I sat in the cockpit for a few moments with Nano. He badly needed reassuring. The business with Davis had frightened him. Nano was a pilot, not a mercenary. He was courageous; he had done as well as could be expected. He felt bad about letting me down.

"They wanted me to go with them and let you fly the plane back alone," I said. "I'm staying with you."

I left Nano and went back aboard the boat.

"My guys don't need to go with us to refuel," I said. "You take them ashore and put them in taxis to the airport," I told our hosts.

They agreed. I gave them a number to call in Madrid.

"Just say Blue Rabbit," I instructed them.

From that, Miguel would know to call my Third Party and say that the operation was sealed and the rabbits delivered. Because I had not said Blue Rabbit Dropped, he would put all payouts in cold storage pending further contact from me.

"Tell the number in Madrid," I continued, "that I want our plane met at Son San Juan in Palma by a closed van. In the van, I want a Spanish Air Force uniform for my pilot and German Air Force fatigues for myself."

Intelligence raised a quizzical eyebrow.

I went below for a final meeting with my men. The first thing I saw was Davis sitting in a chair feeling sorry for himself.

"Are you all right?" I asked him. "Nasty fall."

I passed around the air tickets as if the whole thing had been my idea.

"You are on a six o'clock flight," I told them. "These people are going to arrange taxis and pocket money for you. Any questions?"

We shook hands, said a few quiet goodbyes. I went back on deck to join the Englishmen. They were standing by the stern with the two rabbits. As I approached, Undersecretary was showing them some sort of identification—a ring, a letter, a photo? Rabbit Two sagged and began to sob tears of joy and relief. Rabbit One just smiled.

Both youths were perhaps better men than I had given them credit for. Rabbit Two had shown great spunk in the face of Davis' wrath. It was time for us to part company. I expected no thanks, and they offered none. We shook hands gravely.

My men came on deck to see me off. We threw our webbing into the water and tossed the weapons into the dinghy. I rowed to the plane, slammed the cargo hatch, and climbed into the cockpit alongside Nano.

The boat's engines rumbled and purred. Our engines burst into life. As the boat pulled away, our seven companions stood at the stern. No one waved.

Within an hour, we had refueled. I taxied over the Gulf of Tunis and lifted off to the north. I veered west. We headed for Mallorca.

# EPILOGUE

Because of the complications that developed during our escape and the ramifications of the mission itself in more than one country, it was deemed advisable some time after the operation was closed down to hold a debriefing for all the agencies involved. At this meeting, I learned the purpose of the mission and the reason that the various governments intervened, covertly or otherwise.

If there can be said to be a worldwide center for international terrorism, it would be Munich. This ancient Bavarian capital is a major staging point for Arab terrorists—in particular the PLO and the Libyans—arriving in Europe; sympathy and assistance are readily available from the Arab student community that has been well established in Germany for over twenty years. The massacre of Israelis at the 1976

Munich Olympics was constructed around an Arab terrorist infrastructure as old as some of its victims. The Bavarian people have long been seduced by the politics of terror; witness the history of the first half of the twentieth century. The city continues to offer succor to German political extremists—the remnants of Baader-Meinhof and its younger cousins. The Red Army from Japan and the Red Brigades from Italy convene in Munich to coordinate murder and hijackings.

The costs of maintaining an underground network and mounting an action are enormous. For a fugitive or clandestine operative, the basic tools of survival—food, transportation, lodging, protection, weaponry—became prohibitively expensive. Some of the money for this comes from Colonel Qaddafi, some from taxes on Palestinian refugees, from gifts and loans from sympathetic governments, from bank robberies and kidnappings. A very considerable share is derived from the sale of illicit drugs.

The Munich estate was the headquarters for one of Europe's largest drug wholesalers. The Germans running this drug ring were apolitical insofar as they were dealing drugs purely for profit, though the drugs reached them to a large measure through embassy diplomatic pouches from the Middle East. The Germans then sold the drugs to the dealers *en gros;* it was at this point that crime for profit and terrorism as political implement became intertwined. The drugs were being purchased from the Germans by Arab terrorist organizations—again, principally the PLO and the Libyans. The Arabs were channeling their profits to further both their own activities and those of their Western allies, the fanatical groups that were planting bombs in train stations and shopping centers across Europe. The major supplier of heroin to the Munich organization was the father of Rabbits One and Two.

The escape of the father and, on his death, that of his sons, had been orchestrated in the first instance by the Munich connection. The revolution in Iran and the disruption that followed had interrupted the flow of heroin to Europe, and vast amounts of the drug had gone missing. It was assumed that the father had the missing drugs, or at least knew how to put his hands on them. On his death, his sons became the beneficiaries of his "insurance policies." First were the missing drugs. Second, there were serial numbers and keys to safe-deposit boxes scattered across Europe that contained not only millions in hard currency but, more importantly, details of the Palestinian ring operating within Germany—members, routes, organization—information gathered by the father during the course of his dealings with Munich.

German counterintelligence, having penetrated the Munich organization, knew that if they could obtain this information, they would have a line on Arab operations within Bavaria and possibly a direct conduit to the German and European rings. The use of my contract team was desirable, because this allowed governments to secure this information in "a non-political manner," as it was put to me.

At the Teheran safe house briefing, the boys were made to reveal what they knew about the Munich operation and the PLO prior to our departure, for fear that we might be killed en route to safety. As the boys alone had access to the safe-deposit boxes, they were allowed to leave. Because I had no "need to know," I never learned whether the father worked as well for Israeli intelligence. Nor do I know what actions, if any, have been taken against the Munich operation or the Arabs.

## ABOUT THE AUTHORS

GAYLE RIVERS (a pseudonym) is the European arms dealer who planned and headed the effort to bring the Jewish fugitives to safety.

JAMES HUDSON was born in Dallas, Texas, in 1937. After serving briefly in the army as an intelligence clerk, he went to Paris in 1960, where he studied at the Sorbonne, and then took a job with *The New York Times* International Edition. He has been Paris correspondent for *The Dallas Morning News* and the *Dallas Times Herald*. Working as a free-lance journalist, he has lived in Copenhagen and London. He now lives with his wife and two sons in San Francisco. Rivers and Hudson are coauthors of *The Five Fingers*, another account of a mercenary operation.

# "THE BEST POPULAR NOVEL TO BE PUBLISHED IN AMERICA SINCE *THE GODFATHER.*"

—Stephen King

# RED DRAGON

## by Thomas Harris, author of BLACK SUNDAY

If you never thought a book could make you quake with fear, prepare yourself for RED DRAGON. For in its pages, you will meet a human monster, a tortured being driven by a force he cannot contain, who pleasures in viciously murdering happy families. When you discover how he chooses his victims, you will never feel safe again.

Buy this book at your local bookstore or use this handy coupon for ordering:

# Here are the Books that Explore the Jewish Heritage-Past and Present.

## Fiction

| | | | |
|---|---|---|---|
| ☐ | 22921 | **The Hill of Evil Counsel** Amos Oz | $2.95 |
| ☐ | 20816 | **My Michael** Amos Oz | $2.95 |
| ☐ | 20818 | **Where The Jackals Howl & Other Stories** Amos Oz | $2.95 |
| ☐ | 20570 | **Preparing for Sabbath-** Nessa Rapoport | $2.95 |
| ☐ | 20105 | **Brothers Ashkenazi** I. J. Singer | $4.50 |
| ☐ | 22967 | **Mila 18** Leon Uris | $3.95 |
| ☐ | 20807 | **Night** Elie Wiesel | $1.95 |
| ☐ | 13564 | **Holocaust** Gerald Green | $2.50 |

## Non-Fiction

| | | | |
|---|---|---|---|
| ☐ | 01339 | **The Jewish Family Book** Strassfeld & Green | $9.95 |
| ☐ | 01369 | **Seasons of Our Joy** Arthur Waskow | $8.95 |
| ☐ | 01265 | **The Jewish Almanac** Siegel & Rheins, eds. | $9.95 |
| ☐ | 22500 | **Children of the Holocaust** Helen Epstein | $3.95 |
| ☐ | 13810 | **World of Our Fathers** Irving Howe | $3.95 |
| ☐ | 13807 | **A Treasury of Jewish Folklore** Nathan Ausubel, Ed. | $3.95 |
| ☐ | 20530 | **The War Against the Jews** Lucy S. Dawidowicz | $3.95 |

Buy them at your local bookstore or use this handy coupon for ordering:

---

**Bantam Books Inc., Dept. JE, 414 East Golf Road, Des Plaines, Ill. 60016**

Please send me the books I have checked above. I am enclosing $_____
(please add $1.25 to cover postage and handling). Send check or money order
—no cash or C.O.D.'s please.

Mr/Mrs/Miss_____

Address_____

City_____State/Zip_____

JE—12/82

Please allow four to six weeks for delivery. This offer expires 6/83.